# *The* LAND *of* MILK & HONEY

## A HISTORY OF BEEKEEPING IN VERMONT

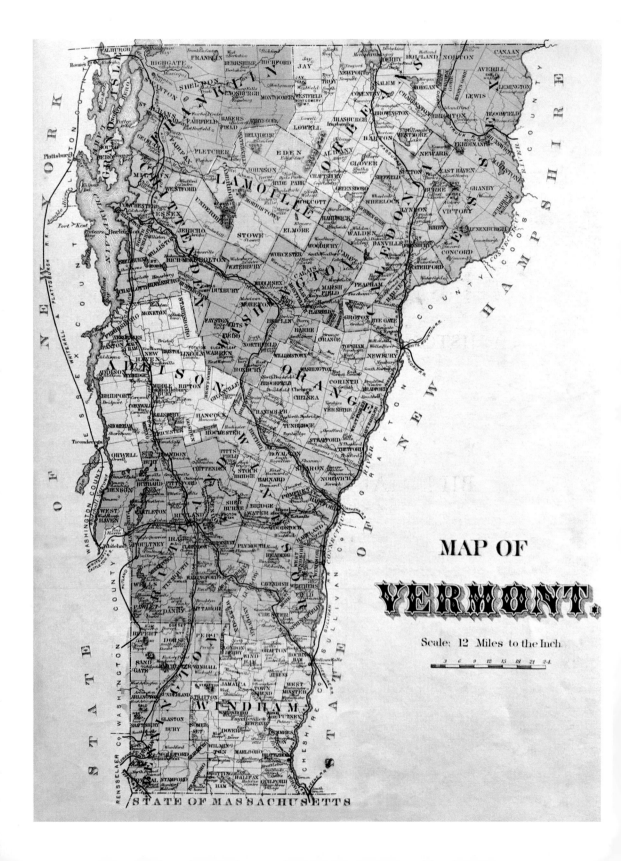

MAP OF

VERMONT.

Scale: 12 Miles to the Inch.

# The LAND of MILK & HONEY

## A HISTORY OF BEEKEEPING IN VERMONT

### BILL MARES & ROSS CONRAD

GREEN WRITERS PRESS | *Brattleboro, Vermont*

Printed in the United States

10  9  8  7  6  5  4  3  2  1

Green Writers Press is a Vermont-based publisher whose mission is to spread a message of hope and renewal through the words and images we publish. Throughout, we will adhere to our commitment to preserving and protecting the natural resources of the earth. To that end, a percentage of our proceeds will be donated to environmental activist groups and conservation/beekeeping nonprofit organizations. Green Writers Press gratefully acknowledges support from individual donors, friends, and readers to help support the environment and our publishing initiative.

GREEN
WRITERS
press

*Giving Voice to Writers & Artists Who Will Make the World a Better Place*
Green Writers Press | Brattleboro, Vermont
www.greenwriterspress.com

ISBN: 978-1-9505841-8-5

ROSS CONRAD PHOTO CREDITS: 38, 63, 64, 68, 69, 70, 125, 127, 128, 176, 243
BILL MARES PHOTO CREDITS: 7, 78, 115, 119, 143, 176

COVER PHOTOS: *The top image, "The Bee-Keeper at His Work" is from "Facts for Farmers" a pamphlet published in 1865 by Johnson and Ward publishers, New York; the middle photo courtesy of Rick Drutchas; bottom photo of Rollin Forbes is from the Chittenden County Historical Society.*

Frontispiece Map: F.W. Beers' Map of Chittenden County, Vermont
(New York) F.W. Beers, A.D. Ellis, G.G. Soule, 1869

THE PAPER USED IN THIS PUBLICATION IS PRODUCED BY MILLS COMMITTED TO RESPONSIBLE AND SUSTAINABLE FORESTRY PRACTICES.

# ACKNOWLEDGMENTS

Scores of people have helped us in this project. We apologize if we have missed anyone in our roll-call of gratitude.

While many assisted the authors in their efforts to create the first beekeeping history book for a state in the U.S., several people deserve extra-special mention. First and foremost for their daily encouragement, editing and good humor we thank Alice Eckles and Chris Hadsel. A huge thank you also goes to Lesley Weisbrot for doing the first (great) edit and cleaning the Augean Stables of our prose and grammar; Dede Cummings, founder of Green Writers Press, herself the author of a bee book, gave us encouragement and ideas in profusion; and Tammy Horn who read the draft manuscript with both academic and practical eyes to make the book palpably better.

We are additionally indebted to the following:

Mary Azarian
Peter Borst
Richard Brown
Dewey Caron
Devin A. Colman, State
   Architectural Historian Vermont
   Division for Historic Preservation
Jeff Cunningham

Reg Dearborn
Prudence Doherty, Public
   Services Librarian, Silver Special
   Collections Library, University of
   Vermont
Rick Drutchas
Jacob Esh
Kim Flottum

James Gabriel
Peter Genier
Hugh Gibson
Jeff Hamelman
Ilsley Public Library
Rebekah Irwin, Middlebury College
    Special Collections
Lynn Lang
Ken Manchester, Jr.
Lee Mayo
Bill Mraz
Chas Mraz
Michelle Mraz
Andrew Munkres
Mike Palmer
Steve Parise
Marilyn Post
Randy and Penny Potvins
Ana Price-Eckles
Jack Rath
Gregory Sanford

Kyle Scanlon
Henry Sheldon Museum
Greg Smela
Abenaki Chief Don Stevens
The family of Enoch Tompkins
David Tremblay
UVM Center for Research on
    Vermont
UVM Silver Special Collections
    Library
UVM Howe Library
Vermont Agency of Agriculture,
    Food and Markets
Vermont Beekeepers Association
Vermont Historical Society
Vermont State Archives
Sam von Trapp
Bill Weatherbee
Kirk Webster
Mike Willard

# CONTENTS

*To Vermont's beekeepers:*
*past, present, and future.*

# INTRODUCTION

## *by Bill Mares and Ross Conrad*

E VERY STATE IN THE UNION has a distinctive beekeeping history, and we hope that each of the other forty-nine will join Vermont in writing their own stories.

Honey bees (or "the white man's fly" to Native Americans) came to Vermont over 350 years ago mostly un-borne and uninvited, preceding the first New England and New York settlers who bracketed the Green Mountains chain. *The Land of Milk and Honey* follows the trials and tribulations of notable and anonymous beekeepers in Vermont from the early 1800s through the next two hundred years. The beekeeping lineage nurtured in the Lake Champlain Valley continues into the present day as apiculturists throughout the world face some of the most challenging times in over two hundred years. In Vermont, many full-time beekeepers passed on their wisdom and experience through experimentation, inventions, breeding, and teaching. Like worker bees spreading the queen's pheromones, they readily shared their knowledge and skills with the larger community.

In its small way, Vermont has joined the worldwide search for ways to harvest honey, maintain these vital pollinators, and save the bees from the predations of the wax moths, American foulbrood, varroa mites, pesticides, loss of forage, and climate change.

The story begins with feral swarms moving into the region now known as Vermont. The story picks up speed with the "Vermont Beehive," patented in 1836 by John Moseley Weeks as Vermont's most prominent entry in a worldwide search to modernize traditional hives. Other Vermont beekeeper-inventors were Augustin Manum and his "Bristol Chaff Hive" and James Crane of Bridport, who pioneered the use of cardboard cases for the packing of honeycomb. Charles Mraz, who bought out the Crane business would go on to become world-famous for his invention of the fume board and his passionate advocacy for apitherapy.

This study provides a microcosm of Americans' relationship with bees, the "farming for intellectuals" in Sue Hubbell's lively phrase. *The Land of Milk and Honey* will explore the relationship between the people of Vermont and the countryside they inhabit: a land and people that shift and change through the centuries in ways that directly affect the health and well-being of bees and beekeepers. One region of Vermont, Addison County, exemplified the matrix between bees, forage, fruits, and dairy cattle, a veritable "land of milk and honey." It would continue to produce roughly half of all Vermont's honey.

To give a broader flavor to the book, its authors come from different parts of the state. Two of them are from ground zero of beekeeping in Vermont, Addison County, and together the authors average twenty-five years' experience in beekeeping.

PREFACE

# *by Bernd Heinrich*

I T's HARD TO IMAGINE, a fellow-creature of more positive influence to us and ecosystems than the honey bee, Apis mellifera. This bee, or practically the "bee" of about 20,000 species world-wide, has influenced and cast a spell on us since pre-historic times, and it continues to be ever-closer tied into our orbit. We keep bees for a livelihood, for fun, health, excitement, and from fascination. The lives of many of us would be vastly different were it not for the bee. It draws and holds many of us throughout life, usually starting from childhood by fun and adventure leading us to the fount of wonder. From there paths lead to scientific discovery, careers, friendships, and to ever-greater appreciation of how the world "works" by way of its various ecosystems, economics, and social systems. Bees inform in all of these, and have also been the gateway to revelations in sensory physiology, social organization, and communication.

The scientific literature abounds with detailed knowledge of the bee that may exceed that of any other animal. Much of it started from the experiences and tentative deductions of bee behavior from early American settlers' bee lining to find wild bee trees filled with honey. Implications of potential recruitment of colony-mates to bee boxes used in bee-lining then led to the amazing experiments of Karl von Frisch that unraveled the bee language, a project that continues in various dimensions into the present day with ever-more surprises of these animals' sophistication. *The Land of Milk and Honey* documents our human involvement with bees and beekeepers, and our evolving relationships with them, by its detailed first-hand coverage of beekeepers and bee-keeping in Vermont spanning some 200 years of contact with and caring for bees. As Jonathan Swift wrote, bees ". . . fill our hives with honey and wax, thus furnishing mankind with the two noblest of things, which are sweetness and light." We have in the meantime co-opted their gift of wax for candles giving light by light-bulbs and substitute sugar for honey, but we have also discovered their role in crop pollination, vastly increasing their perceived and actual value to agriculture and ecosystems. The agrarian state of Vermont, at or near where the bee was introduced into the New World, has through recent centuries been an epicenter of evolution of our handling and use of bees, which however remain genetically as wild as ever.

Vermont was at the forefront of the developments in what was to become today's beekeeping industry for honey production, starting from the pioneer days when the honey bee was introduced to eastern North American and spread in all directions by colonizing hollow trees throughout the forested landscape. Bee-lining to harvest wild honey developed—and long persisted—as a sport for fun and profit, and led beekeepers to efforts to save the bees as well as more efficient ways of obtaining honey than by harvesting bee-trees.

The various innovations of beekeeping banked on intimate knowledge of bee behavior derived from long association with them, to facilitate honey and pollen harvesting, bee handling and survival in relation to climate and diseases. A colorful historical past of the close association of bees with their Vermont beekeepers in the agrarian context of farms and crops and pollination followed. The main ones concerned removable combs for extraction of honey, where the bees build their combs into frames, culminating in the now-near universally-used Langstroth hive. "The Land of Milk and Honey" collects the experience of individual Vermont beekeepers over at least the last two centuries, to provide a fascinating in-depth picture of the mankind-bee symbiosis, as centered in Vermont. This compendium shows where we have been, and what we have learned about beekeeping. It may even yield a model of where we need to go.

JUNE 2019

BERND HEINRICH started bee-lining at age 11 and counts it as one of the most formative experiences of his life, so far! It was amplified by a gift of Karl von Frisch's little book *Bees, Their Vision, Chemical Senses and Language*. It was inscribed by him, "Bernd Heinrich, the beekeeper from his father for Christmas 1956." Heinrich has harvested the honey and the bees from bee trees, and has kept a hive or two as a hobby ever since age fourteen, and still does to this day. A retired professor of biology from UVM, Heinrich is the author or co-author of a wide variety of books and articles including *Bumblebee Economics*, and *The Hot-blooded Insects: Mechanisms and Evolution of Thermoregulation*. He currently resides in Maine.

# *The* LAND *of* MILK & HONEY

## A HISTORY OF BEEKEEPING IN VERMONT

**R. E. Robinson sketch: Early New England Bee Hunters.** Used with permission of Rokeby Museum, Ferrisburgh, Vermont.

CHAPTER I

# The Early Years of Vermont Beekeeping

In 1794, Samuel Williams wrote in "The Natural and Civil History of Vermont;"

*From our earliest acquaintance with Lake Champlain, the honey bee was to be found in the open lands along those shores, at a distance of one hundred miles from the English and French settlements, and long before those settlements had begun to attend to the cultivation of this animal; and from the first settlement of New England hunting for their nests has been a favorite and profitable amusement. But as the chief food of the bee is from the blossoms and flowers of the plants, it does not multiply so fast in the uncultivated parts of the country . . . where the improvements of agriculture and gardening, are constantly producing a greater variety and number of vegetables.*

A LONG, LONG TIME AGO, a distant relative of our modern honey bee winged its way among the blossoming plants of North America. Fossil evidence indicates that this bee lived approximately fourteen million years ago, but for some unknown reason went extinct (Engel 2009). Thus, the honey bees found in Vermont today are not native but are descendants of imported bees, primarily from Europe.

The earliest written evidence we have of the initial importations of honey bees to North America is a letter written December 5, 1621 by the Council of the Virginia Company in London and addressed to the governor and Council in Virginia: "We have by this Ship and the Discovery sent you diverse sorts of seeds, and fruit trees, as also Pigeons, Conies, Peacocks, Mastiffs, and Beehives, as you shall by the invoice perceive; the preservation & increase whereof we respond unto you. . . ." (Kingsbury 1906; Goodwin 1956)

Honey bees apparently spread out from their initial landing site to the rest of the Eastern seaboard. By the time a second wave of honey bees arrived in 1638, the feral honey bee population had already begun to thrive. In 1661, John Eliot translated the New Testament into a Native American language, and then completed the entire Bible in 1663, both of which he published in Massachusetts. He found there was no Native American word for wax or honey (Horn 2005). This, however, does not mean that the First Nation people that lived in this area prior to the occupation of the land by Europeans were unaware of the honey bee.

Four hundred years ago, the land known today as Vermont was inhabited by the Abenaki people who had been living there for thousands of years. Being keen observers of the natural world, the Abenaki were well aware of the honey bee following its importation by the Puritans.[1] Rather than "keep" them in boxes like we do today, the Abenaki traditionally left bees alone to live independently of human interference. By keeping an eye on the bees and noting the cavities colonies and swarms inhabit, they could harvest some of the honey without destroying the colony. Alternatively, they gathered honeycomb that may be left over after a colony is raided by a bear. It is much quicker and a lot less work to gather honey for use as a sweetener than it is to collect and boil sap down into syrup. The Abenaki also have a tradition of using beeswax they gather to preserve (seal) foods, start fires, and wax stone pipes to help waterproof them when they do not have bear grease available.

The Abenaki's relationship with the honey bee has continued into modern times and today's Abenaki descendants often keep bees like any other beekeeper might. Because diabetes is quite prevalent in native communities, due to the difficulty indigenous people tend to have digesting and metabolizing sugar, honey is highly prized as a sweetener since diabetics can handle small amounts of honey much better than they can typically handle small amounts of sugar (Samanta 1985; Shambaugh 1991; Al-Waili 2004). Honey is also revered by the indigenous for its natural preservative and medicinal properties.

Honey bees were commonly found pollinating England's orchards, and so the Puritans wanted them in the New World as well (Horn 2005).

---

[1] Correspondence with Chief Donald Stevens of the Nulhegan Band of the Coosuk-Abenaki Nation.

Thomas Jefferson noted that "the bees have generally extended themselves into the country, a little in advance of the white settlers" and that the Indians recognized the honey bee as a sign of approaching settlers, calling the little insect the 'white man's fly'" (Pellet 1938). It wasn't until 1763 that large numbers of Europeans began to settle in the area that would eventually become the State of Vermont in 1791 (McGrory Klyza 2015).

The colonists kept honey bees for a variety of reasons. Before sugar from the Caribbean became popular, honey was the sweetener of choice for colonists, and some workers were even paid their wages in honey (Robinson 2014). Because hard money was in short supply, honey also became a form of currency known as "country pay," a way to barter for essential commodities with goods from the farm. During the hungry times when crops had failed, honey was a quick and easy way to get energy (Horn 2005).

As bees pushed outward into the Middle Colonies and up into New England, beeswax became "plentiful, cheap, and a considerable Commerce" (Kellar). This commodity could be used for making candles and waterproofing fabric (Robinson 2014). It was also one of the colonies' primary exports; in the eighteenth century, Virginia was regularly exporting beeswax to Portugal and the island of Madeira (Kellar). Compact yet productive, the honey bee supported the livelihood of the American colonies and indigenous communities.

It is uncertain just when beekeeping was first practiced in Vermont. Aside from the feral swarms that entered Vermont from neighboring states, bees were probably brought in from Massachusetts, Connecticut, New York, and perhaps by the French Canadians as inhabitants of those areas began to expand and take up new land. In any event, by the late eighteenth century the honey bee and beekeeping was well established in Vermont since a traveler who visited Dorset around 1795, mentions the great quantities of honey produced there (Anonymous, 1860).

The early settlers throughout New England chased and caught swarms of bees, or found feral colonies in trees. Feral colonies were often killed and the honey harvested. Sometimes wild bees were captured by cutting out the section of tree containing the honey bee colony and placing the log hive in an apiary (such hives were called "gums" or "log gums"). On occasion honey hunters would remove the bees from the tree and place them into portable cavities such as empty gums or skeps.

Bee hunters roamed the woods of New England in search of bee trees through various forms of "bee-lining." They did this often with boxes they themselves had made, since none were manufactured commercially. Bee hunters used the small box to collect honey bees in the act of pollination, then released one bee at a time to watch the path it took to return to its hive. Once a beeline was established, the bee hunter closed the lid of the box and carried it as far as they could along the path leading to the colony. They then stopped, opened the box, and allowed the bees to establish new beelines. The goal was to allow the bees to lead them to the tree where the honey bees lived. Some bee-lining boxes were complex contraptions that allowed bees that were trapped in the box to be manipulated into a second section using glass and trap doors. This second closed-off section of the box contained bait material, be it honey, sugar water, or a combination of both, placed on a small sponge or piece of honey bee comb. Two types of bee-lining boxes are illustrated in Figures 1 and 2.

Unfortunately, this method of collecting honey was not sustainable since the entire tree was typically cut to harvest the honey or the colony. There were also conflicts with ownership of the bee tree as well as that of the honey and bees located inside the tree.[2]

Honey bees were a large enough part of commerce to be involved in a Vermont Supreme Court case in 1827, in which Betsey Farnsworth sued Samuel Farnsworth for divorce for adultery and desertion. The petition held that her "husband now lives with another woman as his wife in Hagerburgh, New York"; the wife testified that he "kept a strumpet" and had "familiarity with other women than his wife." After several dispositions recounting his misdeeds, Betsey Farnsworth was granted the divorce. The alimony included livestock, farm equipment, furniture, kitchenware, "two barrels of pork, thirty-two bushels of wheat, and two swarms [colonies] of bees" (Supreme Court 1832).

The U.S. Census of 1850 shows that nearly 250,000 pounds of honey and beeswax were produced in Vermont that year. Addison County was (and still is) the center of beekeeping for the state.

---

2 See Chapter 3 for discussion of a 1917 law protecting "wild bees."

## BEE-LINING BOXES

FIGURE 1: **Antique Bee Box.**

FIGURE 2: **Modern Bee-Lining Box made by Betterbee in Greenwich, NY.**

## TO BUILD A BETTER BEEHIVE

In the early nineteenth century, New England workshops and mills rang with mechanical innovations as America joined the Industrial Revolution. Vermont had its share of inventors and innovators. Samuel Hopkins of Pittsford received the first U.S. patent for the fertilizer potash in 1790. Among other Vermont inventors were John Deere (the steel plow), Samuel Morey (the steam paddleboat), and Thaddeus Fairbanks (the platform scale). Such inventiveness carried over into beekeeping, at both national and state levels.

For hundreds of years, colonies of honey bees were kept in gums, wooden boxes, straw skeps, pottery vessels, and other containers. Honeycomb built in such hives could not be removed and manipulated like the moveable combs of today. Probably the first hives used in American colonies were straw skeps [Figure 3]. Log gums (i.e., sections of bee trees containing colonies of bees) occasionally were sawed out and used as hives. A few gums may be in use even now, particularly in wooded, isolated areas [Figures 3]. Eventually, the abundance of cheap lumber and lack of trained people to make straw skeps caused a fairly rapid shift to box hives made of wood. Some ingenious farmers built wood box hives with easily removable tops (caps) so that chunks of honey could be removed without killing the colonies.

FIGURE 3: **Examples of Early American Hives (Skep and bee gums).** PHOTO CREDIT: OERTEL (1980)

Adding urgency to the search for improved ways to keep bees was the arrival in the United States of the greater wax moth (*Galleria melanella*), and the lesser wax moth (*Achroia grisella*). The moth's larvae tunnels through wax combs, draws cocoons across combs and woodenware, leaves dirt and excrement in hives, and makes hives unusable. Although they are considered pests to bees and beekeepers, the moth's destruction of the unoccupied comb in hives, which may harbor honey bee diseases, helps to prevent the spread of pathogens throughout local pollinator populations. While today we know the wax moth to be an opportunist scavenging on weak or dead hives, when beekeepers of the day found their bees dead and hives filled with wax moths, they would blame the moth for the death of the colony. For many inventive beekeepers, the wax moths became the biggest enemy, as the beekeepers sought to protect their bees and, if possible, profit from the mechanical devices they could develop.

## EARLY VERMONT PATENTS

While the earliest known patent for a beehive in New England was awarded to John Sweet of Bethlehem, Massachusetts, on April 11, 1810, there were several Vermont beekeepers who developed and received U.S. patents on wooden beehives throughout the 1800s. This is a chronological list of those patent beehives.

Nov. 6, 1834, US Patent #X008488½; Abial Whitman, Jr. Londonderry, VT

June 30, 1836, US Patent #X009815; John M. Weeks, Salisbury, VT

Jul 1,1841, US Patent #US2151A; John M. Weeks, Salisbury, VT

Dec. 31, 1845, US Patent #US4343A; Aaron Colton, Pittsfield, VT

Sep. 19, 1846, US Patent #US4763A; William Whitcomb, Grafton, VT

Oct. 25, 1853, US Patent #US10152A; Wooster A. Flanders, Sharon, VT

Apr. 13, 1858, US Patent #US19,931; K. P. Kidder, Burlington, VT

Mar. 12, 1861, US Patent #US31658A; Ruben Daniels & Gains P. Cobb, Woodstock, VT

Mar. 17, 1863, US Patent #US37,915; K. P. Kidder, Burlington, VT

June 28, 1880, US Patent #US28,871; K. P. Kidder, Burlington, VT

## ABIAL WHITMAN, JR.

In 1834, Abial Whitman, Jr. from Londonderry, Vermont, was the first Vermonter to receive a U.S. patent for a beehive. (Most of the patents prior to 1836 were lost in the December 1836 fire in Washington D.C. so only a description of the hive remains.) He put the moth threat front and center. According to the *Journal of the Franklin Institute*:

> The object aimed at in this hive, is to construct it that millers moths may not deposit their eggs at its entrance, and thus prevent the destruction of the bees and honey by those insects. The hive is to be made of five pieces of board, two of which, forming the ends, are triangular. Two pieces of board, sixteen inches wide, one of them three feet, and the other two feet six inches long, are nailed on to two sides of the triangular ends, but so as to leave an open space of about three-eighths of an inch at the angle, through which the bees are to enter. This angle is to be place downwards, the sides resting against parallel bars. A piece of board nailed on the top forms the roof, which, in consequence of the unequal length of the two sides of the triangle, has the requisite slope. There being no platform, as to heretofore used, to support the hive, upon which, in the filth collected at the bottom of the hive, the millers deposit their eggs. (Whitman 1835)

# JOHN M. WEEKS

The most important Vermont beekeeper to earn a beehive patent was John Moseley Weeks, who was born in 1788 and brought to Vermont from Connecticut at the age of one. As a youth, he worked on the family farm. Although his two older brothers went to college, the family could not afford to send him, so Weeks studied with his brothers. Later, heavy work on the family farm damaged his health and it was necessary for him to hire workers. But on the farm, he kept thinking of improvements and helped to establish the Addison County Agricultural Society.[3]

According to the hagiographic "Memoir of John M. Weeks" chapter in Weeks' *History*

FIGURE 4: **Photo of Weeks Hive**
PHOTO COURTESY OF THE SHELDON
MUSEUM, MIDDLEBURY, VT

*of Salisbury, Vermont*, published in 1860:

> He always cultivated habits of close observation, and took pleasure in philosophizing on what he saw. Through a series of experiments, Weeks successfully developed a beehive that did not attract the bee-moths. From a long and critical observation of the nature and habits of the honey-bee he was led to the invention of the 'Vermont Bee-hive,' which was patented in 1836. This was the first improvement on the old-fashioned hive (in which the honey was obtained at the sacrifice of the

FIGURE 5: **Certificate of Weeks' US Patent #x009815 Patent signed by President Andrew Jackson and John Forsyth, Secretary of State for Presidents Jackson and Martin Van Buren.** PHOTO CREDIT: HENRY SHELDON MUSEUM, MIDDLEBURY, VT.

---

3 Henry Sheldon Museum, Middlebury, VT, Manuscript Collection Inventory, Weeks Family Papers, 1766–1855

bees), and was rapidly introduced into most parts of the United States. It was exhibited at the American Institute in New York in 1839, and received the award of a silver medal from that institution. It was successfully and almost exclusively used everywhere until other inventors sought the same field with other hives, which, though of very similar principle, were sufficiently novel to claim a patent of their own. But even now [1860], after all the changes in beehives, and the great number of them in use, the old Vermont hive meets the eye of the traveler as often as any other. (Weeks 1860)

In 1836, the same year the patent was granted, Weeks published a small treatise on the instincts and habits of the honey bee. The little book had a long title: *A Manual: or An Easy Method of Managing Bees in the Most Profitable Manner to Their Owner: with Infallible Rules to Prevent Their Destruction by the Moth.* He subsequently revised and enlarged the book in several succeeding editions, and eventually sold more than 20,000 copies. The volume gave directions for constructing the "Vermont Hive," management in swarming and hiving, ventilating the hive, and preventing robbing. It also explained Weeks' system of "equalizing colonies," removing honey, raising and introducing queens, and "multiplying colonies." There were additional instructions for combating the bee moth, feeding bees, transferring bees from one hive to another and wintering them.

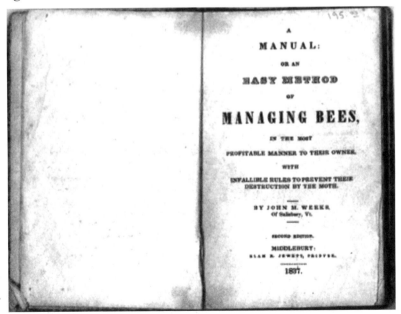

Figure 6: **Second edition of *A Manual: or an Easy Method of Managing Bees.***

Weeks sold many of his beehives, and his efforts were pivotal in launching beekeeping as an American agricultural activity. Weeks' hive, which enjoyed so great an acceptance among beekeepers of the day, greatly advanced the interest in beekeeping in Vermont and nearby states. His Vermont Hive was a great advancement over the plain box hive that was in general use at that time. The Weeks hive spurred competition among beekeepers that experimented and sought to develop new and improved hive designs. James Cutting of Haverhill, New Hampshire, compared his hive design to the Weeks Hive in his *Short Treatise on the Care and Management of Bees*:[4]

> Having taken some pains to procure facts, I will now give a few statistics, of my success in the business for the summer of 1843. I admitted that this season was one of the very best for making honey and rearing Bees. I had in the spring of that season five swarms of Bees in all. These were all in the Weeks Hives . . . I took sixty pounds of extra honey leaving sufficient for wintering them. From the poorest I took 30 pounds. From the best new swarm hived in my kind of hive on the 27th of June, I took 184 1/2 pounds, leaving enough for winter . . . (Cutting 1844)

With *A Manual: or an Easy Method of Managing Bees,* Weeks appears to have been the first to be highly successful in using a beekeeping book to help market a specific hive design; a marketing technique that would soon be imitated by others. While his book and the Vermont Hive were popular in their time, they did not have staying power. As with a number of other books on beekeeping that appeared

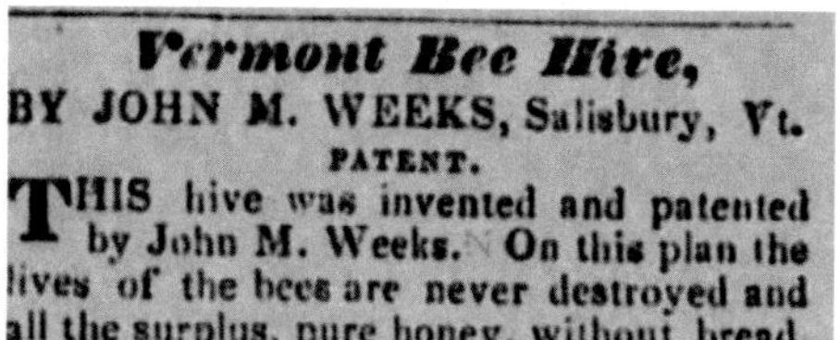

**Vermont Bee Hive,**
**BY JOHN M. WEEKS, Salisbury, Vt.**
PATENT.

THIS hive was invented and patented by John M. Weeks. On this plan the lives of the bees are never destroyed and all the surplus, pure honey, without bread, may be taken from them without danger from stings, or depriving them of any part o' their winter stores, or disturbing the main colony in the operation.

As the success of the bee cultivation depends principally on the management of the queens, and preventing their destruction by the moths, the proprietor has published a book which is designed as an accompaniment to the hive. This book is a concise work, containing only 73 pages, and yet contains all that is necessary to make a skilful Apiarian. It contains 13 plain, concise and easy rules, by which the bees ma be managed in any manner their nature will admit of, and at the same time make them the most profitable to their owner.

Applications for the hive may be made to E. H. PRENTISS, General Agent, Montpelier, or to C. C. ARMS, Waterbury.
Nov. 25, 1836.

Figure 7: 1836 **Advertisement for the Weeks Hive and Book.**

PHOTO CREDIT: HENRY SHELDON MUSEUM OF VERMONT HISTORY, MIDDLEBURY, VERMONT, MANUSCRIPT COLLECTION INVENTORY

---

4 Cuttings published 4 editions between 1844 and 1849.

between 1800 and 1850, "they had contained nothing new and of sufficient importance to impress them upon the consciousness of succeeding generations." (Pellett 1938 pp. 148-149)

Nevertheless, Weeks' book, the hive, and no doubt advice on beekeeping given to those who sought it did much to spread the practice of beekeeping throughout Addison County and other parts of Vermont. In later years Weeks would become a Selectman in Salisbury, a wool buyer, and raise sheep and dairy cows. (Child 1882) He also served as constable in the Town of Salisbury and as executor or administrator of more than sixty estates. Weeks died at the age of seventy in his home in Salisbury on September 1, 1858.

## AARON COLTON

Aaron Colton of Pittsfield, Vermont, obtained US Patent #US4343A, on December 31, 1845 for his newly designed beehive. Colton described the principal advantages of the hive as follows:

> That from its superior convenience and adaptation to the habits of bees, they will accumulate honey more rapidly in it than any other plan; that from the drawers being arranged on each side of the centre (sic) of the hive, the bees will fill from five to six of these drawers in the same time they will fill two placed in the ordinary way, over the top; that the bees more rapidly enter the drawers on the sides without disturbing others, than when they are placed over the top.

Colton's hive received the first premium of the N.Y. State Agricultural Society at its Auburn meeting.

The following is part of an advertisement for Colton's Improved Bee-Hive in the May 21, 1846 edition of the *Green-Mountain Freeman:*

> . . . and such recommendations, from many of the first men in the State (among which are Governor Slade and Lieut. Governor Eaton,). . . Specimens of this Hive may be seen at the residence of the subscribers, in Pittsfield and Stockbridge: Moses F. Weld, East Berkshire; Bennett Eaton, Esq., Enosburgh; and at the Freeman's Office, Montpelier. Application for Town or County Rights from Bennington, Wyndham, Rutland and Addison Counties, and from neighboring states, should be made to Aaron Colton, Pittsfield, VT., and the remaining counties in Vermont to J. M. Bennett, Gaysville. (Colton and Bennett 1846)

## COLTON'S BEE-HIVE

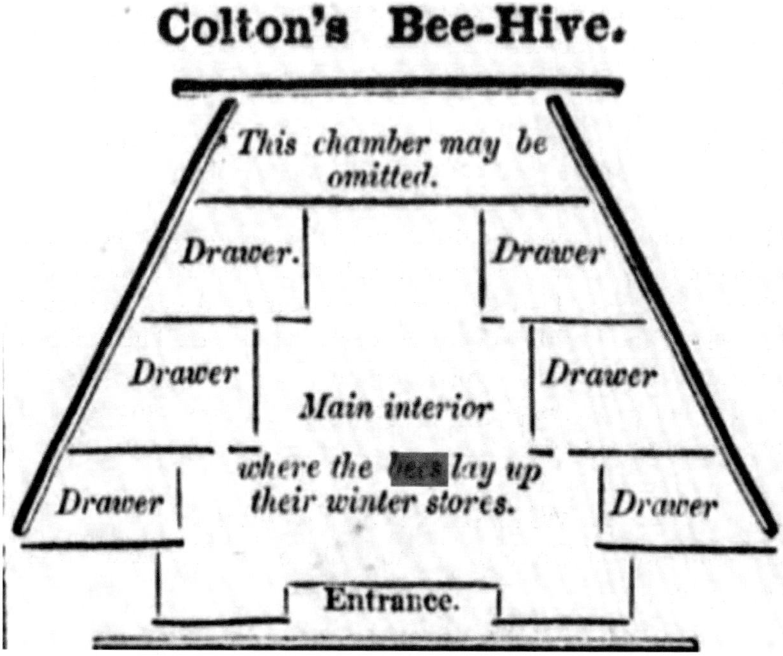

FIGURE 8: **Colton's Bee-Hive.** PHOTO CREDIT: THE VOICE OF FREEDOM, BRANDON, VT, J. HOLCOMB EDITOR & PUBLISHER (1847)

According to an article in the *Green-Mountain Freeman* newspaper of Montpelier, Vermont in 1847:

> The hive patented by Mr. Aaron Colton, of Pittsfield, Vermont is better adapted to the proper management of bees than any other with which I am acquainted. I hived all my young swarms in Colton's hive last year. I find by observation that they readily enter the drawers that no time is lost by the bees when the boxes are changed. I think that, by giving the bees a supply of boxes immediately after the first swarm comes off, they will not be likely to become so much reduced by late swarming as to be troubled with the moth, or be liable to freeze up in the winter. One other great advantage in Colton's Hive is, it is an excellent hive to winter the bees in the double covering keeping out the frost, the comb dry, and the bees in the best condition. I find I am not alone in my opinion of Colton's hive, for

it is already in extensive use in this State; and very many of the oldest and most extensive bee cultivators speak loudly in its favor. I notice, too, in the Cultivator, that the New York State Agricultural Society gave Mr. Colton the first premium. I did not intend to ask for so much space in your columns when I commenced.(A Keeper of Bees, 1847)

In an article in the January 7, 1847 edition of *The Voice of Freedom* of Brandon, Vermont:

We have examined a model of the above Hive and judge it to be superior to anything of the kind we have ever seen, both as to convenience and room for the working bees. The old hives are too contracted and not sufficiently ventilated for the health and convenience of the bees. These difficulties are obviated in Colton's hive being roomy and better protected from the heats of summer. Mr. Joseph Griffin, of Sudbury, has the rights for Addison County. (Voice of Freedom 1847)

## WILLIAM WHITCOMB

William Whitcomb of Grafton, Vermont obtained US Patent #US4763A on September 19, 1846:

New and Useful Improvement in Bee Hives: The peculiar nature of my improvement consists in the manner in which I arrange the cases of the drawers of the hive in the same, the said arrangement although very simple as it may appear enabling me to obtain very great advantages in the management and operations of the bees. I do not claim the employment (in a hive) of drawers or boxes and cases to receive them as I am well aware that such are old and common devices, but that which I do claim is: my improved manner of arranging each box and its case in the main chamber of the hive, as above described, that is to say that so disposing them therein, that two diagonal planes passing through their corners shall be respectively parallel to the bottom and sides of the hive substantially as hereinbefore specified.

In a report, Whitcomb writes:

My first trail was on the parent stock of my bees, which I bought in 1833, having been in the same hive 12 years.

The specimens of honey which I have here produced were made in the hive invented by J. M. Weeks, of Vermont. I have enlarged the chamber of said hive, as you see by the drawer, which weighs more than forty pounds. I know, sir, that there have been objections made here today that the drawer is much too large—that honey together is not so soon sold as the same quantity in smaller drawers.(Whitcomb 1845)

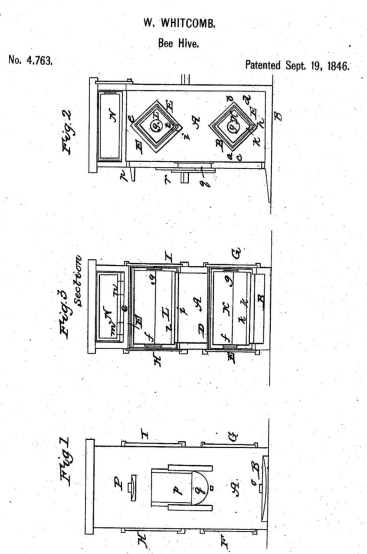

FIGURE 9: **Patent Application Sketch of Whitcomb Bee Hive.**

## WOOSTER A. FLANDERS

The good work started by Weeks was carried on by Wooster A. Flanders of Northfield, Vermont, who received US Patent #US10152A, for a Beehive on October 25, 1853. Sometime prior to 1854, Weeks sold his patent and copyrights on the book to Flanders. In that year, Flanders issued A "Second New Edition, Corrected, Revised, and Enlarged" of the *A Manual: or an Easy Method of Managing Bees*. An appendix by Flanders described the three classes of bees and gave a list of the most common sources of trouble in keeping bees and how to alleviate them by the use of his Vermont Crystal Palace,[5] or Flanders' Patent Bee Hive (patented October 25, 1853).[6]

In 1867, Flanders would release a 64-page, 2nd edition of a book entitled *Nature's Bee Book* that promoted the Crystal Palace hive that he manufactured and sold along with other apiarian equipment. He promised that his hive would prevent both swarming and robbing of honey stores.

Of his hive, he wrote,

> It is often desirable to prevent the issuing of a second swarm from hives, but no efficient method of doing so is known to the apiarian; neither is there any sure method by which to prevent weak families from being pillaged by their more powerful neighbors.
>
> By my invention I am enabled to accomplish with these ends; and it consists in the adaptation of an extra passage to the hive, which is capable of being caged so that while the working bees are permitted to pass and re-pass without hindrance, the passage way is not sufficiently large to permit the queen to leave the hive, she being larger than the other bees . . .
>
> By the use of my invention . . . no bee that is gorged with honey can pass out from the hive, while the inmates are permitted to pass and re-pass freely, all robberies may thus be instantly checked, as no full bee can leave the hive. (Flanders 1867)

---

5 A very tantalizing reference—did Flanders simply name the hive in honor of the Crystal Palace Exhibition in London in 1851, or was that proto-type sent to London for exhibition? So far, we don't know.

6 The Crystal Palace was a cast-iron and plate-glass structure originally built in Hyde Park, London, England, to house the Great Exhibition of 1851. More than 14,000 exhibitors from around the world gathered in its 990,000 square feet (92,000 m$^2$) exhibition space to display examples of technology developed during the Industrial Revolution.

## FLANDERS' PATENT BEE HIVE
### Vermont Crystal Palace, or Flanders' Patent Bee Hive,
(Patented October 25th, 1853.)

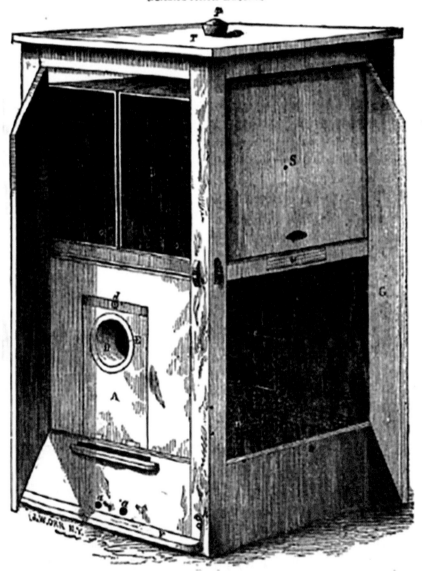

FIGURE 10. **Flanders' Patent Beehive.** SOURCE: *A Manual: or An Easy Method of Managing Bees*; BY J. M. WEEKS & W. A. FLANDERS.

## REVEREND LORENZO LORRAINE LANGSTROTH

While not a Vermonter, L. L. Langstroth, a clergyman and teacher had a huge influence on beekeeping in Vermont and around the world. Born in Philadelphia, Pennsylvania, Langstroth received a patent on October 5, 1852 for the first removable frame hive based on the concept of "bee space" in America. Langstroth's hive along with the publication of his book, *The Hive and The Honey-Bee* in 1853, are credited as foundational events that advanced beekeeping and honey production around the globe eventually leading to the establishment of the beekeeping industry as it is known today. The majority of the hives used by beekeepers in Vermont and in most parts of the world are based on the Langstroth hive. Not all Vermonters, however, appreciated and respected Langstroth's contributions.

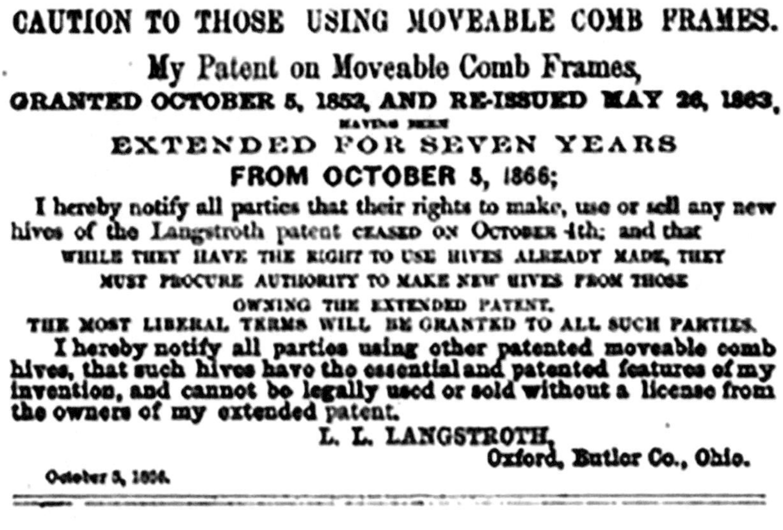

CAUTION TO THOSE USING MOVEABLE COMB FRAMES.

My Patent on Moveable Comb Frames,

GRANTED OCTOBER 5, 1852, AND RE-ISSUED MAY 26, 1863, HAVING BEEN

EXTENDED FOR SEVEN YEARS

FROM OCTOBER 5, 1866;

I hereby notify all parties that their rights to make, use or sell any new hives of the Langstroth patent ceased on October 4th; and that WHILE THEY HAVE THE RIGHT TO USE HIVES ALREADY MADE, THEY MUST PROCURE AUTHORITY TO MAKE NEW HIVES FROM THOSE OWNING THE EXTENDED PATENT.

THE MOST LIBERAL TERMS WILL BE GRANTED TO ALL SUCH PARTIES.

I hereby notify all parties using other patented moveable comb hives, that such hives have the essential and patented features of my invention, and cannot be legally used or sold without a license from the owners of my extended patent.

L. L. LANGSTROTH,
Oxford, Butler Co., Ohio.

October 5, 1866.

**Figure 11: Langstroth patent reissue notice.**

SOURCE: *AMERICAN BEE JOURNAL* 1861

Despite repeated efforts to defend his patents that allowed beekeeping to be conducted more cost-effectively and on a large scale, Langstroth never earned a lot from them.

## KIMBALL PARISH (K.P.) KIDDER

K.P. Kidder of 7 Maple Street (Wharf Street) in Burlington, Vermont (now the Perkins Pier parking lot) obtained US Patent #US19,931 on April 13, 1858.

My invention consists in the construction and arrangement of the parts of the hive, by which it may be converted from a single hive of peculiar construction to a double hive, at pleasure, or when the working of the swarm may require, and it further consists in the peculiar device for regulating the ingress or egress opening, said device being capable of four adjustments.

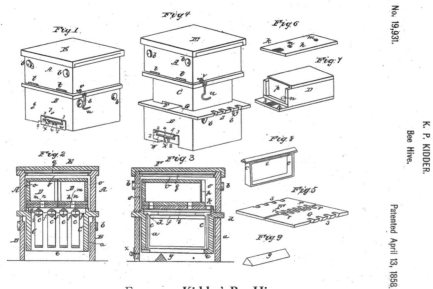

FIGURE 12: **Kidder's Bee Hive.**

As the above diagram clearly illustrates, a removable frame was an integral part of the Kidder Bee Hive that was patented six years after Langstroth's patent. He also received a patent for a bee-escape.

Kidder posted ads that promised prevention of swarming, robbing, the "ravages" of wax moths and "the great loss of bees during the winter." He sold queens by mail with "a liberal discount to Clubs and Agents."

In 1858, Kidder added to the literature on beekeeping with his 175-page book, *Kidder's Guide to Apiarian Science* which promoted the Kidder Bee Hive. On the cover of this book is a picture of the author with a cluster of bees forming a beard on his face. (Figure 14) This bee beard stunt would be used by future beekeepers to capture the audience's attention.

FIGURE 13: SOURCE: *MOORE'S RURAL NEW YORKER*, 20 MAY, 1865

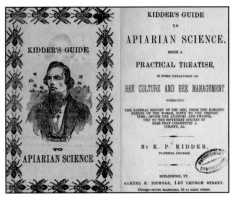

FIGURE 14: **Kidder's Guide to Apiarian Science.**

He was a litigious sort, who promised a lawsuit for anyone using the black and white outlines (or "cuts") in advertisements of three castes of the "Pure Italian or Gold-Colored Bees" he was selling.

FIGURE 15: **Kidder's Queens.** SOURCE: *WISCONSIN FARMER*, 1866

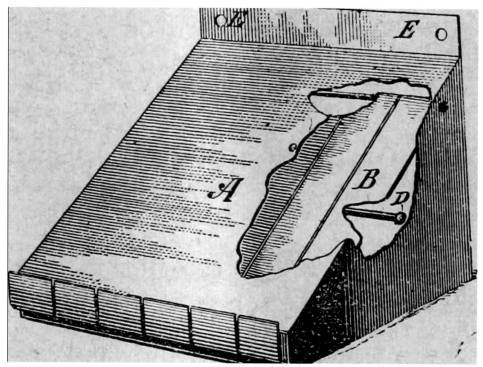

FIGURE 16: **Bee Escape (aka Bee-Guide).** SOURCE: *AMERICAN BEE JOURNAL*, 1861, P. 458

It is likely that since his patented hive included a frame that could be removed, Kidder went into the courts of both public opinion and the law to contest the originality of Langstroth's hive. In the June 3 and July 8, 1865 *Prairie Farmer* newspaper editions, for example, Kidder ran an advertisement: "K. P. Kidder's Advertisement—$500 Reward—Stop Swindlers." He went on to contend that, "The fact is, L. L. Langstroth has no patent hive nor never had his whole patent rests on the movable frame, and I will show, in due time, this claim is invalid."

This advertisement elicited many reactions from readers, especially a Mr. Otis who responds, "That there may be no misapprehension on this point, I will meet Mr. Kidder's assertion by giving the claims granted to Mr. Langstroth, under the patent of October 5, 1852 and the re-issue of May 26, 1863." (Otis 1865)

Kidder also invented and sold a "bee-guide" that worked as a bee escape, creating a one-way passage for bees that eased the job of remove bees from honey combs to be harvested by the beekeeper.

From the July 1891 edition of the *American Bee Journal*:

Bee-Escapes Forty Years Ago . . . I see by the Bee Journal that the bee-escape is causing something of a strife as to who was the first to publish the idea. The idea is an old one, but different in its construction. As far back as about 1853, I purchased one of Mr. K. P. Kidder, of Burlington, Vt., for which I paid him one dollar. It was stamped "patented," but whether it was patented or not, it was a good idea. One thing it had in its favor, it would not smother bees, by getting clogged. He claimed that it would clear the honey boxes, capture robbers, capture bees from a tree, i.e., wild bees, and have them work in a hive, etc. He had a winter-case hive also, or a hive within a hive. I will give a brief description of the K. P. Kidder bee-trap, or box-cleaner. The engraving is a poor representation of it; but it will, no doubt, be readily understood by the readers of the American Bee Journal: It represents a tin box with a slanting top, open at the back and front, with 2 rods running through it, as shown in the engraving. The door, B, is a strip of tin about ¼ of an inch wide, bent up at one end, and hangs on a wire at the other, which runs through the tin box, A, near the top. It rests on rod, D, so that it is held up about ⅛ of an inch from the bottom. (Snow 1891)

As new bee-guides were invented, Kidder tried to prevent their use claiming ownership of the bee-escape idea. The June 1870 edition of the *American Bee Journal* carried the magazine's reply to Kidder: "We have repeatedly advised beekeepers to disregard Mr. Kidder's claims of royalties for the use of Triangular bee-guides yet still inquiries come in regarding the legality of them. We can only state again that he has no valid patent on them and no right to make any claim." (*American Bee Journal* 1870)

Kidder also went to court to defend his use of an "artificial comb guide" also known to beekeepers of the time as an "angular bar" which was used to encourage the bees to build strait combs. A beekeeper named George H. Clark had invented and patented this bee hive improvement. At an 1870 session of the United States District Court in Madison (WI), the jury only needed "a few moments" to deliberate and rule against Kidder, entering a "verdict for the plaintiff, with damages, fully sustaining the Clark patent." (Wisconsin State Journal, January 8, 1870)

Apparently K. P. Kidder was a better beekeeper than he was a patent applicant. No more was heard from Mr. Kidder.

## SHARING KNOWLEDGE

At the time that Kidder was attacking Langstroth's patents, there were still people in Vermont who used and promoted straw hives. In a letter to the *Green-Mountain Freeman,* J. L. Sanborn of Hardwick wrote on April 12, 1860 about his hives that were not patented, and cost "but a trifle."

> Straw, being of a dry and absorbing nature, the moisture is taken up. Now, I have learned that straw hives are as much better in summer as in winter, especially in the season of breeding, when we are subject to frequent and sudden changes of the weather, such as damp chilly nights and hot days. The temperature of a straw hive is more even—especially in damp, chilly weather; bees will breed faster and gather more honey in straw hives than in board hives.
>
> This hive combines all the real advantages of every patent hive that has come to my knowledge, while it obviates all the objections, and retain all the good qualities of the old-fashioned straw hives. I have used this hive for fifteen years, and during this time I have not had a swarm injured in the least by bee-moths, nor have I lost a swarm by flight, nor in any other way by which it could be attributed to a fault in the hive . . . The less a farmer bothers himself with patent hives and bee-palaces, and the less he tries to counteract nature, the better he will be off. I am heartily sick of 'patent bee-hives,' and it is time to abandon them. (Sanborn 1860)

## BEEKEEPING IN VERMONT 1850–1879

Following the arrival of the removable frame hive, fixed-comb hives such as straw skeps and box hives were used less and would eventually be outlawed in various states and provinces since they made it impossible to inspect the combs for diseases. Due to their cost however, the new generation of hives were not as common and slower to be adopted, especially in poorer and more remote communities such as those found in much of Vermont. Beekeeper J. E. Crane of Bridport described what it was like to keep bees in Vermont from 1850–1879:

> Hives for the most part were made of boards of uneven widths, or straw, or sometimes of a section of a hollow log. The size or capacity of these hives varied from half a bushel to two bushels or more [15-60 liters; a 10-frame Langstroth brood box holds 40 liters].

Everyone so far as I remember had a bee-house—an open shed 12 or 15 feet long by 4 or 5 feet wide, open on the south side and boarded up on the north side and also the ends [1 foot = 0.3 m]. There were two shelves, one near the ground and the other about 3 feet above on which the hives were set. Sometimes, setting up at one end of the house, there was the section of the trunk of a tree 6 or 8 feet long that had been brought in from the woods with a runaway swarm in it. . . . For the most part, honey was taken in the fall by killing the bees with sulphur fumes. The best combs were cut out for the table and the dark combs were put through a strainer by the good housewife. (Crane 1999 p. 308)

The killing off of some hives to harvest their honey was in keeping with the common practice of butchering livestock at the end of the season to provide food for the table and only keeping breeding stock through the winter. Growing up on farms on the New England frontier, settlers governed themselves, bartered for necessities, and relied on each other for help and protection. Early settlers learned the agrarian values of hard work, community involvement, and participatory democracy. (Mello 2014) Since those early times, Vermonters have developed a strong sense of community, a Yankee spirit—to do it your own way, and value the landscape for both farms and forests.

Despite the variety of patented hive designs, by the end of the Civil War it was the Langstroth hive that was the pre-eminent means for raising bees and producing honey across the country. And it is to that industrialization of beekeeping in Vermont we will next turn.

FIGURE 17: PHOTO SOURCE: HISTORIC PHOTOS OF VERMONT BY GINGER GELLMAN,
PUBLISHED BY TURNER PUBLISHING CO., NASHVILLE, TENNESEE (2009).

CHAPTER 2

# *Technological and Industrial Advancement*

*No government bonds, bank or railroad stock, no estates, either real or personal, no dairying or sheep husbandry, no stock raising, be it native, Alderney, Ayrshire or Durham, will for the labor bestowed and capital invested, give such rich returns in money.*

—O. C. WAIT

AUGUSTIN E. MANUM WAS BORN in Waitsfield, Vermont in 1839. In his teens he apprenticed in the harness trade and started his own harness business in 1857. In the fall of 1863, Manum returned to Vermont after his momentous service in the Civil War. The twenty-four-year-old from Bristol had fought at Gettysburg with Company G, 14th Vermont Regiment, which helped to break Pickett's Charge on the climactic third day of the battle. Soldiers on either side of A.E. Manum were killed, but he suffered only minor wounds. His nine-month enlistment now up, Manum headed home to his harness business. (Dearborn 2016, pp. 1G-4G)

Seven years later, a friend lent Manum a copy of Moses Quinby's *Mysteries of Bee-Keeping Explained*, and that changed Manum's life. Quinby was possibly the most famous beekeeper in the United States at the time. An inventor, writer, and owner of perhaps 1,000 hives in upstate New York during the 1870s and 1880s, Quinby was arguably the first American to make his living entirely from beekeeping. He is credited with inventing one of the first bee smokers and building a centrifugal extractor for removing honey from combs. Quinby also worked on methods for treating American foulbrood.

Manum purchased four colonies of bees and began the serious study of apiculture. In four years, he had over 150 hives. Once his beekeeping became prosperous, he sold the harness business and went into beekeeping full time. By 1881, Manum had 300 colonies and was selling "apiarist's supplies" out of his shop in Bristol including his hive design dubbed the "Bristol Chaff Hive" which he promoted through the publication of *Bristol Hive*, his contribution to beekeeping literature in 1879. While he was one of thirty people listed as "Apiarists" in the 1881-82 Addison County Gazetteer, only one other person was also selling beekeeping supplies in the county at the time, one Reuben Damon of East Middlebury. (Child 1882) Manum sold his beekeeping supply business to Drake and Smith Company in 1884. (Dearborn 2016) This freed him up to focus on his bees and develop his honey business and by 1890, Manum had grown his operation to over 700 colonies in eight yards spread around Addison County. (Root 1890 p.301)

FIGURE I: **A. E. Manum.** SOURCE: *ROOT* 1908

According to one report:

> He always winters his bees out of doors, packed in the 'Bristol' chaff hive. For the eight years [from 1880-87] his average loss in wintering . . . was only 3½ percent. He uses exclusively a frame of 12¾ x 10 inches, outside measure, which he considers the best for practical purposes in his apiaries. His hive, the "Bristol" is almost entirely his own invention . . . In 1885, his production was 44,000 pounds of comb honey, an average of 93¼ pounds per colony, all made in twelve days from basswood. . . (Root 1890 pp.331-332)

Manum pioneered the use of out-yards to house additional bees when his home yard was overstocked, and was also one of the earliest adopters of the use of scale hives. "Mr. Manum keeps a hive on scales in each yard; and every time he visits one he consults the scales. If they indicate an increase of several pounds, he knows then that the bees in this apiary need more room, and they are also liable to swarm; but if they indicate a loss of several pounds, he infers that the whole yard is losing likewise, and that some colonies may need to be fed." (Root 1908, pp. 318-319)

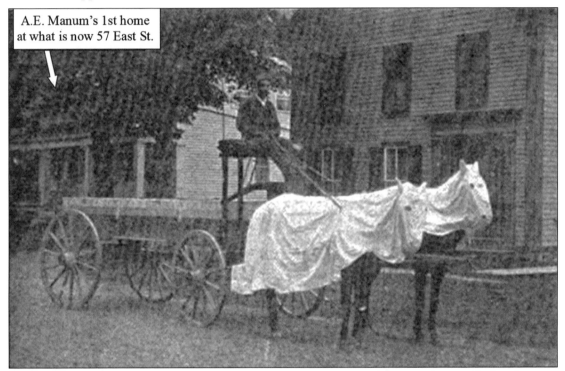

A.E. Manum's 1st home at what is now 57 East St.

FIGURE 2: **To protect his horses from stings, Manum covered them with specially fitted sheets.** SOURCE: DEARBORN 2016

Meanwhile, across the county, James E. Crane of Bridport, who had learned the art of beekeeping from his father B.W. Crane, was running his own prominent and successful honey business. The 1905 edition of *The ABC of Bee Culture* reads:

J.E. Crane was born May 15, 1840 on a farm in the town of Bridport, Vermont. At twenty-five Mr. Crane commenced the study of medicine, but soon felt it necessary to give it up for the free open-air life of the farm.

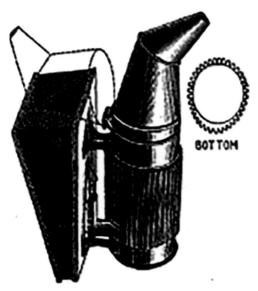

BOTTOM

FIGURE 3: **The Crane Smoker.**
SOURCE: ROOT 1899

(He). . . at once bought one or two hives of bees, hoping to be able to pay for the necessary labor of carrying on a farm. His brother went into company with him. The first year proved a complete failure; but the next year they secured from six or seven hives, hundreds of pounds of comb honey. From this time Mr. Crane's success with bees has been constant, varying with the seasons. He increased his stock until he had nearly 700 hives of his own. He believes it safe to say that he has produced much more honey than any other person in New England. He has produced comb honey almost entirely, leaving to others the simpler method of extracting. (Root 1905)

Among other things, Crane took a stab at improving the bellows smoker that Quinby initiated. Known as the Crane Smoker, it featured a check-valve design that prevented smoke from passing back into the bellows. It was noted that the check-valve would have to be kept free of creosote build-up in order to keep it functional. (Root 1899)

## THE GOLDEN ERA: A LAND OF MILK AND HONEY

The years from 1850 to 1890 were the golden era of technological advancement in beekeeping. Within 10 years of Reverend Lorenzo Langstroth's patenting of a removable frame hive in 1852, there were dozens of imitators who copied the principles he espoused. Meanwhile, former Austrian army officer Franz Hruschka invented the mechanical rotary extractor around 1865, a means of using centrifugal force to remove honey from combs so that the combs could be reused rather than destroyed. This extractor was widely copied and improved upon. Elsewhere, a process to manufacture sheets of wax foundation for comb building was developed in Austria. The bee smoker developed by Quinby was also further developed. In addition, hive tools for manipulating and cleaning hive components, queen excluders for keeping brood out of the honey combs to be harvested, bee escapes for separating the bees from their honey to facilitate honey harvesting, bee veils to protect the beekeeper and improved swarm catching devices all came into common use. These technological advancements helped to form the basis of what was to become a new agricultural industry.

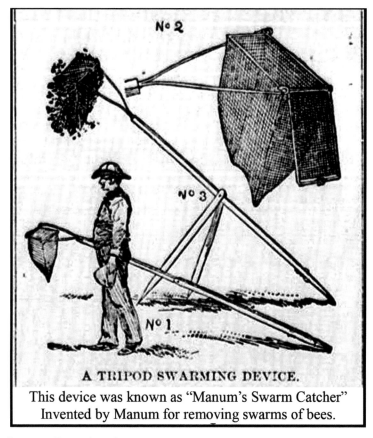

A TRIPOD SWARMING DEVICE.
This device was known as "Manum's Swarm Catcher"
Invented by Manum for removing swarms of bees.

FIGURE 4: SOURCE: *ROOT* (1899) PG. 286

The introduction of Italian, then Carniolan and other races of bees like Cyprian, Palestinian, and Caucasian greatly improved the temperament and productivity of managed honey bees. By the end of the century, few people were still using the original "black bee" from Germany. In 1867 issues of the *American Bee Journal*, C.B. Biglow and K.P. Kidder of Vermont were listed as selling Italian queens which were widely considered to be a much more docile and gentle bee. (Pellett 1938 p.96)

FIGURE 5: **Mrs. R. H. Holmes of Shoreham, Vermont, created a veil that was featured in the 1899 edition of *ABC of Bee Culture*. Of the veil, the authors state "... it is simply a straw hat with a broad rim, the veil being made of mosquito bar, and the facing of brussels net. A strip of cloth lines the lower edge of the veil, and is made just large enough to fit snugly around the shoulders. A couple cloth straps hitched to buttons pass under the arm-pits, and button on behind. Of the veils for women ... this one seems to me to be more desirable."**
SOURCE: *ROOT* 1899, PGS. 304-305.

## AGRICULTURAL TRANSFORMATION

As Vermont was joining the national beekeeping revolution, another agricultural transformation was underway in the state. For forty years before the Civil War (1820–1860), Vermont's dominant agricultural activity was sheep raising. At one point, Vermont had over 1.5 million sheep. But with the opening of the Western lands after the Civil War (1865), it was far cheaper to raise sheep in Montana, Idaho, and Nevada than in New England. This competition, combined with the changes in the country's tariffs and potential inbreeding issues, caused Vermont sheep numbers to drop precipitously over the next several decades.

FIGURE 6: **A.E. Manum's home "side-hill" apiary in Bristol, Vermont, is reported to have held about 100 colonies and produced an average of around 100 pounds of honey per hive.** SOURCE: *ROOT* 1908

Enter dairying. Vermont had the right climate and landscape for dairy cows, which began to replace sheep with their first products of milk, cheese, and butter. By 1880, there were an estimated 35,000 farms in Vermont with a mix of sheep and dairy being dominant. Dairy was on the increase during the 1880s in large part due to the arrival of refrigerated railroad cars, Vermont milk became a large segment of Boston's northern milk shed.

In the wake of sheep farming's decline, Vermont's dairy revolution helped maintain the agricultural paradise of the Champlain Valley. The cattle required forage, hay, clover, and alsike for feed. That same hay provided wonderful forage for honey bees, which beekeepers like Manum sought. Soon enough, beekeepers and farmers (and often they were one and the same) recognized the value of bees for fertilizing (pollinating) fruit trees. The Lake Champlain Valley, and especially Addison County, would literally become a land of milk and honey.

By the 1950s there were still over 10,000 farms in Vermont. The state was able to accommodate so many farms because most were small, family operations with an average herd size around twenty-five dairy cows. Unfortunately by 1963, one-third of those farms had closed. The number was cut again by nearly two-thirds by 1970. And today, the state is home to less than 1,000 dairy farms—barely 10 percent of the total it had in 1953 and less than 3 percent it boasted in 1880. Due to the forage created by farmers growing hay, the success of beekeepers in Vermont has roughly mirrored the success of its herbivore farmers.

To show how quickly and widely beekeeping had advanced during the hay-day of the state's sheep farming, here are some excerpts from a speech in 1872 addressed to the first meeting of the Vermont State Board of Agriculture, Manufactures and Mining in St. Albans. As one can see, such speeches often became a mixture of description and exhortation.

O.C. Wait of Georgia, Vermont suggests in his presentation "Advantages of Bee-keeping" that: "Fear is unnecessary, for even the most timid might learn to handle bees with impunity; that this employment invariably creates a deeper interest in nature than any other department in agriculture . . . Ten good colonies in the best of the season will not only earn more than the daily wages of ten good farm laborers, but they will work for nothing and board themselves. Although honey is sold much higher than sugar, it really costs much less." In his speech, Wait showed a remarkable understanding of the work of the queen, the sequence of jobs followed by the worker bees, and their defense of the colony. He did wax poetic in his anthropomorphism:

> In their civil governments there are no intriguing politicians, no Indian agents and no hangers-on around the public treasury. All alike willingly perform their duties, always working if there is work to do, and cheerfully enjoying in common the benefits. In their armies there are no skedaddlers, no jealousies, no government contractors, and certainly no cowards. But alas! Through some unholy influence or fiendish agency, they, having imbibed one human trait, occasionally depart from the path of rectitude, and, conscious of their own strength and the weakness of an adjoining colony, assume the offensive, marshal their hosts, and conquer them by slaying thousands of their own kind, in which case they take all the accumulated stores. (Poland 1872, pp. 253-265)

He continued his talk on the economic benefits of keeping bees:

It is believed by many that bees injure fruit and grain in gathering honey from the flowers . . . But a little careful investigation on the part of the inquirer would serve to banish this superstition. . . on the contrary, we believe that every fruit-grower or even farmer should keep a few colonies for the more perfect fertilization of fruit and grain. No government bonds, bank or railroad stock, no estates, either real or personal, no dairying or sheep husbandry, no stock raising, be it native, Alderney, Ayrshire or Durham, will for the labor bestowed and capital invested, give such rich returns in money. (Poland 1872, pp 253-265)

With that kind of encouragement from the pulpit and the farm down the road, beekeeping in Vermont rose steadily during the late 1880s.

In a speech he gave in 1874, J.E. Crane urged beekeepers to take advantage of the huge waste of honey out there. He noted a truth that would continue into the 21st century, that Vermont and the Champlain Valley in particular, is one of the finest places to keep bees:

Few portions of our country, I believe, are more inviting to the apiarian than our own State . . . the wants of the bees are met from early spring to late in autumn . . .

[That honey] may be secured by energetic, wide-awake, intelligent beekeepers in numbers sufficient that there shall be at least one in every school district in our state. Of course, such will use movable comb hives, the honey extractor, Italian bees, etc . . . Before the harvest commences, the beekeeper should decide whether he will increase his stocks or take all the profits in surplus honey. If he desires to increase his stock, it can be done most satisfactorily by making artificial swarms. (Crane 1874, pp.695-704)

## COMB HONEY ERA

During the 1870s and 1880s, Manum and Crane were the largest beekeepers in Vermont, with each having more than 600 hives. It was also during this era when reports of the adulteration of liquid extracted honey gave rise to increased demand for honey in the comb, which was seen as more authentic and unadulterated.[1] This led to the Comb Honey Era, the period from 1876 to 1910 when

---

1 It was beekeepers fighting against honey adulteration that ultimately led Congress to pass the pure food law in 1906, (Pellett 1938, pp. 212-213) and the subsequent renewal of confidence in extracted honey that led to the decline in the popularity of comb honey.

the majority of all honey produced in America was sold as sections of comb. (Pellett 1938 p.18)

As a result, demand grew for small wooden boxes (one piece sections) to service the burgeoning comb honey industry. Having a large stand of poplars near his home, Manum set up a business making poplar comb honey sections. He bought a mill relying upon abundant water power from the New Haven River to run the cutting and planing machinery he built. Manum sold his comb honey in basswood section boxes across the United States and even in Europe.

FIGURE 7: **J.E. Crane cleaning a "clamp" (what today we would call a super) of wooden comb honey sections.** PHOTO COURTESY OF THE TOMPKINS FAMILY

## ROKEBY

While most of Vermont's documented beekeepers from the nineteenth century are a result of those that wrote beekeeping books—primarily as a way to promote and sell their patented hive designs—or ran large scale commercial operations, the majority of the beekeepers in Vermont kept bees on a smaller scale, most often as part of a working farm. While some would produce excess to sell or barter with, most simply harvested honey for home use. One example of beekeeping as part of a working farm is the Robinson family.

Thomas and Jemima Robinson were Quakers that moved from Newport, Rhode Island to Vermont in 1792. Once they arrived in the newly formed state, they staked their claim in Ferrisburgh, purchasing land that would become known as Rokeby. In 1810, Thomas purchased some of the first Merino sheep to be imported into the state and the Robinson's went on to become one of the region's largest sheep farmers.

Rowland Thomas Robinson was born at Rokeby in 1796 and while he helped with the farm, he found his true calling as an abolitionist. He and his wife, Rachel, were outspoken opponents of slavery, worked actively in anti-slavery societies, boycotted slave-made goods, and sheltered dozens of refugees from slavery. Rokeby's fame as a stop on the Underground Railroad is what prompted the formation of the Rokeby museum that occupies the Robinson family farm to this day.

Rachel and R. T. Robinson had four children, and it was the youngest Rowland Evans Robinson who left us wonderful documentation that highlighted bees on the farm.

FIGURE 8: **Rowland Evans Robinson.** PHOTO COURTESY OF THE ROKEBY MUSEUM, FERRISBURGH, VERMONT

R. E. Robinson tended to the farm with his older brother George. It was during this time, in the late 1840s, that the sheep industry began to falter. According to Robert Balivet, this was due to three primary factors: the lowering and ultimate loss of protective tariffs on imported wool, competition from western states and problems with sheep inbreeding. (Balivet 1965) When the bottom fell out of the wool market, the brothers diversified their operation and made the transition away from sheep to primarily dairy and pork production. The farm's transition, took place between 1850 and 1880, and it was in 1849 that the Robinsons planted an apple orchard. It was likely the recognition of the value of bees for pollinating fruit trees, which prompted the Robinsons to add bees to their farming operation. At the time it was common to procure bees through the capture of swarms and the hunting of feral colonies. R.E. Robinson was undoubtedly an avid bee hunter judging from the numerous drawings he created of bee hunting and the bee-lining box that he left behind and is on display at the Rokeby museum.

FIGURE 9: **Bee-lining box believed to be built and used by Rowland Evans Robinson.**

FIGURE 10 & 11: **Bee-lining sketches by R.E. Robinson.** USED WITH PERMISSION OF ROKEBY MUSEUM, FERRISBURGH, VERMONT

It does not appear that the Robinsons kept many hives and most of the honey that they did produce probably was consumed on the farm. Federal Census figures for the years between 1850 and 1880 only indicate one year where honey production was recorded at Rokeby, and that is 100 pounds in 1860.

From 1850–1889, Rowland Evans Robinson used his early training as an illustrator to create numerous scenes of beekeeping on the farm. (See Figures 10 and 11 and Chapter 1 frontispiece illustration.)

## THE FOUNDING OF AN ASSOCIATION

On March 10, 1875, several dozen of Addison County's established beekeepers came together in the offices of Dr. Henry Kingsley of Middlebury, to "organize and aid in extending the discoveries and improvements in the methods of managing bees and securing honey that in the hands of a few has been such a wonderful success."

A constitution was drawn up and signed by thirty-three founding members "to promote the interest of bee culture."(Poland 1878 pp. 287-288) The Addison County Bee Keepers Association was to meet annually and the dues were twenty-five cents. Mimicking the newly formed (1871) national organization, the North American Beekeepers Society, association dues applied to everyone "except ladies who shall be admitted free." (Pellett 1938, p.115) Also, in words that arguably should have been in *Robert's Rules of Parliamentary Procedure*, Article 6 of their constitution noted that "No member shall be entitled to the floor more than three minutes in the discussion of any motion, resolution or petition without the consent of the Association." (Poland, 1878, p. 287) The first officers of the newly formed Association included the following people:

- **President:** Dr. F. Bond, Cornwall
- **Vice Presidents:**
  - A.E. Manum, Bristol
  - B.W. Crane, Bridport
  - A.C. Hooker, Middlebury
- **Secretary:** E.A. Sturdevant, Middlebury
- **Treasurer:** A.H. Hubbard, Whiting

FIGURE 12: **Members of the Vermont Beekeepers Association at the residence of V.V. Blackmer, Orwell, VT.** SOURCE: *ROOT* 1895

FIGURE 13: **A.E. Manum's apiary in winter.**  SOURCE: ROOT 1895

One interesting feature of the early programs of the new association was the Question Box. Members placed slips of paper with written questions that were to be discussed into this box. Another common practice was the reading by some member of papers on some aspect of beekeeping.

In January 1879, the name of the association was changed to the Champlain Valley Bee Keepers Association to take into account the increasing honey harvests that stretched from the Grand Isle and Franklin Counties down to Rutland County.

Some of the larger apiaries in 1884 were the following:
- H.B. Isham, Weybridge: 108 colonies
- A.E. Manum, Bristol: 520 colonies
- J.E. Crane, Middlebury: 500 colonies
- H.L. Leonard, Duxbury: 100 colonies

At a Middlebury meeting of the Champlain Valley Bee Keepers Association held in 1884, J. E. Crane, as if in answer to O.C. Wait, gave a quick summary of beekeeping in general—of which Vermont was by then so much a part:

As showing how its importance had increased, he stated that in 1862 the value of honey produced in the U.S. was $2,000,000, and in 1882 it was

$32,000,000. He contrasted the old style of hives and method of handling bees with the present, and exhibited a little book, which was the first book on beekeeping published in the United States. Now there are a dozen or more journals devoted to this interest. About 1850 the moveable frame hive was invented. It had been the most valuable addition to the facilities of the bee-keeper ever produced, as it gives the keeper entire control of the bees. In 1860, Mr. Parsons of Flushing, L.I. imported the first Italian bees, which have proved very valuable. The Cyprian bee, the Egyptian bee and the Palestine bee have all been tried, but in the speaker's opinion, none of them was as good as the Italian. In 1867, the honey extractor was brought out. By its use the honey is extracted and the comb returned to the hive. This has largely increased the honey product, as it costs the bees as much labor to make the comb as to make the honey. . .

Bees can be handled perfectly by smoke so there is no danger from stings. Among the appliances of the apiary are bee cages for sending queens to a distance, and wax extractors which do away with all the disagreeable features of making wax by the old methods. Bee-keepers have long looked for a hive that would not swarm, but as yet no one has ever succeeded in planning such a hive. (Crane 1884)

## THE VERMONT BEEKEEPERS ASSOCIATION IS BORN

At the twelfth annual meeting of the Champlain Valley Bee Keepers Association held in the basement of the Town Hall in Middlebury on January 21, 1886, members voted to change the organization's name again, to Vermont Bee Keepers Association[2]. Prizes were awarded for best bee hive, honey boxes, and shipping crates, extracted honey, and comb honey. (Tuttle & Co. 1895 p. 45)

From these early days of Vermont beekeeping, there were many people, mostly farmers, who took up the craft on their own, without joining the Association. By definition, there are no numbers for this cohort, but it was likely two-thirds to three-quarters of all Vermont's beekeepers. It is probable that the craft spread through informal mentoring and sharing beyond the Champlain Valley, but documentation for this is sparse.

---

2 The spelling would later be changed to Vermont Beekeepers Association.

# THE STATE UNIVERSITY GETS INVOLVED

In 1878, the Vermont legislature established a State Board of Agriculture " . . . for the improvement and the general interests of husbandry and the promotion of agricultural education throughout the State."[3]

In 1886, the legislature established a State Agricultural Experimental Station at the University of Vermont and State Agricultural College in Burlington. The station's farm was located several miles south of the university (at what is now the corner of Swift and Spear Streets in South Burlington).

In 1892 the Vermont Beekeepers Association (VBA) petitioned the Experimental Station to begin practical experiments with bees. Sometime in the 1890s, a "bee house" was constructed with hives donated by members of the VBA at the university farm some three and a half miles south of the main campus. The Apiary House had workspace for twenty-four hives with an extractor, honey knives, brood boxes, observation hives, queen nursery, etc. (Watchman & Journal Press, 1884)

That year, 15 donated colonies were taken into the winter with a variety of insulation, both indoors and outside.

Various experiments were conducted at the Experimental Station over the next decade. For example, those run in 1895 included the following:

- The relative value of different frames types, for building up in the spring and for production of honey. No perceptible difference was noted.

- Stimulative spring feeding—this was determined to be "positively injurious" and not "allowed until enough young bees have hatched to maintain the heat of the colony."

- Will bees use bits and scraps of wax in comb and construction during the honey flow? Yes, reported Crane. The bees "pounced" upon the wax and 36-48 hours later the cappings were mottled, being white and yellow.

- Experimenters tested whether swarming could be prevented by removing all drones and drone brood from the hive every ten days. The bees still swarmed.

---

3 Beekeeping continues to be one of the more economically accessible agricultural pursuits to this day since a beekeeper does not have to own land to keep bees, as long as permission to place hives on another's property is granted by the owner.

A report stated that colonies wintered indoors were in better shape than those wintered outside on summer stands. The VBA committee to the Experimental Station observed:

> A word in conclusion on spraying. The horticulturalist, mindful of the necessity of the proper fertilization of his fruit blossoms, should consult his own interests as well as those of the bee keeper, by refraining from spraying his trees during their bloom. It is moreover unnecessary to spray at this time, since it has been shown that the proper season for spraying is immediately after the petals fall. (Lowery 1896, pp. 146-148)

Further experiments in 1898 concluded the following:

- There was no conclusive improvement in production using double brood chambers.
- Leaving queens undisturbed during honey flow, rather than removing her, gave forty percent more honey.
- Feeding back extracted honey at the end of the season gave no tangible increase in overall production. (Peck 1898, pp. 308-9)

## THE 1892–1896 VBA MEETINGS

At the 1892 meeting of the VBA, dues were increased to 50 cents per year and new races of bees were discussed. Also discussed during the meeting were queen excluders. C.J. Lowery and several others favored their use in the production of extracted honey. W.G. Larrabee reported that he was selling extracted honey in 60-pound cans for large shipments and 5-pound pails for retail sales. He said there was more profit in producing comb honey. Other topics discussed were problems with shipping, careless handling of honey by railroad workers and shippers, overstocking, and ventilation for wintering.

Professor L.R. Jones of UVM spoke on the potential danger to bees of the practice of spraying potatoes with "poisonous mixtures." Following his talk, the VBA passed the following resolution: "Resolved that we as beekeepers apprehend danger from the addition of sugar to poisons used in spraying potatoes." Members reported that the past season had been a poor one. Porter bee escapes were discussed and many thought they were the best yet put on the market.

In 1894 at the Agricultural Institute in Pawlet, Crane presented a paper on bees and fruit. After noting the well-established principle of the benefits of cross-fertilization, including references to Charles Darwin, he quotes other sources across the country that indicated "cross-fertilization was carried on often and most efficiently by honey bees." Crane quoted the Ontario Bee Keepers

Association as lobbying the provincial government to "ban spraying while trees are in bloom, as the bees were being poisoned in various places, and the spraying at such a time was unnecessary. . . as well as injurious to the bees . . . Thus we see that our horticulturalists and farmers alike, with the apiarist, are dependent for the best prosperity on the presence and well-being of the bees. They should realize this fact, and should demand that our legislators not only become informed, but act accordingly."(Crane 1894, p. 16-25)

A resolution against the proposed lowering of the tariff on honey was passed and sent to Vermont's Congressional delegation.

Reports from VBA members present showed an increase from 1,883 colonies (spring count) to 2,291 (fall count) with a honey crop of 57,863 pounds of comb and 1,550 pounds of extracted honey. (This averaged 25 pounds per colony.) It was thought this 58,000 pounds was less than one-half the state's total production.[4] (Crane 1894, p. 16-25)

In the 1895 meeting, the VBA discussed "how to raise queens in upper stories and the best time to raise good ones" and "how to clean wax and make foundation." "Solar wax extractors" were another topic. H.H. Burge spoke of his house apiary, which contained fifty-two colonies and cost $50 to build. (Lowery 1896)

Minutes from the 1896 meeting in Burlington show a discussion about the size of hive best for Vermont. A. Everest of Vergennes advocated for a hive with 10 frames and 14 x 8 ½ inches with a long entrance on the side. W. I. Leonard of Brandon preferred a medium-sized hive with 10 frames and 10 x 13 inches. Lowery of Jericho used a hive for nine or twelve frames and 11 ¼ inches square.

Further discussions compared comb honey from three different sources, the comparative cost of comb and extracted honey, and honey plants and spraying. Members reported a light honey crop, averaging only nineteen pounds per colony, and very little increase in colonies into the fall.

## THE 1897–1910 VBA MEETINGS

Bee Association meetings had evolved into an amalgam of beekeeping educational opportunities, camaraderie, and a way to air issues and challenges facing the beekeeping community.

For example, at the VBA meeting in 1897 a resolution passed approving a legislative act making it illegal to spray fruit trees while in bloom. Another resolution was passed, asking railroad officials to "notify their employees to handle comb honey as carefully as they would eggs." Since almost all honey sold out

---

4 According to the US Department of Agriculture statistics, in 1889, Vermont produced 379,000 pounds of both comb and extracted honey!

FIGURE 14: **While comb honey was the norm in the late 19th and early 20th century, today is it a seasonal item produced in limited amounts by a small subset of beekeeepers and the majority of all honey produced is in the extracted form.** PHOTO CREDIT: AMY CAREY

of state was in comb form, the caution was well-founded. A discussion topic that did not result in a consensus and action was, "Will it pay to place our comb honey in warm storage in seasons of plenty to prevent over-supplying the market?" Honey production reported by members amounted to 44,600 pounds of comb and 4,600 pounds of extracted honey from 912 colonies (spring count). This was an average production of forty-nine pounds of comb and five pounds of extracted honey per colony.

At an Agricultural Institute in Grand Isle in 1898, Thaddeus L. Kinney Jr. sought to calm prospective practitioners and reassure his audience of the simple pleasures and profits of beekeeping: "Most people seem to have a prejudice against the honey bee. Farmers who ought to grow all the honey they need for their own use actually buy it at the store. Some are so frightened they run before they are even stung . . . A plain unpatented frame hive is the best for a farmer . . . [e]quipped with a wire screen veil, thin gloves with wraps around the wrists and a good smoker, one is prepared not for battle but for good work." (Kinney 1898, pp. 38-39)

According to meeting minutes, the 1898 VBA meeting returned to Burlington. After an opening prayer, the secretary reported a balance of $5 in the treasury. R. H. Holmes spoke on "The Comparative Value of Italian and Black Races of Bees." He observed that few of the original black bees remained in the state. "The large majority were already Italians and hybrids. The Italians were deemed preferable because they gathered honey faster; they were better at defending their comb from wax moths; they defended their stores better; and they flew further for honey." (Holmes 1898, pp. 38-39)

In his talk on spring management, Crane predicted great advances in breeding desirable characteristics in bees and breeding out undesirable ones. He thought that the productiveness of bees could be doubled through selective breeding.[5]

The 1899 VBA meeting was held in Middlebury, and the association's finances showed a balance of $11.62. Professor George Perkins, entomologist at the Experimental Station, lectured on the relationship between some other insects and bees.

Several orchardist beekeepers commented on spraying apple trees and the resulting yield of fruit. They saw little increase in fruit from spraying. Mr. H.L. Leonard spoke of travel stain on comb honey. (Burlington Free Press Association 1899)

Production of honey increased, with 1,779 colonies producing 80,000 pounds of comb and 6,000 pounds of extracted honey, an average over forty-eight pounds per colony. Even though the extractor had been in use for over thirty years, the statistics on VBA production shows a wide disparity still between the production of the two forms of honey. Only seven percent was in extracted form.

According to bee historian Frank Pellett, there were several reasons. One was the readiness of granulation of the liquid variety. A second problem was that some beekeepers, in their enthusiasm for the amount of honey they could extract, pushed the process and left too much moisture in the honey which caused fermentation. Another and larger issue was that liquid honey was prone to adulteration. (Pellett 1938 Ch. XXV) For a score of years, Vermont had a law against the adulteration of maple syrup and honey and a possible fine of "not more than two hundred dollars nor less than fifty dollars for each offense," with one-half of such fine going to the complainant. (Tuttle Company 1895) The

---

5 This prediction would prove prophetic as bees would not only eventually be bred to be gentle and more productive, they have also been bred to resist diseases and pests.

Crane honey company would eventually sell both forms. (Pellett 1938 p. 211) But this would change significantly in the decade of World War I.

According to Everett Oertel, between 1875 and 1915, approximately one-third of the honey produced in New England was section honey. This declined rapidly after World War I. The product was fragile and difficult to ship, the shelf life was short, and combs were likely to leak or granulate. Production of section honey required a heavy nectar flow of several weeks' duration and a great deal of hand labor for cleaning, weighing, and grading. In addition, beekeepers were unable to provide the intensive colony management needed in out yards miles from their homes. The Pure Food Law of 1906 gave buyers more confidence in the purity of extracted honey, thereby increasing demand for it. (Oertel 1980, p. 71)

## CONTINUING EDUCATION

One interesting question is how did the average beekeeper learn their craft? As Crane recounted in one of the last of his numerous articles in various leading bee journals like *Gleanings in Bee Culture*[6] and the *American Bee Journal*:

> We had no bee books or bee journals in those days and our knowledge of bees was very limited. Some enterprising persons made some changes in their hives, had them patented and sold farm rights. Very few of them were any better, if as good as, a plain box hive.
>
> There were few large apiaries in those days, but many small ones. When farmers got together, they would discuss the mysteries and wonders of their bees from the "great king bee" to the drones that were supposed to lay eggs. (Crane 1931, Pgs. 427-429)

All indications are that while a few folks learned from reading books and journals, most learned from lectures and presentations given at association meetings. However, networking with other beekeepers (at meetings or in the neighborhood) appears to be one of the primary ways new beekeepers learned. Some also learned from traditional apprenticeships and from mentors, friends, and family . . . or, as R.H. Holmes puts it, "an occasional visit to some practical apiarist." And of course, folks learned from trial and error and by their own direct observation. Basically, they learned the same way we do today, only

---

6 Gleanings in Bee Culture would eventually change its name to "Bee Culture" in January 1993.

today we have greater access to books and journals and have the internet, as well as organized classes and workshops.

On January 27, 1899, Lowery spoke before the state Board of Agriculture in New Haven, Vermont. He described what can be considered a four-part matrix of skilled beekeeping, fruit, pasture forage, and cattle that made Addison County an agricultural paradise:

> Addison County is a great place for bees and honey. If we need to use brains as well as muscle in the production of grain, milk and butter, or in the production of fruit for that business, we need also proper methods along the line of bee-keeping.
> . . . Close observation and study are necessary in bee culture. A person that keeps bees should know their habits and understand the flora of his locality. If we expect the honey flow to begin June 15th, we should strive to have a large working force at the right time as it takes about 35 days from the egg before young bees go into the fields to gather honey.
> . . . Many do not understand the great good the honey-bee does in the fertilization of fruits and flowers, the fertilization of the clover blossoms especially, the white or Dutch clover, which together with the Kentucky blue grass makes our finest pastures for growing stock . . .
> It has been clearly proven by many of our leading entomologists that bees are a necessity in cross-fertilizing the blossoms of fruit crops." (Burlington Free Press Assoc. 1899, pp 68-71)

In a speech presented in Manchester on January 2, 1900, R.H. Holmes, VBA president from Shoreham, added his voice to a chorus of praise for the craft and profit from bees:

> The occupation of beekeeping and production of honey, although not a new industry, is comparatively little known by the general public. Vermont only produced a small percentage of the US total of 150 million pounds, but in quality, she stands in the front rank in regard to honey, as well as horses, dairy cows, sheep, butter or even maple syrup.
> Besides the undoubted benefit of this most wholesome and healthy sweet, another advantage is the cross fertilization of blossoms . . . it is becoming known that better fruit is obtained when the best methods of fertilization are used. Although nature has provided other agents to carry out this purpose, there is no means practically so effective as the honey bee as it visits the blossoms of all our fruits from the tiny bloom of the raspberry to that of the mammoth squash that adorns the table of our

country fairs . . . the honey bee is the friend and not the foe of the farmer and fruit grower. (Holmes 1900)

Holmes then demolished two erroneous clichés of bee culture: first, that they "work for nothing and board themselves"; and second, that the business does not pay. One must put in the time and attention for proper management. He sought to encourage the hobbyist by stating that:

. . . the keeping of a few swarms of bees by individuals who have other sources of income and might with advantage take up the occupation as an adjunct of fruit growing, farming or even housekeeping, for some women have found the keeping of a few swarms of bees quite as profitable and much easier than rambling over the hillsides to keep the turkeys out of their neighbors' grain field or the young chicks out of the wet grass. It is true that bees have the faculty and sometimes will sting, but the danger from this sources (sic) is often magnified beyond necessity or actual facts. The beginner should protect the face and hands while manipulating the bees and the most timid can train themselves to deliberate and careful movement and gather interest and enjoyment in the work . . .

Holmes' comments may be understood as start small with a few hives, or swarms, as they were often called.

An occasional visit to some practical apiarist will aid materially to success... Study the habits and requirements of the bees. Observe the flora of your vicinity. Find out where the bees get the most honey and from which source and how long it continues . . .
Swarms should be kept strong in numbers and in normal conditions. How to have a hive full of bees and ready for action is as important as that a general of the army have his men in good health and spirits and under good discipline when the enemy approaches . . .
The honey season in Vermont is short at the best and the time for procuring surplus honey is sometimes limited to a few days, and in no occupation is the old maxim more true that our dish should be right side up when it rains porridge.
. . . I have already said enough to convince you that bee keeping is no child's play; that it requires skillful labor and good judgment . . . But many farmers have added this branch to their other interests and found it the most profitable of any for the amount of labor and expense involved. Many who have not strength to grapple with the heavier farm labor have taken up this

work and found a healthful and pleasurable occupation with remuneration sufficient to induce them to continue the business for the profits alone . . .

The old saying holds true, 'that any business is good business, provided that it is well followed.' (Holmes 1900)

## A THESIS ON BEEKEEPING IN VERMONT

While attending UVM in 1910, Henry Ward Beecher wrote a senior thesis on beekeeping in the state. Based upon a mailed survey (there was no state apiarist at the time), Beecher concluded that Addison County produced nearly as much honey as all other counties together. J.E. Crane of Middlebury with 635 hives was the ". . . king of beekeepers in Vermont, and possibly of New England." (Beecher 1910)

Beecher noted that beekeeping was a long-standing component of Vermont agriculture, with some beekeepers practicing the craft for more than 50 years.

### Collective Data of all Beekeepers Reporting:

| DATA | NUMBER |
|---|---|
| TOTAL NUMBER OF BEEKEEPERS REPORTING | 70 |
| AVERAGE NUMBER OF YEARS IN BUSINESS | 23 |
| NUMBER OF COLONIES REPORTED | 4,447 |
| AVERAGE NUMBER OF COLONIES PER PERSON | 64 |
| AVERAGE YIELD PER COLONY OF 38 PERSONS REPORTING | 37 LBS. |

SOURCE: BEECHER 1910

### Large Commercial Beekeepers in Vermont—1910:

| NAME | IN BUSINESS SINCE | NUMBER OF COLONIES |
|---|---|---|
| J.E. CRANE, MIDDLEBURY | 1866 | 635 |
| W.G. LARRABEE, SHOREHAM | 1890 | 120 |
| R.H. HOLMES, SHOREHAM | 1885 | 195 |
| S. PRESTON, VERGENNES | 1885 | 220 |
| L.O. THOMPSON, WEYBRIDGE | 1860 | 450 |
| H.J. MANCHESTER, MIDDLEBURY | 1860 | 150 |

SOURCE: BEECHER 1910

In 1910, by Beecher's count, Addison County had three times as many colonies as all of Vermont's other counties put together: 3,285 versus 1,125.

## ROLLIN FORBES

The most well documented example we have of a beekeeper who kept bees as so many people did back then, as part of a working farm, is Rollin Forbes of St. George, Vermont. Forbes kept a farm diary, copies of which are part of the Special Collections Department at Middlebury College. The diaries cover most of the years from 1895–1940.

In the fall of 2010, Danielle Meiners documented Forbes' success one season in a paper on the agricultural history of St. George:

> ... the season is over and the honey all sold. I got 2,200 one-pound sections filled and about 200 pounds of extracted honey. I began the season with 45 colonies, rather weak. I had 22 natural swarms and one that came to me and one that I took out of a tree and put thim (sic) in a hive all ready for housekeeping. I got 65 lbs. of nice white honey out of the tree, gathered this season, and have 69 colonies in the cellar with sealed covers. I raised the back end of the hive up a little that gives thim (sic) plenty of ventilation and a good chance to keep the (entrance) clean. The rest are outside in mannour (sic) hives packed with planed shavins and sawdust mixed. I make all of my hives and crates. I made some 10 frame hives but I think the 8 frame hive is large enough for my locality if they have plenty of surplus room and by raising the hive a little from the bottom board I am not bothered much with swarming. Today Jan 3rd bees are having a good fly, the only times since November 27. (Meiners 2010)

## INSPECTION LAW COMES TO VERMONT 1910

Wax moths had long been a problem in Vermont, and there were hints of intestinal disease (nosema) causing problems for the state's beekeepers.

People also talked about a mysterious "disappearing disease." In the latter 19th century, the whole country was afflicted with a disease called American foulbrood, so named because of the rotten smell emitted in afflicted hives during the later stages of the disease. Quinby had recognized it in the 1870s. It would eventually affect colonies in every part of the globe.

American foulbrood disease (AFB) is caused by the bacterium *Paenibacillus larvae*, which exists in both a spore and vegetative stage. The disease is transmitted by the spore, and the infected brood is killed by the vegetative stage,

FIGURE 15: **Rollin Forbes and his son, Benjamin pictured in their home apiary in St. George 1894. Besides honey, the Forbes family farm produced vegetables, fruits, grains, milk, eggs, meat, maple syrup and the occasional live animal for sale primarily in the nearby communities of Burlington and Essex.** PHOTO CREDIT: CARLISLE 1976

when the spore germinates in larval guts. This is the most destructive and most contagious of the brood diseases and is the reason why apiary inspection laws were first passed . . . Spores can live in hive products (honey, pollen, wax, and propolis) for up to eighty years. (Sammataro & Avitabile)

The disease is carried from hive to hive by robbing bees, through use of old equipment, and by the use of infected honey for food.

As it destroyed more and more hives, beekeepers across the country began to urge state agricultural departments to empower inspectors to enter an apiary and force beekeepers to clean up or destroy infected hives. Around 1900, a number of states began enacting laws to allow for such inspections. (Pellett 1938, p. 191) Correspondence between two leading Vermont beekeepers shows their concern. Larrabee of Shoreham wrote to Crane to ask for help in researching other states' experience. Crane obtained the relevant Ohio statute from E.R.

Root who advised the Vermonters not to seek an appropriation, as this could slow the legislation's passage.

Larrabee also asked Crane if he could help lobby for the bill. "We have not got a (state) representative that I would care to let introduce and push this bill . . . Possibly a petition signed by the beekeepers of the state would be of assistance but the trouble would be to get such a petition in the hands of the beekeepers. [It is possible] you could reach most of them in Addison County with your auto in a day or two . . ." (Larrabee 1910)

In what must be considered warp speed for a legislature, the law was enacted 5 weeks later. It was "An Act for the Suppression of Contagious Diseases among Bees."

In part, it read:

Section 1. The commissioner of agriculture shall, by virtue of his office, be inspector of apiaries, and he is hereby authorized to appoint one or more assistants, as needed, who shall be practical bee-keepers, to carry on the inspection under his supervision.

Section 2. The inspector, or his assistant, shall, when notified in writing by the owner of an apiary or by any three tax-payers, examine all reported apiaries and others in the same locality not reported, and ascertain whether or not the diseases known as American or European foul brood or any other disease, which is infectious or contagious in its nature and injurious to honey-bees in their egg, larval, pupal or adult stages exists in such apiaries, and if satisfied of the existence of any such disease, he shall give the owners or care-takers of the diseased apiaries full instructions how to treat such cases as in the inspector's judgment seems best.

Section 3. The inspector or his assistant shall visit all diseased apiaries a second time twenty days after his first inspection, and, if need be, burn all colonies of bees that he may find not cured of such disease, and all honey and appliance which would spread the disease, *without recompense* (emphasis added) to the owner, lessee or agent thereof.

Section 4. If the owner of an apiary, honey or appliance where disease exists, shall sell, barter, give away, or move, without the consent of the inspector, any diseased bees, colonies, honey or appliances, or expose other bees to the danger of such disease, said owner shall on conviction pay a fine of not less than ten nor more than fifty dollars, or be imprisoned not less than ten days nor more than thirty days in the county jail.

Section 5. For the enforcement of the provisions of this act the state commissioner of agriculture or his duly authorized assistant shall have access, ingress and egress, to all apiaries or places where bees are kept, and any person or persons who shall resist, impede, or hinder in any way, the inspector of apiaries or his assistant in the discharge of duties under the provisions of this act, shall on conviction be liable to a fine of not less than ten nor more than fifty dollars, or imprisonment not less than ten days nor more than twenty days in the county jail. (Vermont General Assembly 1910, pp. 11-13)

And so we end this chapter, which starts with the beginnings of a possible new industry thanks to Langstroth's invention of the removable frame hive, and ends with a well-developed beekeeping industry in place by 1910. The passage of the inspection law and the state's investment in an inspection program were watershed events for Vermont beekeeping, as they were in other states that adopted similar measures.

FIGURE 16: **Mr. C. H. Carpenter of Enosburg Falls, Vermont bee inspector, early 1930s.**
PHOTO CREDIT: BILL WEATHERBEE

CHAPTER 3

# Of Foulbrood, Inspections, Switchel, and Apitherapy

*Somebody wanted to call 'em the Vermont insect. I don't want anybody calling 'em an insect. They're something much more than that. I call 'em little heavenly creatures.*

—KERMIT MAYO

IN THE SPRING OF 1911, James E. Crane of Bridport, arguably the most successful beekeeper in Vermont, took up new duties. He became the first state bee inspector with the right and duty to inspect bee hives for the presence of brood diseases and to educate the beekeeping public. Crane established a precedent that would continue until 1980: the state would contract with certain professional beekeepers to inspect all known hives in the state and report upon their condition. Reading the biennial inspector reports reveals a tone that mixes the teacher and the parent. In his first report to the Commissioner of Agriculture, Crane showed a teacher's instinct for improving—not "re-proving"—his students:

I have inspected some 92 yards, containing 1,417 hives of bees from Alburgh and Swanton to Bennington and Pownall. Of these I found disease in 61 yards and 280 colonies [*a 20 percent infestation rate—Ed.*]. Of the 280 diseased colonies, I have treated or destroyed 20, leaving the rest for the owners of the bees to attend to after instructing them as to methods, and doing it myself where necessary to prevent the spread of disease.

To destroy every colony found diseased after giving the owner time to free them of disease would doubtless be the quickest way to rid the state of disease but I doubt if it would form the best way, as it would in many instances almost completely destroy the industry in many sections where the disease has taken a strong hold. Too much, it seems to be, like burning a barn to get rid of rats, and not necessary. It has seemed to be better to go a little slow perhaps, carefully instructing beekeepers in better methods of beekeeping, and the danger that comes from brood diseases.

While brood diseases are a great hindrance to profitable beekeeping, I find the ignorance of the average beekeeper to be even greater. Many seem to think that knowing how to hive a colony cluster on a tree or bush and to put on and take off surplus boxes is enough to fit one to keep bees. (Crane 1913, pp. 14–16)

In a companion report to Crane's, the assistant inspector J.P. Rock observed that,

The number of beekeepers who believe there is no such thing as foul brood of bees is surprising, and usually this class of people keep but a few colonies and realize but little from them... (Crane 1913, pp. 14–16)

Rock also recognized the problem of irresponsible neighboring beekeepers, which continues today:

... this same class of beekeepers are a menace to their neighbors who are striving to stay in the business, as it is by compulsion only that they will do anything toward treating their bees after they are condemned...

While Rock had burned hives because the owners were endangering others' bees through their own inaction, he wrote, "... it is not the intent of the law or the inspectors to condemn and destroy but to assist in suppressing disease and to give instructions in the most modern methods of beekeeping." Making matters worse, Rock wrote, that about 90 percent of the Vermont beekeepers he saw still had the original German black bee (*Apis mellifera mellifera*). According to Rock, these bees were more susceptible to foulbrood than the Italian or Carniolan bees. On another note, he went on to praise the bees' industry in pollination:

... a great many people think that honey gathered by the little fellows is the only product. Such is not the case as the work which they do in pollinating the fruits and flowers is hard to estimate. In fact, the intelligent fruit grower has long known that without the work of the bee, he cannot look for the best results. Fruit growers should do all they can to encourage the keeping of more and better bees. (Crane 1913, pp. 15–17)

In 1914, Crane wrote to Elbert S. Brigham, Commissioner of Agriculture:

> . . . I am satisfied from my four years' experience as an inspector that the permanent elimination of bee diseases will come quite as much from the intelligent efforts of beekeepers as from the work of the inspector . . .
>
> More and more the work of the inspector is appreciated by the beekeepers of the state as is proved by their increasing friendliness, hospitality and helpfulness. (Crane 1914 p. 21)

Two years later, "friendliness and hospitality" were the not characteristics Crane and Rock expressed in response to petitions from some beekeepers that they be reimbursed for the loss of diseased hives:

> "Foul brood is a curable disease and anyone who will follow the instructions given by apiary inspectors may at small expense cure bees of these diseases. The careless owner who will not take pains to treat his bees should not have a premium placed upon his negligence by having the State pay him for swarms destroyed." (Crane 1916, p. 9)

And in the next report (1918), Crane bemoaned the lack of interest in beekeeping among farmers:

> I believe there is no branch of rural industry that will pay better . . . than beekeeping if intelligently followed . . . The demand for honey this year is greater than ever before and we cannot begin to supply it. Much more honey has gone un-gathered for lack of bees and intelligent beekeepers in western Vermont than has been gathered. (Crane 1918, pp. 47-49)

But, on the other side of the state, assistant inspector Rock observed in the same report that beekeepers had greatly improved their beekeeping techniques and equipment:

> I am quite sure that this cooperation [*between beekeeper and inspector—Ed.*] means that in time every beekeeper will act as his own inspector, by being forever on the lookout for bee diseases of all kinds. (Crane 1918, pp. 47-49)

## PROTECTING WILD BEES FROM POACHERS

In the Middle Ages, beekeepers were some of the only people allowed defensive arms, (e.g. crossbows) to protect against marauding bears. From 1917 to at least 1947, Vermont had a law to protect wild bees and honey, which presumably meant swarms on one's property. The law provided that to prevent the taking of such bees and honey, the owner "shall maintain a notice not less than two feet long by one foot wide stating that the taking of wild bees or honey is prohibited and giving the name of such owner or person, upon every twenty-five acres of the premises sought to be protected. A penalty of $25 shall be levied on violators of this statute by the land owner." (State of Vermont 1917)

## THE CRANE HONEY COMPANY

In our focus upon Crane's role as state inspector, we must not forget his own large business. He and his son Philip continued to run one of the largest honey operations in the state—and perhaps in New England. From their 700 hives, they sold honey either directly or through wholesalers to hotels, resorts, country stores, and even summer camps throughout the region from New York City to Maine and across all of Vermont. Their honey came primarily in comb form, though they produced some extracted honey as well.

By this time, comb foundation was readily available commercially. Manufacturers competed to have strong enough containers to ship multiples boxes of comb honey. The Cranes were in the thick of this competition, pioneering the use of cardboard shipping boxes instead of wooden crates. They promoted their honey with pictures of a man standing upon boxes. Reinforcing the public preference for comb was a

**"Hawkeye" Corrugated Comb Honey Shipping Cases**
The up-to-date case for the progressive beekeeper.
For full particulars and samples write
**THE IOWA FIBER BOX CO., Keokuk, Iowa**

FIGURE 1: **The Cranes were the first to use cardboard shipping cases for honey. Beekeepers traditionally had shipped their honey in wooden crates and it took time to convince them that a cardboard box was strong enough to keep the contents safe during shipment.**
SOURCE: *ROOT* 1908, P. 125

widespread customer fear of adulteration in this and other foods. The Pure Food and Drug Act (1906) gave customers more confidence to buy extracted honey. And unquestionably, jars and cans with tight lids were far more secure, stable, and unlikely to drip than the widely used Basswood comb honey boxes.

Over the years James Crane wrote scores of articles for *Gleanings in Bee Culture* and the *American Bee Journal* until his death in 1931. Just a few of his monographs were: "Shipping Comb Honey," "Swarm Control," "Comb vs. Extracted Honey," "Will Breeding Change the Honey?" "The Double-Walled Hive for Winter," and in the month of the Great Crash of 1929, "Must We Drown in Our Own Honey?"

## HONEY MARKETING

While Vermont's small number of commercial beekeepers mounted their own modest advertising campaigns, the industry at large participated in two state-sponsored efforts beyond its borders by rail. In 1927 and 1929, the State of Vermont sent special promotional trains around the East Coast, the Midwest and into Canada to show off Vermont products ranging from cloth and lathes, to cheese and honey, the latter from Addison County.

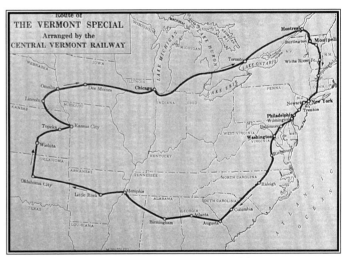

FIGURE 2: **Map showing the route taken by 'The Vermont Special' promotional train.** SOURCE: KEN MANCHESTER, JR.

In 1930, honey was among four Vermont agricultural products authorized to use the "New England Quality" label. Although we do not know their names, the four Vermont beekeepers who received certification, according to the report of H. A. Dwinell, director of the Bureau of Markets,

> . . . represented a considerable portion of the honey production of the state. Interviews with producers indicate that the use of the label has been a distinct advantage in the marketing of the honey graded and labeled. Labeled comb honey has been found for sale in many of the local stores both within and outside the state. (Dwinell 1930)

FIGURE 3: **Vermont honey was one of the featured items on the special promotional train that traveled the country in the 1920s. The train carried honey produced by both the Crane and the Manchester families.** PHOTO COURTESY OF KEN MANCHESTER, JR.

With the advent of World War II in 1941, Vermont saw a 50 percent increase in the number of honey bee colonies to over 6,000 as sugar rationing took effect. To quote the World War II Museum website:

> Never underestimate the honey bee. The influence of these creatures on our world is enormous, and the aid of bees and beekeepers during World War II was necessary to winning the war. The Dept. of Agriculture deemed the honey industry essential during wartime and even requested a 20 percent increase in production just to keep up with demand for both honey and beeswax.
>
> The U.S. lost access to sugar supplies from countries occupied by the Japanese, which led to shortages and rationing. Honey was an easily accessible substitute. In addition, beeswax was used to coat airplanes, shells, drills, bits, cables, pulleys; used in adhesive tape, varnishes, canvass and awnings. Beeswax prevented rust and waterproofed a variety of materials. On occasion, beekeepers were exempted from military service. (Tayler 2015)

## CHARLES MRAZ
## COMES TO VERMONT

The son of Czechoslovakian immigrants, Charles Mraz (1905–1999) kept bees in Woodside, Queens, New York City during the early 20th century. He started working for other beekeepers, moved to Middlebury, Vermont in 1928, and bought Crane's honey business when Phil Crane retired in 1930. Mraz named his new company Champlain Valley Apiaries (CVA). Three generations of Cranes and three of Mraz's would eventually keep bees in Vermont for over 145 years.

As if to bless this succession, the two of them appeared in same July 1931 issue of *Gleanings in Bee Culture* (the precursor to today's *Bee Culture* magazine). James Crane, who had written dozens of articles for this and other beekeeping publications, titled his article, "Building an Industry." (In a footnote, Ernest Root, the son of company founder A.I. Root, said, "Mr. Crane has given a true

FIGURE 4: **Charles Mraz**
PHOTO COURTESY OF THE MRAZ FAMILY

picture of conditions as they were. I was a witness to much of the later history.") Mraz, who would also write scores of articles for *Gleanings* and the *American Bee Journal*, had a piece about a novel approach to harvesting honey by applying carbolic acid to a "fume board" that sits on the top of the hive above the honey. As the carbolic acid evaporates, the fumes drive the bees down and out of honey supers so the honey can be removed from the hive free of bees and extracted.

In the mid-1940s, Mraz moved his business to a modest three-story building on Washington Street Extension in Middlebury. He went

FIGURE 5: **The Fume Board resembles an undersized outer cover that sits on top of the hive with absorbent fabric attached to the inside. The metal covered fume board on the left has seen about 50 seasons of use while the newer fume board on the right, with the plastic top showing under the detaching cloth, has been used for roughly 15 seasons.**

FIGURE 6: **The Mraz honey house in Middlebury.**

on to become a world-famous beekeeper. Not only did Mraz invent the fume board for removing bees from honey supers at harvest time, but he developed a chain uncapping machine (a variation of an older machine), and collaborated with Alan Benton of Vespa Labs, the man who is credited with developing the first bee venom extractor/collector. Mraz traveled extensively to South and Central America, Europe, Asia, and the Middle East consulting with beekeepers on beekeeping methods and technologies. In 1992, the American Beekeeping Federation (ABF) recognized Mraz as one of the five most distinguished beekeepers in the United States for his advances in commercial beekeeping.

Mraz is perhaps most famous for his work in apitherapy, the therapeutic use of bee products. Most notably, he spent over sixty years treating people with bee stings for relief from arthritis and worked tirelessly to try to get the medical establishment to recognize the potential healing benefits of bee venom therapy (BVT). Mraz went on to treat people with multiple sclerosis and other autoimmune diseases with BVT. He also helped found the North American Apitherapy Society in 1979 (which changed its name to the American Apitherapy Society in 1989) and is still active today acting as a clearinghouse for information on the use of bee products for healing and health. He published *Health and the Honey Bee* in 1994, recounting his years working with bee venom in the treatment of many degenerative diseases that modern medicine has so far been unable to effectively cure.

BEEKEEPER MARIANNA HOLZER OF HINESBURG, picked up her first bees from Kirk Webster in 1994. She explains her journey to beekeeping this way:

"About twenty-five years ago, I suffered a mysterious health crisis. One day, without warning, I went completely blind in my right eye. Gradually, my vision came back and then it happened again—six months later I lost the vision in my other eye.

After much testing and a few other episodes, I received the diagnosis: Multiple Sclerosis (MS). This was a condition I knew nothing about, but after learning as much as I could, I became quite depressed and fearful of when it would strike again. Fatigue is a common problem in MS, and I had that in spades. I had always been a very healthy person and loved being outdoors, counting gardening, hiking, and bicycling among my favorite activities.

A friend told me about a man in a town not far from us who had helped folks with MS by stinging them with honey bees. This sounded pretty far out, but I was ready to try anything in order to feel better. My husband, Rik Palieri, and I drove down to Middlebury from our home near Burlington to meet this man, Charlie Mraz, and to learn about the bees.

FIGURE 7: **Marianna Holzer pictured here describes her greatest beekeeping successes as, "wining a blue ribbon for light honey at the Farm Show in Barre after our first harvest, and the great improvement in my MS due to stinging myself with my bees."** PHOTO CREDIT: RIK PALIERI

Charlie ushered us into his home where he was helping a woman with severe arthritis by holding bees against her hip and her leg until she received several stings. He then turned to us. He asked me a few questions about my symptoms, allergies, and medications. He gave me a test sting on my leg and waited a few minutes to see if I would have a severe reaction. While we waited, he told me about acupressure points and meridian lines (healing pathways in the body), pressing on these points to see if I was sore. Every time I said 'ouch!' he chuckled and marked the spot with a red wax pencil. He gave me seven or eight stings, telling me to start out slowly with only a few stings, and then he taught us how to handle the bees ourselves.

The next step was to go out to his bee yard to collect bees in a jar to take home. We walked up a few steps to go outside, and the woman he had treated when we arrived turned around and went down the stairs, paused, climbed up them again and paused once more, a quizzical look on her face. After going up and down several more times, she turned to us with tears in her eyes and told us that this was the first time she had been able to climb stairs without pain in many years. It gave me hope.

Honey bees and their healing venom have changed my life. My husband, Rik noticed a lightening of my spirit right away. I have more energy, more hope, and feel empowered, as I have now found something I can do for myself. To keep up with my treatment, I became interested in beekeeping and soon had hives of my own."

Like Crane before him, Mraz served as chief state apiary inspector in the late 1930s and early 1940s. In his report of 1940, Mraz wrote:

> Compared to the industry in many other states, beekeeping in Vermont is a small though old enterprise. Presently, there are about 10,000 hives of bees in the state, kept by over 1,000 small and large beekeepers.
>
> Over a period of years, beekeeping has kept at a fairly steady level in much of the state. Beekeeping is a hobby, with most beekeepers having fewer than 100 hives. Commercial beekeeping is practical mainly in the northwest corner of the state where the best honey is produced from clovers growing in the limestone soil of the Champlain Valley. Here the largest beekeepers are located, one operating almost 700 colonies.(Mraz 1940, pp. 18–9)

FIGURE 8: **Charles Mraz operating the uncapping machine he invented.** PHOTO COURTESY OF THE MRAZ FAMILY COLLECTION

FIGURE 9: **Charles Mraz hives a swarm.** SOURCE: MRAZ 1940, P. 18

When he wrote these words, American foulbrood (AFB) was preventing the expansion of beekeeping into other parts of the state, even though many stated, and the federal government had proven, that resistant stock could control the disease. Mraz would regularly purchase queens from a New York beekeeper named Lockhart, who was one of the pioneers in this technique. Mraz said that the common use of resistant stock would reduce bee losses to almost nothing and encourage the expansion of beekeeping into many other parts of the state. According to his son, Bill, before the antibiotic Terramycin was developed for treating AFB disease, it was standard practice to burn infected hives. However, Bill says that when Charles found a hive with AFB that was still strong and well populated with bees, he could put a Lockhart queen in the hive and within a couple of months, the disease would clear up.

After Lockhart died and his bees were gone, Mraz established a queen rearing yard in the area near Lockhart's bee yards off Lockhart Mountain Road in Lake George, New York. He hoped that there might be some surviving feral bees with AFB resistant genetics that his breeder hives might tap into, but nothing ever seemed to come of it and the AFB resistant bee appears to be lost to history.

Around 1976, Charles's son William (Bill) Mraz, began the transition of taking over the business. Bill, the younger of two sons, is a mechanical engineer. Once he transitioned to CVA full-time, Bill rebuilt and made improvements to Charles' venom collector, built a new wax separator that was a lot smaller than the old Cook & Beal's version and didn't require the heating of the honey (Maxant would produce and market it), and invented a reversing jig that raised the hive off the ground and provided an easy way to catch the burr comb scrapings when reversing bees. Unfortunately, Bill's taking over the helm of the company coincided with the tracheal mite's arrival in Vermont and CVA winter losses jumped from 5–10 percent in a bad year to regular losses around 30 percent. After suffering large initial losses, Bill got the beekeeping operation on an even keel just in time for the Varroa mite invasion at which time losses jumped up again, only this time to 30-40 percent.

It was around 2004-2005 that Bill's son, Charles (Chas) Mraz, transitioned into running the business. Chas had been a construction supervisor in New York City but was familiar with the bees having grown up around them. Bill had built the business up to around 1200 colonies, and CVA lost approximately 45 percent of their bees the winter of 2004 and Chas came on board that spring. "It was a wild start but my father and I worked side by side to build our numbers back up," he says. The numbers have been up and down ever since.

A practice that Chas has carried on from his father and grandfather, which is different from most operations their size is

FIGURE 10: **William (Bill) Mraz (left) and Charlie (Chas) Mraz outside their honey shop in Middlebury, 2015.**

to winter the bees on honey. "Back in the '50s Charlie would do what everybody did, take the honey and feedback sugar syrup," explains Chas. "One year winter came very quickly and they only had a chance to feed half the bees. They were taking the supers off and feeding, and had gotten through about half the hives, when snow fell and temperatures dropped and Charlie said 'Well, we can't feed them, it's gotten too cold so we'll just leave a super of honey on that half of the operation,' and the next spring, that half of the operation was just boiling out of the hives and the other half was not. So he said, '. . . well if this is the result, we are going to leave honey on all of them from now on.'" Chas goes on to explain, "We probably leave about $80 of extractable honey on every bee hive and it is expensive, but we're not buying syrup and we're not going back to the yard and investing in the labor to feed them, or wash the feeders afterwards, which we don't have time for anyway. There is a definite payoff. That honey is valuable, but I think it is more valuable for the bees."

FIGURE II: **Chas Mraz displays a jar of honey by the bottling stations in Champlain Valley Apiaries honey house.**

Despite his best efforts, Chas recognizes that the bees don't have the kind of vitality that they used to have. "We moved to Middlebury when I was 12, but before that we lived in Georgia, Vermont," says Chas. "My father always had bees in Georgia. I can't remember if I went out and worked with the bees with him (Bill) or not, I probably did when I was a kid, but we always had bees there and in fact my father said one bee hive was there for twenty-five years just continuously, re-queening itself and just going on and on like many of them used to do."

Chas has worked to make each branch of the business (production, packing, bee venom) independent and profitable. The most challenging area has been the bee venom side of the business. Pharmaceutical compliance is extremely stringent and sales are unreliable and irregular. Pharmaceutical companies use the venom primarily for creating the desensitization shots doctors provide to folks who are hyperallergic to bee venom.

His devotion to beekeeping also extends outside his business. Chas served for three years as the President of the Vermont Beekeepers Association, and has worked with faculty at the University of Vermont to develop ways for farmers to improve the amount of pollinator friendly forage on their farms as a way to bolster pollinator health, while improving farm income at the same time. And he has worked with Vermont Public Television on a documentary focusing on the impacts neonicotinoid pesticides are having on bees.

Chas reflects on the changes he's seen during his year's beekeeping..."The farmers certainly cut hay more aggressively than they used to and they have the machinery to do it. They didn't have the machinery when I was a kid to cut hay like they do now. But perhaps the biggest change is all the extra work that comes with the diseases and varroa mites, that's really the most significant thing that has changed... the problems." According to Chas, "We used to have a problem come along every ten, fifteen, twenty years or so, there would be a new bee problem. Now it seems like every few years there's a new issue and it is a lot more expensive to keep bees

FIGURE 12: **Mraz memorial, Middlebury, VT.**

today. There are more operations to do with the treatments and we spend more time checking the hives."

In 2004, a marble bench memorializing Chas' grandfather, Charles Mraz, was erected on the green in front of the Middlebury Inn known as Court Square. A little way up the hill from the memorial, an American Linden (basswood) tree was also planted in Charlie's honor and to provide forage for pollinators.

## ENOCH H. TOMPKINS: "A MAN OF HUMBLE ROOTS"

Around 1950, Enoch H. Tompkins, a combat engineer during World War II, came to the University of Vermont (UVM) to teach agricultural economics. He was employed at the university until 1976 as Assistant, then Associate, Agricultural Economist. An avid beekeeper for much of his life, Tompkins served as president of the Eastern Apicultural Society (EAS) and as secretary and president of the Vermont Beekeepers Association (VBA). He also co-authored a book on beekeeping titled: *Practical Beekeeping*. A meticulous record keeper, Tompkins also wrote a 60-page booklet about the beekeeping industry in Vermont at mid-century. (Tompkins 1961) His collections of beekeeping equipment were the cores of two major exhibits at the Shelburne Museum. Tompkins was also an inveterate tutor of new beekeepers. One, Rick Stoner of Shelburne, wrote:

FIGURE 13: **Sister Mary Angela works one of her hives at St. Mary's Convent in Burlington under the tutelage of Enoch Tompkins. A sixth grade teacher at St. Mary's Academy, Sister Angela has twenty colonies and finds an observation hive in her classroom in the spring, "one of the most effective ways of teaching science."** (WEED, 1962)

I first meet Enoch Tompkins while serving on the Natural Resources Committee for the Town of Shelburne. He was a man of very few words, but when he did speak he spoke in a humble manner that was, more often than not, spot on. A Mainer born and raised in the 'County' meaning Aroostock County, Maine.

As a boy he kept bees so as to earn money by pollinating the blueberry crops and selling the honey. It was a bare bones upbringing, but instilled in Enoch an appreciation for bees and the wild world around him.

When I made the connection with him on the Committee I learned a bit of his upbringing and his passion for bees. As a result, I asked Enoch if he would mentor me in starting bees. He agreed, and in spite of his failing health, he guided me always with a steady, encouraging demeanor.

To a man of humble roots, I am forever in his debt. (Stoner 2017)

FIGURE 14: **Enoch Tompkins.** PHOTO COURTESY OF THE TOMPKINS FAMILY

In 1956, Tompkins and his team interviewed 100 beekeepers from all but one of Vermont's fourteen counties. The results reported in a paper titled: *Honey Production and Marketing Bulletin*, gave a statistical snapshot of beekeeping in Vermont in the mid-20th century. With an average of forty-two pounds each for 6,700 colonies, overall Vermont honey production was 281,000 pounds. Vermont led all of New England in total honey produced and per colony average. (Tompkins 1961)

Beekeeping and honey production was a part of many working farms. Of 6,600 total farms in the state, 579 reported an average of 12 colonies each. Of those, 448 farms had 1-9 colonies, 95 had 10-40 colonies and 1 farm had over 300 colonies. Addison County had one-third of the total colonies in the state.

One-quarter of the beekeepers were also dairy farmers, and retirees accounted for nine percent. Five percent were teachers and stone workers, and six percent were women. One-quarter had over thirty years' experience; one-third had over twenty years; and one-third had less than ten years. Eighty percent were over fifty years of age and most were backyard beekeepers (hobbyists).

As Tompkins wrote, the surveyed beekeepers were not "joiners." Only 20 percent belonged to the VBA. When asked to enumerate the causes of their winter colony losses, the beekeepers listed starvation, cold, and poor management. None, however, mentioned diseases, although AFB had been found in seven percent of Vermont colonies only four years earlier.

The surveyed beekeepers reported spending an average of $1.02 per colony per year. This expenditure was broken down in the following way: forty-six cents for frames, foundation, and other hive equipment; forty-five cents for bees; seven cents for queens; and four cents for extracting equipment.

Eighty-seven percent of those who sold honey estimated they spent eight hours per year per colony on removing honey, extracting, packing, and selling. Sixty percent spent less than 1 hour per colony. As Tompkins observed dryly: "Some hobbyists enjoy observing their bees and spend many more hours with them than needed. Others, of course, could profitably spend more time than they do." (Tomkins 1961, p. 14)

Tompkins' team also interviewed all nine Vermont beekeepers who described themselves as "professional." They averaged 440 colonies each and had an average age of fifty-four. Their per colony honey production averaged sixty pounds, almost fifty percent higher than the state average of all beekeepers. Per colony expenditures were $2.10 and they estimated they spent five to six hours per year on each colony. Interestingly, all reported that they pasteurized their honey at between 130°F and 180°F, presumably to delay crystallization.

The prices they received for a one-pound jar were: roadside stand, 42 cents; home, 45 cents; stores: 30 cents; and jobbers, 28 cents. Three producers bought additional honey to sell from other beekeepers. In sharp contrast to the honey market at the turn of the century, only 9 percent of their total honey sales of 62,000 pounds was in the form of comb.

## MANCHESTER FAMILY

One of the beekeepers Tompkins and his team would have interviewed were the Manchesters of Cornwall: a four-generation Vermont beekeeping family. By 1910, Henry J. Manchester of Cornwall had kept bees for 50 years and had around 150 hives. His son and daughter-in-law were Frank D. and Vivian Manchester. They were Cornwall dairy farmers who kept about 110 hives, and also had pigs and horses, and harvested maple syrup. The pair founded Clover Leaf Apiaries in the 1930s.

FIGURE 15: **Frank Manchester of Clover Leaf Apiaries in his bee yard.**
PHOTO COURTESY OF KEN MANCHESTER JR.

Their son Kenneth and his wife Maxine, also of Cornwall, would eventually run upwards of 600 hives in 10-12 yards in the Addison County towns of Cornwall, Bridport, Middlebury, Whiting, and Shoreham. They produced liquid and comb honey, and they also pollinated and raised queens. After Kenneth was crippled

FIGURE 16: **Maxine Manchester shows the inner workings of the hive to a young Ken Manchester Jr. and the daughter of the photographer.** PHOTO CREDIT: JOSEPH NOONAN, *VERMONT LIFE*, 1967

due to illness, Maxine ran the operation. (She would become deeply involved in the establishment of the EAS and served as its first secretary-treasurer.)

Kenneth and Maxine Manchester sold honey at the State Fair in Rutland, and honey produced by various Vermont beekeepers in the Vermont building at the Eastern States Exposition (the Big E) in Springfield, Massachusetts. Among their children was Ken Jr., who started selling honey at the VBA booth at the Addison County Fair and Field Days.

Ken Jr. ran his parents' operation himself for a number of years after his parents retired. He eventually left his parents' operation to work as a trucker. After he returned to beekeeping around 1980, Ken built up to about 200-300 hives. He recalled how he had to cut his honeymoon short to get back home to receive a shipment of packaged bees.

In 1980, he bought the Dadant & Sons stock being sold through a local Agway store and became the local Dadant representative. Several years later,

FIGURE 17: **Kenneth Manchester Jr.**
PHOTO CREDIT: JOAN MANCHESTER

he added the Betterbee franchise, which specialized in serving backyard beekeepers. Ken produced eight to ten tons of honey per year and did some local pollination for hire, moving everything by hand and at night. (Fellow members of the Cornwall Volunteer Fire Department would help him move bees during pollination.)

In the 1980s, Ken along with Cornwall residents Ed Peet and Sid Gingras converted Ed's cellar to overwinter 150 hives. This allowed them to harvest more honey, since they fed sugar. They had a beekeeper from Quebec famed for this technique come down and look at it, and he was reportedly impressed. But they only did this for a couple of years.

Ken's bees in Middlebury got hit by bears. In one incident, two bears destroyed eighteen out of twenty hives in one yard, then came back the next night and finished off the other two. Ken got an insurance payment of $1,200, but no indemnity from the state because the land was posted.[1]

Ken mentored Ed and Sid in beekeeping, and they then went their own ways. As Ed Peet noted to his interviewer, "There are not many businesses where, if you pollinate, and get a good honey crop in a good year, you can make back your investment in a single season."[2] Eventually, Ken tired of his beekeeping duties, including harvesting honey, pollination for hire, and selling equipment. Ken eventually sold his bees to Kirk Webster, a young and rising beekeeper who built up and runs his own operation after having worked for the Mraz's at Champlain Valley Apiaries.

---

1 Interview with Ken Manchester, Jr. 2017
2 Interview with Ed Peet, 2017

## NEW STATE INTEREST IN BEEKEEPING

In his biennual report to the legislature in 1956, Agricultural Commissioner Elmer Towne began a decades-long debate about the need for a full-time bee inspector:

> Apiary inspection—the limitation of $1,000 annually for the eradication of foul brood limits our service to spot checks in areas where the disease is known to exist and to investigate requests for help in new areas.
>
> Consideration should be given to furnishing the services of a full-time expert for at least eight months each year. This industry should be built up. It furnishes one of nature's best, high quality, health-building, nutritious foods with very low capital investment. In addition, fruit and seed crop pollination [*by bees—Ed.*] is a basic requirement if those industries are to prosper.
>
> The interests of the beekeepers should be protected and coordinated with the interests of forests, orchards and field crops either by law or by the development of regulations by the Civil Aeronautic Authority concerning the widespread use of pesticides which may be injurious to bees. (Towne 1956 p. 7)

It would be another 24 years before improved inspection came to pass.

## SWITCHEL AND DR. JARVIS

In the late 1950s, Vermont honey leapt to the top of the national charts. This sudden fame came about through the writing of a mild-mannered Barre doctor who did not even keep bees: Dr. DeForest Jarvis. Over his forty years of practice, however, Jarvis gathered backcountry nostrums, proclaimed the benefits of natural and unprocessed foods, and gave special emphasis to a liquid mixture of water, honey, apple cider vinegar, and perhaps ginger for flavoring. Known as switchel, this mixture was a common hayfield thirst-quencher and pick-me-up. In the pre-script to his book *Folk Medicine*, Jarvis wrote:

I believe the doctor of the future will be a teacher as well as a physician. His real job

FIGURE 18: **Dr. DeForest Jarvis.**
SOURCE: VT HISTORICAL SOCIETY

will be to teach people how to be healthy. Doctors will be even busier than they are now because it is a lot harder to keep people well than it is just to get them over a sickness. (Jarvis 1958)

Jarvis' book would stay on the *New York Times* best-selling list for over two years and sell over 1 million copies.

There were skeptics—even some who called Jarvis a quack. But the doctor presented these remedies not as cure-alls, but as Vermont's medical inheritance. As Jarvis told *Vermont Life* magazine in 1960, "They are safe remedies, for if they do not do any good, they will not do harm."(Carroll 1960)

*"Look! If honey and vinegar was better than aureomycin, I'd be selling honey and vinegar and not aureomycin, wouldn't I?"*

FIGURE 19: **Dunne (1960).**

## EASTERN APICULTURAL SOCIETY (EAS) COMES TO VERMONT

The EAS is like few other organizations. It is not an academic society, a trade association, or a fraternal organization, but a mixture of all three. Its members include backyard, sideliner, and professional beekeepers, scientists, equipment vendors, and state inspectors—all dedicated to sharing information about better beekeeping. The EAS covers North America's eastern twenty-plus states and three Canadian provinces, and its central event is an annual conference and short course in a member state or province that changes location on a rotating basis. One proud tradition is a rigorous Master Beekeeper program (along with tests) that gives successful candidates much knowledge and bragging rights.

The EAS was formed in Rhode Island in 1955, and a founding member and the first secretary-treasurer of the society was Maxine Manchester of Clover Leaf Apiaries in Middlebury. Seven years later, in 1962, Manchester and Tompkins, the UVM Associate Agricultural Economist, spearheaded the first EAS conference in Vermont. Their program brought together over 350 beekeepers and researchers from the eastern United States and Canada. There were talks on beekeeping in Canada and Europe and a discussion on the history of Vermont beekeeping. Dr. Frank E. Todd of the US Department of Agriculture discussed bee research, Dr. James Hambleton spoke about professional beekeeping in the United States, and Dr. Joseph Saine of Montreal lectured on bee venom and royal jelly. Robert Mead, then the chief Vermont apiary inspector, gave demonstrations for new beekeepers on hive assembly, installing packages, making splits, extracting and bottling.

The keynote speaker was best-selling author and doctor, DeForest Jarvis of Barre. Charles Mraz of Middlebury spoke about his beekeeping work in Mexico.

As was clear from the headline in a local paper, events were planned for "beekeepers' honeys," also known as wives. These included tea, a short lecture, and discussions on cooking with honey and field trips to the Kennedy Brothers woodenware plant in Vergennes, the Shelburne Museum, and the UVM campus.

## ROBERT MEAD, INSPECTOR

In 1950, after the state bee inspectors said their pay was too low, the VBA membership voted to ask the State to raise the inspector's pay to $1,500 per year plus expenses. One year later, Robert Mead of Bridgewater became State inspector, and served until 1972. One of his first complaints was about the number of beekeepers who refused to register their hives.
Bill Mraz recalls him this way:

> Bob Mead was an old Vermonter, very low key, but a very nice and well-mannered guy. He was very tall, almost scrawny, and his skin looked like paper. According to my father, (Charles Mraz) he got into bees because he

had some serious disease and the doctors told him he had at the most, a year
to live. He started keeping bees and of course, he started getting stung, and
a year went by and he was still alive. Two years went by and he got more
bees, kept getting stung, and when he died, he was an old man. But he
always looked like he had something seriously wrong with him.

He used to make great comb honey. He had quite a few hives for those
days, a couple hundred. In the fall, he was always hunting and trapping, so
he'd drive all over the state and since the inspector's job was part-time, he
could find good spots. He liked the logging operations, where they'd cut a lot
of big areas fairly heavily and it would all grow back into berries. He would
wait until just before the blackberries and raspberries started to bloom and
then take 10 hives or however many he could get on his truck and he would
go down these logging roads and place them. He would make this beautiful
blackberry comb honey. Its cappings were white as a piece of cake, and the
reddish brown honey, two-color combination was just delicious.[3]

Newsletters through the period were encouraging members to act in their own
self-interest and sell their honey at the Eastern States Exposition, the Vermont
State Fair and Champlain Valley Fair.

In 1954, Mead expressed another pet peeve:

Our experience at the fairs this year reflect the difficulties of bee-keeping in
general. Everything we buy is terribly high and our product does not find
an enthusiastic market even with short crops. As I see it, the whole future
of beekeeping is tied up in getting a greater public acceptance of honey. We
are being called the "backbone of agriculture" but nice names are a poor
substitute for adequate income. (VBA 1954)

In the 1960 VBA Newsletter, Mead reminded members that their dues of
$1.00 per year did NOT cover the basics of running the organization. That gap of
$150+ was filled by the sales of members' honey at the Eastern States Exposition
in Springfield, Massachusetts which was itself dependent upon volunteer work
from Vermont beekeepers. "This money cannot be raised by wishful thinking, so
the Eastern States booth still seems to be the best bet until someone comes up
with a better idea." (VBA 1960)

Some excerpts of Mead's inspector reports follow:

- 1958 report: "Most of the AFB-infected colonies were found in bee yards of
  hobby or part-time beekeepers. The commercial apiaries continue to have a

3 Interview with Bill Mraz, October, 2015

low incidence of disease. Beekeepers who have not had the inspection service are urged to write to the Department." (Mead 1958)

• 1960 report: "In addition to regular inspections, some sixty-five orchards were visited at blossom time to check on approximately 1,300 hives brought into the state for pollination.[4] Besides inspection, some work has been done on marketing and instructing a great many beginners. A beekeepers' registration law is still badly needed. Much of the foul brood of the past two years has been traced to unknown and out of the way beekeepers who are difficult or impossible for the inspectors to find." (Mead 1960)

• 1962 report: "During the biennial period the apiary inspectors have provided a variety of technical services to beekeeper's organizations, individual beekeepers and farmers including advice to beginners, assistance in marketing, and information on pollination services." (Mead 1962)

In his 1967-68 biennial report, Mead reported he had inspected 5,123 colonies in Vermont, and ninety-one were infected with AFB [*a one percent infection rate—Ed.*]:

Over-all, this biennium has not been good for Vermont beekeepers. Some pesticide poisoning occurred in Grand Isle and Addison County areas in 1967. A very cold and long-delayed spring in 1967 was largely responsible for a small crop. In the fore part of 1968, little trouble with pesticides was reported but beekeepers had a hard winter and it appeared that the honey crop might be the smallest in a decade.

The number of bee hives in Vermont is about the same. There is increased interest in renting bees for pollination, and beekeepers are certainly looking forward to an improved honey crop situation in the coming years.

American foulbrood, the principle infectious disease of honey bees in Vermont, does not seem to be much of a problem where beekeepers give proper care and learn to recognize the disease as soon as it shows up. We are having trouble with some neglected apiaries and the disease will occasionally show up even in the best-kept apiaries. (Mead 1968, p.84)

In the 1969–1970 biennial report, Mead and assistant inspector William Matson of White River Junction, inspected 5,350 colonies and found 250 infected with AFB. [*a four percent infection rate—Ed.*]

---

4 This is perhaps the first time that pollination for hire was reported, although Agricultural Commissioner Elmer Towne mentioned it as an important local bee service four years earlier in 1956.

Vermont beekeeping suffered setbacks during the biennium as a result of two severe winters which killed a large number of colonies. Not all of the lost colonies have been replaced. Winter kill of bees and low return from the honey crop have helped to reduce the number of colonies in Vermont, which once numbered some 10,000 in the early 1960s. Honey crops in the past two seasons have been only fair in quantity.

About 1,000 colonies are used in Vermont orchards each spring for pollination of the apple crop. Strength of some of the colonies; that is, the number of bees per hive, have been reported as low, or weak. The Vermont Beekeepers Association, the apple growers and the beekeepers who supply the rental pollination hives are working on this problem. There is no easy solution in sight because the strength of bee colonies at that early season of apple blossom will vary greatly because of several conditions. The average rental of a bee colony for pollination purposes seems to be about eight dollars each. (Mead 1970, p.74)

## REPORT OF THE VBA, 1970

| Title | Name and Location |
|---|---|
| President | Rene Nolet, East Dorset |
| Vice President | Kermit Mayo, Milton |
| Treasurer | James Warren, N. Springfield |
| Secretary | Connie Mayo, Milton |

Source: Mayo (1970)

Despite the challenges, Vermont's beekeepers did what they have always done, keep on plugging along making the best of the situation as indicated by VBA Secretary Mayo's 1970 report:

The Vermont Beekeepers Association held winter and summer meetings during this biennium and also participated in educational and public relations activities at the Eastern States Exposition, West Springfield, Massachusetts . . . The winter meetings were held at Barre, Vermont, in conjunction with the Vermont Farm Show. [*a tradition that continues today—Ed.*] Programs featured speakers on pesticide controls, bee indemnity payment, apicultural practices and market development.

Summer meetings were held at Westminster and North Hero. Programs included the election of officers, competitive exhibits of honey products, selection of a Honey Princess and demonstrations of beekeeping practices.

The following girls have served as Honey Princess during the biennium: Ginette Mailloux, Ferrisburg and Cecilia Dodge, Middlesex. The Association is indebted to these young ladies for the fine public relations functions which they have performed at the Vermont Farm Show and the 1970 Exposition activities.

The Association has encouraged and supported interest in beekeeping by youth through organizations and also individual contacts. (Connie Mayo 1970, p. 105)

In the 1971–1972 biennial report, Mead wrote that 5,000 hives were inspected throughout Vermont, 527 were infected, [*a ten percent infection rate—Ed.*] and 400 were treated with antibiotics.

During the biennium, action has been taken to develop better records of Vermont beekeeping. Beekeeping is in a state of constant change making it difficult to obtain reliable figures as to the number of apiarists and hives in operation in any one year, as often some small beekeepers are not discovered. However, the new apiary registration law, plus extended inspection work has given us a more correct picture.

There were still outlaws who refused to register their hives, but this new legal requirement brought in many who had been merely neglectful, not willful, in their non-action. Mead explained:

While not all beekeepers have registered, I believe that 5,250 colonies and 250 beekeepers would cover most of the bees in the State. Of the 250 beekeepers, only four depend on beekeeping alone for a living. Between thirty and forty more keep from 20-100 colonies as an intensive sideline, but receive most of their income from other sources. When it comes to pollination (mainly apple orchards) again only four of the larger beekeepers are renting bees on a commercial basis.

It should be noted that many small beekeepers make a considerable contribution to Vermont beekeeping because of their enthusiasm for honey and their support of the Vermont Beekeepers Association.

During the biennium several changes have taken place which may have an important effect on the future of the bee industry. First, the apiary law has made it possible for your inspectors to find many more beekeepers.[5] This, in time, should help to lower the incidence of American foulbrood. Second, a much greater awareness of the use of poisons and the enactment of new pesticide regulations give the beekeepers a much better chance to survive the threat of these substances to their industry. Third, a complete about-face in the honey market occurred. For the last 30 years, the price of honey remained almost stationary, while everything else went up [*in price- Ed.*]. Then, late in the fall of 1971, due to local and worldwide shortages, the price of honey increased dramatically. At present, it seems to have stabilized nicely at a level more in line with other products. This price increase gives Vermont producers a much-needed incentive to replace worn-out equipment and to maintain a reasonable number of colonies. Fourth, a greatly increased interest in the use of health foods has attracted much favorable attention to honey... there were an unusually large number of new beekeepers in the spring of 1972... (Mead 1972)

In the 1973–1974 biennial report, Mead wrote:

During this biennium, beekeeping in Vermont continued to be centered on a large number of beginners. Prices for honey have continued at unusually high levels because of a sustained interest in health foods, short crops, and an interest in a back-to-the-land movement. It is further evidenced by a heavy demand for bees, bee hives and equipment and also by a large attendance at the beekeeping course conducted by Enoch Tompkins of the Rural and Farm Family Rehabilitation Project.[6]

---

5 The new law said, in part, that "The inspector of Apiaries or his assistants shall examine all apiaries as necessary and ascertain whether or not the diseases known as American or European foul brood or any other diseases . . . and if in his opinion any such diseases exist, he shall give the owners or caretakers of the diseased apiaries written order to treat, burn or otherwise handle infected bee colonies in order to prevent the spread or dissemination of any and all contagious diseases of honeybees." Section 2, 6 V.S.A # 3002 Section 9, 6 V.S.A. #3011 reads: 'It will be the duty of any person or persons having one or more colonies of bees in his possession or under his control to report to the apiary inspector the locations of such colonies, at such times and in such manner as the commissioner by regulation shall prescribe."

6 Among its components was one that distributed hives of bees to members of a targeted population of rural poor.

Vermont has a great potential as a honey-producing state, but the weather offered during the biennium has been one of overly-frequent rains, flooding and unseasonable cold. Honey crops were disappointing and bee activity was diminished. Good crops can produce honey of the very highest quality and Vermont honey is in demand throughout the eastern half of the nation.

The required registration of bee hives by Vermont beekeepers with the Commissioner of Agriculture is the only means that the bee inspectors have of finding the bee hives. Examination of the bee colonies is necessary to detect possible outbreaks of foul brood disease so that preventive action can be taken before it becomes an epidemic. (Mead 1974)

Two years later, the trend of more "newbees" continued. Mead noted, "As in the past, the number of beginning beekeepers was on the increase. The trend of people wanting to return to the land was probably part of this motivation for continued enthusiasm in apiculture." (Mead 1976)

The back to the land movement that Mead kept referring to would spur growth and change that would engulf Vermont and have a huge impact not just on Vermont beekeeping, but Vermont in general. While old-time Vermonters often griped about the influx of these "hippies," Yvonne Daley suggests that in many ways, it was precisely these "transients" that saved Vermont.

. . . it could be argued that by the mid-1960s what Vermont needed most was people, specifically young people, to stop the brain and energy drain of young Vermonters leaving the state for jobs elsewhere. For while the rest of the nation had experienced a dramatic population growth, especially following World War II, Vermont's population had grown by less than 9 percent between 1930 and 1960. Between 1950 and 1960 alone, 15,000 Vermonters between the ages of twenty and forty-four left the state. With an increasingly aging population, how would Vermont raise enough revenue to pay for education, road maintenance, and other services?[7] The so-called invasion changed everything. By 1970, approximately 35,800 hippies were estimated to be living in Vermont, representing roughly 33 percent of the total population of 107,527 Vermonters between the ages of eighteen and thirty-four. The 1980 census showed that Vermont's population grew even more dramatically over the decade, from 444,732 to 511,456, making it the

---

7 The problem of an aging population and declining workforce would surface again during the Administration of Governor Phil Scott in the latter half of the second decade of the 21st century.

largest increase since the Revolutionary War; 57 percent of that growth were people from out of state. (Daley 2018)

The profound influence that these newcomers ended up having on Vermont was social, political and economic and the beekeeping industry would not elude their impact. Many of them came to escape the cities and suburbs harboring visions of a simple live that included living close to the land and naive ideas about growing their own food inspired by Helen and Scott Nearing of *The Good Life* fame.

While many of the newcomers who became beekeepers were buying equipment from A. I. Root, Walter T. Kelley, Dadant and Sons, Inc., and F. W. Jones and Son in Bedford Quebec, there was enough interest that locally grown beekeeping suppliers sprung up such as John Tardie in Essex Junction.

A few books geared to these beginners were penned by Vermont authors during this period including the Garden Way publications booklet *Starting Right With Bees* (1980), *Practical Beekeeping* by Enoch Tompkins and Roger Griffith (1977) and the *Beekeeper's Manual* by L.A. Stephens-Potter (1984). The new crop of beekeepers were welcomed into the fold.

## AN APIARY OF CHARACTERS

The graduation of beekeepers from anonymous to celebrity, and from complete amateur to full-time professional has always been a continuum, not a clear division. From the mid-forties to the mid-fifties, Agathe von Trapp, at the urging of her father Georg, kept a few hives at the Trapp Family Lodge in Stowe. According to Johannes von Trapp, some of the honey produced went to the family and the rest to guests at the Lodge. Then, in 2018, employees at the Lodge bought several hives, and the Stowe hills rang again with the sound of buzzing bees. Unlike Agatha von Trapp, the sampling of Vermont beekeepers below tends toward the middle group of sideliners and are not as well known, though they deserve to have been. With the exception of Ed Hazen, the following are part-timers for whom honey production was outside their day jobs, or a sweet retirement exercise.

## BEA AND CASSIUS GUYETTE'S BEEHIVE COTTAGES

Cassius Guyette was raised in New York, but as his parents were originally from Addison and Bridport, Vermont where he had spent his youthful summers at his grandparents' farm. As a young adult, Cassius became very ill. It was recommended that he leave his office job in New York and go live the rural life in Vermont. In 1937, the Guyettes purchased a small farm along Route 7. Cassius had kept bees since the age of fourteen, so beekeeping and honey production were part of the plan. With the help of a local contractor the Guyettes gutted and renovated the farmhouse, then built cottages and a gas station. They named their business The Beehive DeLuxe Cottage Court.

They pumped gas, rented cottages, and made honey from hives on the farm. With the fields of alfalfa and clover all around, production was good. In their best year, the Guyettes harvested 5,000 pounds of honey that was sold right there at the gas station to passersby and by word of mouth. Signs in the Burma-Shave tradition were put along the roadside. Jeanne Wisner, the Guyettes' daughter, remembers four such signs: "Like Honey," "Sure you do," "Made for sale," and "At the Beehive."

In 1948, the Guyettes' honey was selected among products representing Vermont at the opening of the UN General Assembly building in New York City. The Guyettes made honey at the farm for 33 years, until 1970. Cassius died at the age of 83.[8]

## KERMIT MAYO OF MILTON

Another beekeeping character was Kermit Mayo of Milton. Born in 1909, he did a lot of bee-lining with his grandfather and great uncle. He told an interviewer, "We used to cut bee trees in late November, take all the honey and leave the poor bees to starve to death." Because Mayo felt sorry for the bees, he began keeping them in Langstroth hives to help them get through the winter. That hobby-business lasted over sixty

---

8 The story as told by Jeanne Wisner, the Guyettes' daughter, with extra research by Silas Towler.

FIGURE 20: **Kermit Mayo.** PHOTO CREDIT: ELAINE ISAACSON, *BURLINGTON FREE PRESS*

FIGURE 21: **Kermit Mayo capturing a swarm.** PHOTO COURTESY OF LEE MAYO

years. He made his living from honey, sugaring, chickens, trapping, vegetables, and fruits. Mayo used to sell vegetables and fruit and maybe honey from a truck at the corner of College and St. Paul Streets in Burlington, where Ben Cohen and Jerry Greenfield launched their iconic brand of ice cream. He put some of his bees in the Missisquoi Wildlife Refuge in Swanton, for which he paid the US Department of the Interior rental of 25 cents per hive. (Strickland 1998)

In the early 1960s, Mayo ran his own beekeeping workshops, where he encouraged VBA members to come visit him and talk bees. He would provide cider and donuts, and they held meetings in his root cellar. He was a VBA president from 1968 to 1970 and his wife Doris was treasurer. In the early 1980s, he told an interviewer:

> We have the best tasting honey in the world along the Champlain Valley. You get the lightest honey right around the longest day of the year, the 21st in June.

Why shouldn't anyone become fond of bees? Scientists can't make a comb of honey . . . Only a honey bee can make honey . . .

Somebody wanted to call 'em the Vermont insect. I don't want anybody calling 'em an insect. They're something much more than that. I call 'em little heavenly creatures. (Strickland 1998)[9]

FIGURE 22: **Comb honey specialist, Arnold Waters of Waterford.**
PHOTO CREDIT: RICHARD BROWN

## ARNOLD WATERS

Among the new beekeepers in Vermont in the early 1970s was Dr. Arnold E. Waters of Lower Waterford. He grew up in Baltimore, where he kept bees as a boy. Waters went to Johns Hopkins University for his bachelor's and doctorate degrees in geology. In the 1930s, during the middle of the Great Depression

---

9 The legislature would make the honey bee the Vermont State Insect in 1978.

the only job he could find was in colonial British Africa prospecting for copper, zinc, and later, diamonds. Waters went on to become one of the world's premier diamond geologists.

Within two years of his retirement to Vermont in 1973, he had an apiary of twenty to twenty-five colonies. He made only traditional comb honey in basswood boxes, which frequently won the Best of Show at the Vermont Farm Show. In this style of honey, Waters joined Ed Hazen and Robert Mead as notable practitioners.

Waters' great gift to Vermont beekeeping was less his example than it was his tutelage of novice beekeepers. Like doctors of yore, he made house calls, and his green Mercedes became well-known on the dusty back roads of Caledonia County. Waters often left his own bee yard and drove to answer emergencies with his veil on. He gave countless hours to helping beginners to dissect the catalogues that read like Greek and understand how to assemble hives, replace queens, treat for AFB, and a host of other newbee concerns.[10]

## ED HAZEN

Among the professionals, the best beekeeper in the state, by common agreement, was a quiet retired school teacher named Ed Hazen who kept upwards of 500 hives in the Lake Champlain Islands. A Dartmouth College graduate, he taught school in New Hampshire for thirty-eight years before retiring to Vermont. He and his wife Ethel specialized in comb honey. He would collect it and Ethel would package it, and they would take it around to country stores all over Vermont and New Hampshire. "When you have over 400 swarms of bees, you have to get an early start, particularly during the honey-harvest season," he would say. According to Rick Drutchas, a future Vermont bee inspector, Hazen made an average of 125 pounds per hive:

Ed would take hives that were about to swarm, go in and find the old queen, kill her, leave one or two queen cells and keep the hive. That was a lot of work! And with 500 hives![11]

---

10  Bill Mares, one of Waters' tutees, swore that if he were keeping bees at Waters' age, he too would take up teaching. He was, and he did.
11  Interview with Rick Drutchas, October 2017.

FIGURE 23: **Franklin Heyburn.**
PHOTO CREDIT: CLAIRE HEYBURN

## FRANKLIN HEYBURN

Franklin began beekeeping in 1977 while living at the Hudak farm in Swanton and teaching science at Sheldon Elementary School. An elderly beekeeper, Curtis Moynan, lived down the road and Franklin sometimes helped him with his hives or to catch swarms. He received some of his first hives as pay for helping Mike Palmer move some colonies that Mike had bought in southern Vermont. Not long after that, Franklin purchased twenty-five or thirty colonies, and a large pile of mostly homemade Canadian equipment, from Jacques Clermont, a retired bee inspector from Stanbridge, Quebec.

In 1980, Franklin worked during the winter in Minnesota, and while there he took the beekeeping course, taught by Basil Furgala, at the University of Minnesota Graduate School of Agriculture in St. Paul. After returning to Vermont in the early 1980s, Franklin worked for Todd Hardie helping him to care for the 500 colonies at Chazy Orchards in New York (this was before Mike Palmer bought up the bees there). Todd was living in Morses Line, was the state bee inspector and had about 125 colonies at the time. When Todd went into the chewing gum business, Franklin bought him out. Another "nice guy and wonderful man" who helped Franklin out a lot was John Craighead, who co-owned F.W. Jones beekeeping supply with his brother Billy, in Bedford, Quebec. It was during the 1980s that Franklin served a year as President of the Vermont Beekeepers Association.

At his height, Heyburn kept about 400 colonies spread out among about twenty locations in Highgate, Franklin, West Swanton, Georgia, the Burlington Intervale, and South Burlington. The colonies in South Burlington had formerly belonged to his old friend, Pat Broderick.

One of his early mentors was Ed Hazen, a master comb honey producer from Grand Isle. "One of the great things I remember from conversations with Ed, which always struck me as indicative of the good teacher that he was, was that you would start out by asking him questions, but he would always turn it around and ask you questions. This showed his life-long interest in learning (he never tried to come across as the authority)," Franklin recalls. "As I think about it, it was a subtle sort of way of bolstering your own confidence in learning about bees. You would be thinking, 'Gee whizz, Ed Hazen is asking me what my opinion is. Maybe I could be getting somewhere with this after all . . .' His manner of discussing bees and beekeeping caused you to take your powers of observation more seriously, and to be more thoughtful and careful in your observations on the subject, because if Ed was going to be asking you what you thought and saw out in the beeyard (which he always did) then you better be paying attention and looking closely."

Other beekeepers who answered his beekeeping questions included Peter Genier (Old Mill Apiaries, Fair Haven), Mike Palmer (French Hill Apiaries, Saint Albans), Kermit Mayo (K.E. Mayo Honey, Milton), and Bill and Charlie Mraz (Champlain Valley Apiaries, Middlebury). Franklin has tried to answer questions and help other beekeepers, including his nephew, Eloi Ferland, who has a beekeeping operation near Portneuf, Quebec close to Quebec City.

Franklin kept his bees near some of the same locations as Fannie Borossi, a somewhat legendary figure in Vermont beekeeping, who was highly thought of by some of the older beekeepers including Ed Hazen. Ed thought it was because her equipment always was full of holes that helped to vent moisture during the winter. Fannie lived in Alburg Springs, the same town as Charlie Ferree. It was Charlie who bought Ed Hazen's bees when Ed got out of beekeeping, and Charlie ended up selling out to Rick Drutchas, who eventually sold out to Josh

FIGURE 24: **Bill Matson capturing bees while bee-lining.**
PHOTO CREDIT: RICHARD HOWARD, *VERMONT LIFE*, 1979

White who had established North Woods Apiaries after helping Franklin move bees, extract honey and build equipment.

## BEE-LINING AND THE MATSONS

Following Mead as Vermont's chief bee inspector in 1972 was former assistant apiary inspector, Bill Matson of White River Junction. He and his brother Louis were legendary bee liners. "Lining wild bees was the natural way to get started," he said. (Khouri 1979)

Historically, before bees were available for purchase, the beekeeper was limited to lining bee trees, collecting swarms, or splitting colonies, to build up or replenish an apiary. Swarming was a sign of health, not pathology. Capturing swarms and putting them in new boxes on new comb or foundation was a way to hold colony numbers steady—even if the beekeepers lost honey production for that year. Indeed, in A.E. Manum's and Crane's, day, the word "swarm" was commonly interchangeable with "hive" or "colony."

To line bees is a skill going back at least to the early 19th century. Henry David Thoreau wrote eight pages in his journal about bee-lining around Fair Haven Pond, near his home in Concord, Massachusetts. According to Thoreau, the practice was to follow foraging bees home to their hive in the wild, often a hollow tree or a log, and the techniques varied (some active and some passive). Bee liners aimed to get at least the honey and sometimes the bees that went with it. The construction of bee boxes was almost a folk art, with farmers designing their own. These boxes could include from one to three chambers, spring-loaded doors, and glass windows.[12] (Thoreau 1906)

## BUDGET SQUEEZES BEE INSPECTIONS

The flurry of new interest in bees in the early 1970s was threatened as the recession of 1973–1975 rippled through Vermont. The Federal government and State legislature looked for programs to cut, large and small. One of them was the apiary inspection service along with its contractual employees' pay and travel expenses for the two bee inspectors. The total cost of inspections in fiscal year 1974 was $5,264. (Mead, 1974)

Hearing from some beekeeper constituents, Vermont Senator Herbert Ogden (R-Windsor), who was himself a beekeeper, wrote to the state Department of Agriculture:

*Dear Sirs:*

*I understand there is some prospect that Vermont's bee inspection may be suspended for lack of funds—barring increased taxes. This would be too bad, for a number of reasons.*

*I assume that the inspection is now supported from the general fund on the grounds that the bee population benefits a great number of people in addition to the owner(s) of the bees. Yet, rather than see foulbrood make any kind of a comeback in the next year or two, I wonder whether the bee owners might not be agreeable to the payment of a license fee, per hive, to fund the bee inspection. It might even be feasible, in case insufficient funds could be raised through a fee, to cut down on the inspection without suspending it entirely. It does seem as though it will be most important to continue a degree of inspection because of the newcomers in the bee business—the back-to-the-land folk who buy used equipment and know next to nothing about bee keeping. (Ogden 1975)*

---

12 The definitive book on bee-lining today is *Follow the Wild Bees, the Craft and Science of Bee Hunting* (Princeton University Press, Princeton, NJ, by Thomas D. Seeley, 2016).

In reply John W. Scott, director of the Vermont State Plant and Pest Control Division of the Department, wrote back to say that a fee system would not be practical:

> . . . the cost of collecting inspection fees from over 300 beekeepers would likely offset any advantage that might be obtained over the use of State General Funds . . . for some beekeepers with 3, 4, 6 or 8 hundred hives this would be quite a burden. We also feel that we would have a more difficult chore to locate all the bee colonies in the state as individuals would not be inclined to state that they have bee hives if they were charged an inspection fee.[13]

In an undated hand-written letter to Scott, Robert Mead, the longtime and newly-retired inspector decried the cuts and, simultaneously, voiced skepticism that a fee-for-service proposal would work.

> . . . the real sore spots would not be touched. This is something that has to be a state program with the force of some authority behind it to be effective in disease control.[14]

Like everyone else in the state, beekeepers were on tenterhooks as the Governor and Legislature wrestled with the effects of the oil crisis of the 1970s that resulted in gas shortages and the worst economic crisis up to that time since the Great Depression. What would happen to their vital inspection program?

---

13 Letter from John W. Scott to Senator Herbert Ogden, February 5, 1975.
14 The fee for service/inspection idea became moot when a full-time inspector was hired in 1979. The idea would resurface however in 2015 during another recession.

FIGURE 25: **Crane Honey Circular.** IMAGE COURTESY OF THE TOMPKINS FAMILY COLLECTION

## CHAPTER 4

# Battling Budget Cuts, Diseases, and Pests

*. . . It seems that there are as many varied ways of keeping bees as there are beekeepers, and each will stand by his or her method.*
—CORALIE MAGOON

IN THE NATIONAL BICENTENNIAL YEAR OF 1976, beekeepers around Vermont breathed a sigh of relief when the legislature decided to continue the inspection program. That year the state hired Todd Hardie, a young graduate of the Cornell University College of Agriculture and Life Sciences, to be the new apiary inspector. He recalled his three years as an inspector in the late 1970s this way:

> My plan since I began a life-long relationship with honey bees was to be a beekeeper in Vermont.
> After Cornell Ag School, I was working with older beekeepers in the Finger Lakes of Upstate New York. I heard that there was an opening to be the bee inspector for Northern Vermont. The prerequisite was that one had to train for a month in Erie County, New York. American Foulbrood was at a high level in Vermont, and New York State wanted to invest in her Eastern border and slow down the spread of AFB into her Eastern Counties.

I trained with New York inspector Ben Gabbert. He was a gentle man in his seventies and had seen the glory days of the '40s, '50s, and '60s, when the big crops were made. Sometimes we would go days without seeing AFB. When we found the disease, the colonies were always burned. This experience was instrumental in preparing me to be an inspector in Vermont.

I covered Chittenden, Lamoille, Washington and Caledonia Counties, north to the Quebec border. It was a broad territory, a beautiful land with many fine people who kept bees. Besides helping to reduce the high level of AFB in our state, I feel that my most important work was to set up a record keeping system, with cards and maps that made this work more efficient.

I truly believe then, as I do now, that the best thing to do with bees that are found with AFB is to burn them. This was not an easy path to be on, but it did help in time to dramatically reduce the percentage of infected hives each year. We had seen the spread of this bacterial disease in China when drugs are used in colonies found to have AFB.

As this was only a seasonal position, after three years I felt that I had to move onto work with bees and the marketing of their products year round.[1]

## A POLLEN AND NECTAR SURVEY

Just before he left his inspector's job in 1979, Hardie was instrumental in uniting the Vermont State Department of Agriculture with the Vermont Beekeepers Association (VBA) on a survey of nectar and pollen plants across the state. The goal was to thoroughly document the main plants that honey bees work and the dates they bloom. From this work, two large benefits would ensue. First, the planting of various trees, shrubs, legumes, and other flowering plants could increase pollen and nectar availability for the bees. Second, by knowing the flowering dates of these bee-friendly plants, beekeepers could improve their management of bees. This information would be shared across the state, by county. (Hardie 1979)

Enough surveys were returned in the first year to allow Hardie's replacement, Rick Drutchas, to assemble a rough chronology of plant blooms. It included early blooms such as willow, poplar, and red maple, then dandelion through midseason plants like, apple, white clover, basswood, black locust, and milkweed, and late bloomers like asters and goldenrod.[2]

---

1 Interview with Todd Hardie, January 27, 2018.
2 See VT Pollen and Nectar Survey, pp. 248-49.

FIGURE 1: **Todd Hardie with his daughters Charlotte (left) and Meriwether (right) in a Honey Garden Apiaries' bee yard located in Charlotte, VT.** PHOTO CREDIT: SCOTT DOSCHER

## THE VERMONT STATE INSECT

In 1978, led by students from the Barnard Central School, the Vermont Legislature voted to recognize the honey bee for its production of honey and its importance to pollination by making it the State Insect. That year, Governor Richard Snelling signed the bill to make it law.

## FROM FAMINE TO FEAST

At the end of the 1970s, recognition of the important role bees play in pollination, an expanding honey market, a wave of new beekeepers, and some federal aid combined to spark interest in hiring a full-time state apiary inspector. What a change this was from the dark days in mid-decade, when Vermont almost lost all inspection services! The state's first full-time inspector was Rick Drutchas, who recalls his story:

I grew up in Michigan and went to Wayne State University where I got a degree in acting. After graduation, I bought and operated a 24-foot straight-bodied box truck. I trucked a wide variety of things, from scenery for the Wayne State traveling Children's Theatre, the Mc5 punk band, welding rods for the Ford Rouge Plant, to food for the Ann Arbor Food Co-op. The trucking systems for food co-ops were just beginning to form back then and oddly enough that's what brought me to Vermont and a lifetime career as a beekeeper.

I moved to Pittsford, Vermont in 1972, and picked up my first beehive from a neighbor who was involved with some beekeeping welfare program that Enoch Tompkins had started. It was then I also started hauling honey to the burgeoning Rutland Food Co-op from Myers Apiaries in Granville New York. I became more and more interested in honey and beekeeping and fate would have it that I went from that first hive to over 700 hives in about 20 years, in a process that involved taking over the selling of Hammer Handle honey from Martin McKlusky, who grew up in Illinois next to Dadant, trucking Vermont Honey Yogurt for Peter Genier and Roland Smith, bussing people to a sheltered workshop for Rutland Community Mental Health and making maple syrup at a farm in Wallingford and selling it out of a station wagon in NYC.

All that time, I was building up my hive count and beekeeping 'chops.' I had 100 hives and was selling honey at the new Rutland Farmers Market when I got my big break. It was 1978. I was at the Vermont Beekeepers Associations summer meeting, sitting on the grass with Todd Hardie, who had just graduated from Roger Morse's Cornell beekeeping course. He was supposed to be going to Alabama for a job with Louis Harbin, a master queen breeder, but he'd just started as Vermont state bee inspector. Was I interested in going to Alabama? I leaped at the opportunity, which became much more then queen breeding. It turned out Louis had been wiped out by American foulbrood and my job became burning it up and starting anew for him. I came back to Vermont the next year. With some experience with the U.S. Soil Conservation Service, that gave me the credentials to pick up the newly created Vermont State Apiculturist position.

As the first full-time bee inspector I wore three hats—with extension, marketing, and regulatory responsibilities. After ten years we'd cleaned up most of the then prevalent foulbrood but by then the tracheal mites had arrived. I quit the state's apiculturist job in 1990 and went commercial, buying out Charles Ferree on the Champlain Islands. This meant I had the Hunger Mt. and City Market Co-op accounts and I began to pollinate for Chazy Orchard in NY and Hackett's and Allen's Orchards on the Champlain Islands. This allowed me a modest life as a small commercial beekeeper for the next 20 years. In 2010, I sold most of Bee Haven's existing apiaries and all of our accounts to Josh White of Northwoods Apiary in Troy, Vermont. I intended to keep a smaller scale operation going with 150 hives. With the help of my wife, Genevieve, we transitioned to specializing in raw, unfiltered honey we continue to sell to New England health-conscious families, herbalists and medicine makers who come to our farm each season to pick up bulk buckets.[3]

In his first year as inspector (1979), Drutchas wrote the following:

Beekeeping is rapidly becoming a very popular and rewarding hobby for many individuals. Everywhere you look, beehives are popping up like mushrooms—new beekeepers, commercial operators and part-timers. As a hobby, it fits right into the 'back-to-the-landers' dream of a large garden, a few goats, and a beehive or two.

FIGURE 2: **Drutchas and bees.**
PHOTO COURTESY OF RICK DRUTCHAS

---

3 Personal communication with authors.

Due to this rapid increase, the apiary inspection program must continue to increase public awareness as to the importance of such a program. Bee diseases result in losses of several thousands of dollars each year. American foulbrood, European foulbrood, Sac brood, Chalk brood, and Nosema are the major diseases our inspectors search for. Infections can be transmitted from larva to larvae by nursing bees but can also spread from hive to hive by robber bees. Early detection and control are the best means of limiting the spread of these diseases. (Drutchas 1980)

Presciently, Drutchas pointed out the coming plague of varroa mites, which had already caused havoc in bee yards throughout much of the world. (Varroa would arrive in Vermont during 1992.)

In his biennial report to the Vermont Commissioner of Agriculture, Drutchas wrote:

Previous to making diagnoses, we have generally had to wait six weeks for reports from the USDA laboratory in Beltsville, MD. Now the USDA is set up to identify AFB and nosema from samples sent in from the field.

Bee disease lectures are also being provided. These types of lectures and workshops will continue to raise public awareness on bee diseases. Along with technical assistance and inspection, work has been done with the VBA on a quarterly newsletter, the summer and winter meetings, and the Eastern States Exhibition.

The 1979 crop was reported to be the best in over 10 years with a one-hundred pound average reported all across Vermont. It was estimated that a total of 500,000 pounds of honey was produced in the Champlain Valley.

It was a different story in 1980. The crop yield varied from region to region. Commercial beekeepers in the Champlain Valley reported averages of 15-40 pounds while those in other areas averaged 30-100 pounds.

The open winter of 1980 turned out to be a good winter for the bees. They came through the winter strong with very few winter kills and in good shape to pollinate the apple orchards. The 1980 bad crop can be attributed to cold weather in June and a dry summer, in other words, the snowless winter." (Drutchas 1980)

| 9 | VERMONT COMMERCIAL BEEKEEPERS OWN 4,000 HIVES |
|---|---|
| 5 | OUT-OF-STATE COMMERCIAL BEEKEEPERS OWN 1,300 HIVES |
| 28 | PART-TIME COMMERCIAL BEEKEEPERS OWN 1,700 HIVES |
| 50 | REGISTERED BEEKEEPERS WITH 20-50 HIVES: 1,200 HIVES |
| 1,394 | NON-COMMERCIAL APIARIES (WITH 1-5 HIVES) |
| 252 | NON-COMMERCIAL APIARIES (WITH 5-10 HIVES) |
| 106 | NON-COMMERCIAL APIARIES (WITH 10-20 HIVES) |
| 12,172 | TOTAL REGISTERED HIVES |

TABLE 1: **1980 Statistics [locations not reported]**
SOURCE: DRUTCHAS (1980)

## VBA REPORTS: 1980–1982

Drutchas worked with the county extension agents to establish bee clubs in every county, although only a few of the clubs really took. The agents welcomed the professional help with a topic that was increasingly popular with the back-to-the-landers. Drutchas launched a series of beekeeping lectures and workshops across the state for beekeeping clubs, as well as other groups like Future Farmers of America (FFA), 4-H, the University of Vermont (UVM) Plant Club, the Vermont Institute of Natural Science, and the Vermont State Grange. The ones that really took were in St. Johnsbury, Morrisville, and Bennington. He appeared on radio and television talk shows and wrote articles in Extension Service newsletters and Vermont's Department of Agriculture *Agriview* newsletter. All in all, in 1981 and 1982, Drutchas conducted over 110 programs on good beekeeping management across the State.

In a 1979 report, VBA president Grace Hill of Hinesburg wrote:

All Vermonters benefit from the 10,000 or so colonies in the state. Not only do we depend on bees for honey production, but they are also important in pollinating the following plants that grow in the state: Fruit—apples, blueberries, cherries, pears, raspberries, and minor fruit; vegetables—cucumbers, melons, pumpkins and squash; legumes— alfalfa, alsike clover, birds-foot trefoil, Ladino clover, sweet clover, and vetches; flowers—domestic and wild; and buckwheat, soybeans and sunflowers. Bees are invaluable to dairy farmers as they reseed their legume crops and cut down on the times in which fields need to be mechanically re-seeded. The apple industry depends upon bees to insure a properly pollinated crop with about 2000 hired hives . . .

Vermont is not the easiest place to keep bees. Colonies are lost each year to over-wintering problems, swarming, diseases, and pesticides. Members of the association are currently researching more efficient overwintering.

The Vermont Beekeepers Association works with the Apiary Inspection program of the VT Dept. of Agriculture to teach beekeepers about disease and its control, mainly American Foulbrood. Outbreaks of the disease throughout the State in recent years have been controlled but there is still much education and vigilant inspection to be done yearly. (Hill 1980)

In a 1982 report, VBA secretary Coralie Magoon of Colchester wrote that there were 12,000 hives in the state tended by hobbyists with a few, to professionals with hundreds. Through the VBA newsletter and one-day seminars and workshops around the state, members were kept current on such topics as queen rearing, new research, improved methods for wintering, disease control, and other topics. About 200 were members of VBA. Magoon noted, "And it seems that there are as many varied ways of keeping bees as there are beekeepers, and each will stand by his or her method."

## AMERICAN FOULBROOD (AFB): A CONTINUING THREAT AFTER MORE THAN 100 YEARS

Of AFB, Drutchas said:

There was a lot when I began. I burned hundreds of colonies. There were barns of used equipment full of it. The old timers didn't know much. It wasn't on their radar, and that became my big crusade to educate these guys about the destructiveness of AFB. When I started there were beekeepers in the back woods that didn't have a basic understanding of bacteria and how it could spread, made for some interesting discussions. Even basic stuff like how bees collect honey. I remember this fellow showing me how hard his bees where working he said look at that bee it's carrying honey on its head, he was referring to chicory pollen on the bee head thinking they made honey out of that white stuff.[4]

4 Drutchas interview 2017.

In 1980, I found 233 cases of AFB out of 4,100 hives inspected, for a 5.6 percent rate, much too high, when it should be about 1 percent.

Drutchas wrote at length about treating for AFB and the limitations of the antibiotic Terramycin which only works to kill the bacteria in the growing stage, but not the resting stage. (Drutchas 1982)

## THE OLDEST BEE HOUSE STILL STANDING IN VERMONT

FIGURE 3: **This one-story hexagonal bee house was known as the Badger Apiary. The building was originally painted yellow and is believed to have been built by Alden Badger of Hardwick, VT c. 1900. The building was originally sited on property owned by Edward Utton in Mackville (Hardwick) but was moved down the road several lots to the property of Marc and Joyce Bellavance. Joyce is the grand-daughter of Alden Badger.**
PHOTO CREDIT: HISTORIC PRESERVATION CONSULTANT, ELIZABETH PRITCHETT, 1986

FIGURE 4: **American foulbrood levels were kept in check during the 1980s thanks in part to a foulbrood sniffing dog named Max.** PHOTO COURTESY OF RICK DRUTCHAS

# MAX THE AFB DOG

Based upon experiences in Maryland and Michigan, Drutchas and the Vermont State Police Canine Corps trained a dog named Max to sniff out the distinctive rotting larvae smell of AFB. The dog had been too rambunctious to be a drug sniffer, but for a couple of years, he was good at identifying AFB. Drutchas would lead him through a yard and he would stop and sniff at the offending colony. Max could only be used during cold weather when the bees were not flying. During the spring of 1986, they ran the dog past 890 hives in 44 apiaries. Max sat at 21 hives, of which 14 were verified as being diseased.[5]

When it came to actually destroying hives, Drutchas said:

Yes, we had the law's requirement and a police power to go and burn hives, but you never wanted to come in like a cop and say 'Do it or else!' You had to talk people into it. I'd explain why we had the law. I'd do the toothpick demonstration. I'd promise to send the sample off to the U.S. Department of Agriculture laboratory in Beltsville, Maryland. When they understood the law, most people complied readily. And if we had to burn the hive, I always had the beekeeper light the match!

One year I spotted an abandoned hive on one farm I passed. I stopped, and it was full of AFB. When I looked in the barn there were a dozen other hives, loaded with foul brood. I went and told the farmer's wife that we'd have to come back and burn the hives.

In about two weeks I came back with my assistant.

We knocked on the door and the farmer's son comes to the door. I told him we were here to burn the hives and we'd talked to his mother about it.

He turns and pointed toward the living room and there she was laid out on the sofa, dead.

Really embarrassed, we said, "Oh, my Gosh, we'll come back later!"

But outside, my assistant said, "Let's not wait, let me talk to this guy."

So gently but insistently he tells the son that we'll dig a hole and burn all this equipment and cover it up and he wouldn't have to worry about it.

Then the son said, "Well, we could use our tractor to dig the hole."

"That's good," we said.

"And would this be today?" the son asked.

---

5 Alas, the dog came to a grim end. In his second year, Mack broke loose at Drutchas' home in Worcester and was struck by a car on Route 12. Drutchas said, "He couldn't walk so I had to put him down. To this day it's hard to think about Max without breaking down. I really loved that dog."

"'Absolutely!" we said.

Then the boy looked up with a big smile and said, almost to himself, "Won't that make the neighbors think!"[6]

## EASTERN APICULTURAL SOCIETY (1980)

In 1980, the VBA hosted its second EAS Summer Conference. John Tardie of Essex Junction was president of the VBA and became president of EAS for that year.

Tardie was born in Jericho and served in the US Marines during the Korean War. He built an extensive bookkeeping and tax preparation business and was also passionate about beekeeping. Tardie established Vermont Beekeeping Supply to sell equipment and bees to northwestern Vermont beekeepers. Along with the equipment, he supplied free guidance and answers to countless questions from his customers.

In organizing and hosting the conference, Tardie had help from numerous Vermonters, including Charles Mraz, Mike Palmer, Enoch Tompkins, Grace Hill, Peter Genier, Rick Drutchas, Charles Ferree, and many others. Altogether, 580 people attended the conference.[7]

In his conference report, Tardie noted:

EAS was founded in 1955 by a group of beekeepers, USDA scientists and university extension specialists who put together a two-day meeting about current beekeeping problems. Today, the membership includes folks from 21 states and 5 Canadian provinces and lasts for a week. Its board includes directors elected or appointed by their state associations. The summer conference is held each year in a different State or province and is attended by 400-700 people. Attendees came from 22 states and two Canadian provinces. Seventy-four attendees were Vermonters.

Although some attendees have thousands of hives, most have fewer than 20. Some have kept bees for 50 years, some are rank beginners. You can always find someone to talk to at your level. Everyone is very open and willing to answer questions. There are no cliques. You are free to mingle or sit at any table, which may have a beginner, a world-famous apicultural scientist, a seasoned sideliner, a pollination beekeeper with 5000 hives, a PhD in entomology, or even the American Honey Queen sponsored by

---

6 Interview with Rick Drutchas, October, 2017.

7 Vermont would not host another EAS until 2012.

the American Beekeeping Federation. (This year's queen, Renee Blatt of Pennsylvania has 20 hives of her own.)

At the short course in beekeeping (on Monday & Tuesday) led by Dr. Dewey Caron of the University of Delaware (and a UVM graduate), attendance grew to over 150 attendees for two levels, one for beginners and one for advanced beekeepers. There were 11 instructors in all. About 20-25 hives are brought onto the grounds for visual and hands-on experience.

The E.A.S. main conference lasted from Wednesday noon to Friday evening. There were a series of 15-45 minute talks with slides and/or films on some of the most pertinent topics in beekeeping. Examples from this year's conference were: Revisiting American foulbrood, vine crop pollination, integrated pest management, apple pollination and hive quality assessment. Ralph Gamber of Dutch Gold Honey, one of the largest honey packers in the country spoke of industry efforts to stop adulteration of honey with corn syrup. Dr. Roger Morse of Cornell University spoke about the impending peril of varroa mites, which, he said, would be worse than the foulbrood diseases and a peril for which there were no remedies to date. (Tardie 1980)

## IMPORTS AND PROMOTION

In 1984, Drutchas wrote, "about 100 million pounds of honey was imported into the U.S.[8] With the strong U.S. dollar and cheap foreign labor, foreign honey bulk prices dropped as low as thirty-three cents per pound, about half the cost of production of domestic honey." (Drutchas 1984)

In response to this flood of Mexican, Argentine, and Chinese honey, the federal Department of Agriculture began a loan program based on 64 cents per pound. The majority of American honey producers reneged on the loan repayments, leaving the federal government with 100,000,000 pounds of honey. Subsequently, the government let the producers pay back the loans at 47 cents per pound, thus swallowing the 17 cents difference. Drutchas wrote that the better solution would be a tariff on imported honey.

In his 1983–1984 report, Drutchas continued to lament the effect of low cost foreign honey.

Until recently, Vermont honey producers have been exempt from this foreign honey problem. Vermont honey, like Vermont maple syrup, has a

---

8 By 2015, that number was 380 million pounds.

'mystique' that keeps it in demand for the tourist trade. The Vermont name has kept Vermont bulk honey prices between 60-70 cents per pound.

[But now] lower-priced foreign honey is keeping domestic honey prices down, making it harder for Vermont honey producers to keep up with infla- tion and stay out of the red. Foreign honey producers and rich honey pack- ers are not encouraging the growth of Vermont agriculture. They are not increasing Vermont honey production and not pollinating Vermont fruits and vegetables. They are simply making money by fraudulently labeling honey. (Drutchas 1984)

In response to the competition from low-cost foreign honey, a Vermont Honey Promotion Board was set up in 1984 to help promote consumption of Vermont honey. It produced, among other things, a honey commercial and poster, and a standard Vermont honey label available for use by all Vermont Beekeepers. Vermont beekeepers also looked to increase the number of bee pre- sentations presented to local groups, county fairs, schools, and service clubs.

In May 1986, a National Honey Board (NHB) was established to fund proj- ects in research, promotion, and consumer education to expand honey markets in the United States. Beekeepers and importers around the country who pro- duced or imported over 6,000 pounds of honey would be assessed 1 cent/pound to support the program. Drutchas hoped that some of that money would come back to the Vermont Honey Promotion Board. Eleven Vermont producers con- tributed to the NHB.[9]

## MAPLE GROVE HONEY MUSEUM
*Now the site of WW Building Supply (434 VT Route 100, Wilmington, VT)*

From 1978 to 1984, the Maple Grove Honey Museum (a museum and store) served as an extension and promotional arm of Maple Grove Farms of St. Johnsbury, VT. They sold honey, maple syrup, candy, salad dressing, pancake batter, and other Vermont goodies. They also processed honey for mail order. Honey would arrive in 55-gallon drums to be bottled and shipped from the back room. The store had some beekeeping equipment and at least four observation hives with exit/entrance tubes to the outside. Three of the four full-time employ- ees were beekeepers in their own right (Connie Robinson, Chris Chapman, and

---

9 The next twenty years saw progressive increase in imported honey to where two-thirds of the honey consumed in the United States is foreign.

Julie Moore). A part-time tour guide was employed in the summer to talk about bees to the bus tour people and to sell honey.

This venture was primarily directed at tourists, as it catered to senior citizen bus tours, which helped keep the Deerfield Valley ski lodges full in the summer.

Bus drivers would pull up and let the seniors off right in front of the door. One time after pulling up to the museum to unload passengers, a driver did not move the bus or close the door. An hour later, the bus was full of confused bees. It took several hours to get them all off the bus.[10]

## THE VBA'S MOST USED . . . AND LONGEST LIVED PROMOTION

In the mid-1980s, Rick Drutchas oversaw a collective effort by the VBA and the Vermont Honey Promotion Board to publish *The Vermont Beekeeper's Cookbook.* The information and recipes in the pocket sized book for meals and body care products were compiled by members of the VBA. Jane Wilson volunteered the typing, and David Ambrose and Charles Ferree (a former VBA president) contributed the information on honey bees and nectar-producing plants in Vermont. Susan Marno collected and tested numerous recipes, and facts about both honey and cooking with honey were submitted by Grace Hill of Hinesburg, a former president of the VBA. Linoleum block print illustrations of bee forage plants were done by Jane Eddy of

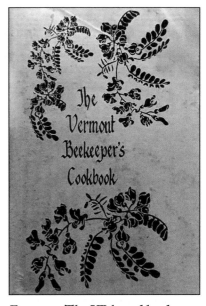

FIGURE 5: **The VBA cookbook was first published with seventy-three pages in a small format (a little over 4″ x 6.5″) in 1985.**

FIGURE 6: **An updated version of the VBA cookbook utilized a larger (8.5″ x 8.5″) format. At the time of this writing there is talk about possibly updating the cookbook once again.**

---

10 As related by Connie Robinson, next-door neighbor and manager.

Middlebury, and the woodcut print on the cover was the work of well-known artist Mary Azarian of Plainfield. The first edition of the cookbook was bankrolled by the Honey Promotion Board and published in 1985. Subsequent editions were paid for by the VBA from the book's sales proceeds. To date, the cookbook has gone through two revisions selling 1,000-1,300 copies a year while providing a modest but regular profit for the VBA.

In the midst of all this promotional work, Drutchas persuaded the Vermont legislature to give the inspectors more authority in dealing with the expected arrival of tracheal and varroa mites. He told the lawmakers that he expected the tracheal mites to arrive first through package bees and queens shipped from the South.

## TRACHEAL MITES

First came tracheal mites, which were identified in the United States in 1984 and washed over much of the country within a few years. By August 1986, they were reported in twenty-seven states.

Tracheal mites are microscope mites that reproduce in the trachea (airways) of the bee. The mites feed through the walls of the trachea, causing scarification of the tracheal tubes. Such injuries limit the bees' ability to acquire oxygen and can also physically obstruct the airway.

At Drutchas' urging, Vermont established a quarantine in 1985 barring all shipments of bees into Vermont from mite-infested areas. Years later, Drutchas confessed that the quarantine was a mistake:

> Due to the inaccuracy of the mite detection techniques, it was impossible to determine mite-free areas from which to get bees. Tracheal mite infested colonies from supposedly mite-free areas poured into the State. The quarantine was a disaster.[11]

The first tracheal mites detected in Vermont were in Chester in March 1987. During the following fifteen months, seven more apiaries with a total of fifty colonies located in four counties were found to be infested. Twenty of those colonies died during the winter; the others were killed in the belief these cases were isolated.

It took about twelve more months for the mites to build up to detectable levels statewide. Positive samples taken in October 1988 from large apiaries in

---

11 Interview with Rick Drutchas, June 2016.

Figure 7: **An adult Varroa mite sitting on the thorax of a young worker bee.**
Photo credit: Steve Parise

the Champlain Valley made it clear that eradication of this pest was impossible. There were simply too many infested colonies, and the mites had spread to neighboring apiaries and undoubtedly to feral bees. Some beekeepers lost as many as 30-60 percent of their hives.

A few beekeepers, led by Kirk Webster of Bridport, went cold turkey on mite treatments and took losses well over 50 percent in an effort to build a resistant strain of bees from surviving stock.

In the midst of tracheal mite challenges, a much greater threat emerged on the horizon: what would become named *Varroa destructor*. The parasitic bee mite, *V. destructor* is one of the most serious pests of the western honey bee, (*Apis mellifera*). About one hundred years ago it jumped species from its primary host, the eastern honey bee (*Apis cerana*), to *A. mellifera* and has since afflicted most honey bee colonies across the world.

Adult bees serve as intermediate hosts when little or no brood is available and as a means of transport. The female mites attach to the adult bee between the abdominal segments on the underside of the abdomen, making them difficult to detect. These are also places from which they can easily feed on the bees' fat bodies.[12] As a consequence, the adult bee suffers from an impaired immune system making it harder for the bee to detoxify pesticides, more vulnerable to microbial invasion, and leading to reduced life expectancy. (Ramsay 2018)

In his 1987–1988 Inspector's Report, Drutchas, like a 4th century Roman watching the approach of Vandals and Goths, described the inexorable march of varroa destruction across the land:

> The first mite was detected in Wisconsin in September, 1987, but was probably brought there by a migratory beekeeper from Florida. The mites probably came from South America. It attaches to the body of the bee in both the pupal and adult stages and weakens the bee by sucking its hemolymph. In the process RNA viruses such as Deformed Wing Virus (DWV) and Israeli Acute Paralysis Virus (IAPV) spread to bees. Experts estimated that half of all hives in the U.S. will die from this pest in next few years if the experience in Europe was a guide. Some chemicals have been developed which might reduce these numbers. Fluvalinate, a synthetic pyrethroid impregnated in plastic strips like a flea collar, have been approved by the EPA for use with queen bees, and eventually for all bees. They are not 100 percent effective and the mites are expected to develop resistance to almost any chemical in three to four years. It will be an on-going battle. (Drutchas 1988)

After ten years in harness, Rick Drutchas left in 1990 to go into "private practice." Meanwhile his words would be fully justified during the next few years as Vermont beekeeping became irrevocably tied to that of the entire world through the varroa mite.

---

12 For two decades following its arrival on U.S. shores, researchers thought that varroa fed on the bees' blood (hemolymph) but this would be proven to be a false conclusion.

FIGURE 8: **A modern view inside the Badger Apiary** (SEEN ON PAGE 105).

FIGURE 9: **From right to left, Charles (Juna) Mraz, Jr., William (Bill) Mraz, and a friend.**

## CHAPTER 5

# *Adapting to a Changing World*

*As for beekeeping education, there was next to none, except at the bi-annual Vermont Beekeepers Association meetings. There were no workshops, no certification program, no mentors, no best practices. There were no local clubs and when UVM did away with extension work, there was nothing except the bi-annual VBA meetings.*

—MIKE PALMER

### A NEW INSPECTOR

In 1990, the State of Vermont went in search of a new inspector, but due to budget tightening in Montpelier, they now would have reduced beekeeping duties. Whoever was hired would spend half their time on apple inspections. The next year, after a nationwide search, the state hired Steve Parise.[1]

Parise came with broad experience. He began keeping bees as a teenager in suburban Detroit. As a student at Michigan State University, he managed the university apiary under the renowned Roger Hoopingarner. After graduation, Parise took a job at the University of Illinois under Professor Elbert Jaycox, where

---

1 Parise described the evolution of his job this way: "Yes, when I was hired in 1991, I was spending about half on bees, half on the apple export program. However, as the export apple industry in VT gradually declined, my 'apple' time was shifted to the pesticide program. Once the apple export program died completely, the food safety programs (nationally) were getting started, and since I was already licensed by USDA as a program cooperator, it was logical for me to take that program on. With the slow but steady growth in food safety issues, I was shifted from the pesticide section to the consumer protection section where I was assigned other food safety, food related program responsibilities."

FIGURE 1: **Steve Parise.** PHOTO CREDIT: MARILYN McCLURE

he helped with classes and publications. His next job was working in a big commercial operation in Idaho with over 10,000 hives, which produced honey and then pollinated alfalfa and almonds. After five years, Parise went back to Michigan and cobbled together jobs with bees, a post office, a bakery, and state bee inspection work. Then he left for Hawaii to work for a company that did three harvests a year and millions of pounds of honey, of which he said, "Whew! That was a young man's job. We were always pulling honey!" It was then that he saw an ad for the Vermont inspector's job in the *American Bee Journal*. Parise applied, and after several phone interviews across seven time zones, he was hired. Parise arrived in Vermont just ahead of a new pest that would dramatically change the face of Vermont beekeeping.

## VARROA ARRIVES

In his first biennial report, Parise wrote that winter losses were slightly higher than normal, with commercial beekeepers losing more hives to tracheal mites and backyard beekeepers losing more to starvation.[2]

In that report Parise noted that as of June 30, 1992, varroa had not appeared in Vermont, but that it would surely come. He laid out a plan of defense against the mite that involved monitoring and sampling twice a year and examining both adult bees and drone brood:

> If one colony in an apiary is found to have varroa mites, the beekeeper should assume that all colonies have mites. This is because bees frequently drift into the wrong hives and take the mites with them . . . Beekeepers in Vermont who are aware of what is going on in their hives will be able to handle this new pest. Others will not be so fortunate, because once these mites get established, it will take only two-three years before the colonies succumb . . . Experience in other states has shown that these mites can be controlled, but beekeepers must be vigilant and keep track of mile levels in their colonies.

---

2 Said professional beekeeper Peter Genier of Fair Haven: "I lost 40 percent of my hives two years in a row from tracheal mites. Those were sparse pickings; it selected out the people who weren't hard working."

FIGURE 2: **Steve Parise (middle) leads a workshop at Burlington's Intervale.**

Today, the only approved chemical control is Apistan®, a synthetic pyrethroid. While not 100 percent effective, a high level of control will be achieved when used according to the label directions. (Parise 1992)

However, Parise further warned that the mites could become resistant to fluvalinate—the active ingredient in Apistan®—particularly through misuse of the chemical.

In the fall of 1992, varroa mites made their ominous debut in Vermont and began to spread to most parts of the state, bringing weakened colonies and other mite-induced bee diseases.

Most of the large operations adjusted to the infestation. Unfortunately, this meant another $3 expense per colony to pay for Apistan strips, the only US Environmental Protection Agency (EPA) approved miticide to control the mites, and additional trips to the bee yards to administer the strips.

Two years later, Parise warned:

Many hobby beekeepers are still unaware or unconcerned about the dire consequences of this pest and will soon see weakened or dead colonies as a result. Fortunately there has been no evidence, as of yet, that varroa are developing resistance to Apistan®. This will allow time for researchers and industry to work on additional control strategies and/or resistant strains.

Tracheal mites are still present in most areas of Vermont, but for the most part, are not as serious a pest as they once were. It appears that the most susceptible bees have died out, and the current bee population appears to be holding its own. Resistant lines are also becoming available, most notably the 'Buckfast' strain, which are showing natural resistance to the mites. (Parise 1994)

## MORE THAN HALF VERMONT'S BEES AFFLICTED

During the biennium of 1995–1996, 5,238 hives were inspected and 58 percent were infested with varroa mites. Parise wrote a lucid and sobering assessment of what was the greatest crisis to hit beekeeping in the 20th century:

As reported in the last biennium, varroa mites are having a greater impact on Vermont's (and the nation's) bees. Hobby beekeepers (those with less than 20 hives) have been especially hard hit. With the 1995 crop coming in so late, control measures for varroa were applied later since the material used, Apistan, can only be applied after the harvest. Many beekeepers reported colonies dying late last year after removing a good honey crop from apparently strong colonies. Many beekeepers that did not lose colonies in the fall were dismayed to find heavy losses this spring (1996). For Vermont, there are several apparent explanations:
  • Delayed mite treatment allowed the last several brood cycles to be parasitized, which resulted in a shorter life span and higher mortality for the bees that would become the "winter" and "spring" bees to get the colony going in the spring;
  • A prolonged winter;
  • A cool wet spring;
  • Tracheal mites.
Add the effects of several minor bee diseases, which by themselves are not serious, with the stress of continual feeding of both tracheal and varroa mites and the results were devastating to many colonies. Many hobbyists lost all their colonies and those that survived were often weak.

There has been much speculation in the bee industry that the mites are spreading a disease or several diseases. This theory is based upon how the mites feed. Both types of mites have biting mouth parts with which they frequently puncture the bee's body. The microscopic tracheal mites feed on the inside of the bees and varroa feed on the outside, both producing many puncture wounds that serve as sites of infection. Since both mites are capable of movement from bee to bee, it is possible that they are spreading diseases from one colony to another, either through robbing or when colonies are split by the beekeeper.

The loss of many colonies has several direct results, including a reduction in the number of colonies available for commercial pollination for crops such as apples, melons, squash and cucumbers which result in lower yields (higher prices) and reduced quality. Indirect results include fewer bees to pollination plants used by wildlife as food sources. Many gardeners have noticed a big decline in the number of bees in their gardens in Vermont and elsewhere.

Also, many 'wild' bee colonies have died off, due to the mites, resulting in a significant decline in pollination.

Apiary program activities will continue to emphasize working with bee-keepers to identify and control varroa mites, monitoring miticide use inside hives, providing educational information and materials to beekeepers (especially new beekeepers), monitoring mite populations and spread, and monitoring the incidences of other bee diseases, including American foulbrood and chalkbrood." (Parise 1996)

In his next biennial report (1997–1998), Parise sounded a bit less pessimistic:

The honey crop for the 1996 season ended up a bit below normal due to the rather wet season. Wholesale prices were up significantly, approaching $1.00/lb. This allowed most of the larger operations to post a profit, which was a pleasant change. . .

Varroa mites had a lesser impact on Vermont's bees during the biennium due, in part, to a greater awareness by beekeepers, and the proper use of Apistan to control this mite. Even though varroa is found in most apiaries, the numbers of mites in individual hives is relatively low and the bees are able to survive and still be productive. (Parise 1998)

He also noted a decline in tracheal mite predation:

Ongoing surveys indicate a low level 'background' population in most apiaries, but a steady decline in the lethal populations seen in the mid-1980s. The reason for this decline is not clear. Possibly the most susceptible bee populations have died off, the remaining population has a degree of resistance to the mite, or perhaps the mite itself has undergone some change. Whatever the reason, it appears *for now, that tracheal mites are not a major problem for Vermont beekeepers.*" [*Emphasis added—Ed.*]

While varroa mites continued to be a problem for VT beekeepers, there was a new twist. Some mites were found resistant to Apistan®, the only EPA-approved chemical for treating varroa. This development was expected, as resistance to Apistan® had already been noted elsewhere in the country.

Parise then applied to the EPA for an emergency one-year permit to use CheckMite™ pest strips with the harsher organophosphate pesticide, coumaphos. Unfortunately for some beekeepers, Apistan-resistant varroa had already established themselves in their hives, causing losses of 30-75 percent. And, as Parise noted, varroa would inevitably become resistant to this harsher chemical, which indeed happened within three years.

During the 1999-2000 biennium there were 1,423 registered beekeepers operating 9,400 colonies in 1,862 locations. Parise performed 6,198 hive inspections throughout Vermont during the two years. Varroa mites were found in 70 percent of the colonies and tracheal mites in 62 percent. Both numbers were similar to those in the last biennium. AFB was found in 2.7 percent. (Parise 2000, p. 30)

## MIGRATORY BEEKEEPING

During 1995–1998, a significant change that occurred in the Vermont bee industry was the movement of bee colonies out of state for the winter. Several large commercial beekeepers adopted this practice. About 15 percent of the state's bees were moved south for the winter, with Florida the most popular destination, followed by South Carolina and Maryland.

Of this practice, Parise wrote:

The reasons for migration are several. In the case of Florida, there is an opportunity to make a significant honey crop during the winter, from the blossoms of orange trees. The move also eliminates expensive and time-consuming activities such as feeding bees or wrapping them for winter protection. Since the bees are in a warmer climate, they tend to maintain stronger populations during the winter, allowing the beekeepers to make divisions of stronger colonies to replace losses, increasing their hive counts or offering nucs for sale to other beekeepers. Also, they are able to supply consistently strong colonies for apple pollination in the spring.

FIGURE 3: **Photo of Peter Genier loading hives to send to California.**
PHOTO CREDIT: STEVE PARISE

The downside is the logistics of picking up several hundred hives, loading them on trucks and successfully moving them hundreds of miles south. There is also increased wear and tear on the equipment, as well as the additional stress on the bees and beekeepers, and exposure to potential disease and parasite problems. [*Also, there was the increasing fight for space to place the bees, and later, the Africanization of bees.—Ed.*] The trend in the moment is for increased migratory activity as commercial beekeepers look for ways to make their operations more profitable and efficient. (Parise 1998)[3]

---

3 Interestingly, only one or two Vermont beekeepers ever joined the vast mid-winter migration of two-thirds of all American honey bee colonies to California to pollinate almonds.

Some of those migratories were Roland Smith of Singing Cedars Apiaries, Orwell, Todd Hardie of Honey Garden Apiaries, Hinesburg, and Josh White of North Woods Apiaries, Fairfield.

Old Mill Apiaries owner, Peter Genier of Fair Haven, who took his bees to Florida, describes that experience:

> I grew up on a dairy farm in Pawlet. My sister was related to a beekeeper who had over 200 hives. When I was 12, I started going there for a month in the summers. It was only harvesting, but I still learned a lot about bees and enjoyed the experience. When I was 18, I got a job as a part-time New York bee inspector. It was a great summer job for college kid. It gradually dawned on me that I could make a living with bees.
>
> In 1970 I bought out a beekeeper in Rupert who had about 80 hives, but still kept my inspector's job. My first full year as a beekeeper was 1974. By 1985, I had 500 colonies and kept it that way until the 1990s. Ninety percent of the business was honey, and the other ten percent was selling nucs to other beekeepers. I rented about 300 colonies for apple pollination, which we loaded by hand. That was really insane!
>
> After our kids were out of school, I began taking bees south. In 1995 I first rented, then bought a honey house in Florida. At first it was a miraculous experience. You had all winter to re-queen, and get an orange blossom crop. One year we got 200 barrels on 1000 colonies. We came back here raring to go on May 1. Did that for ten years and got up to 1,500 colonies. But the development came, wiped out many orange groves and we lost places to put the bees. Then the tracheal and varroa mites came. Being in Florida was less and less fun.
>
> We had a small, diverse group of professionals who got together periodically and enjoyed each other, talking bees without talking politics. Nice quality to meetings. If we had to make a run to Dadant's warehouse in New York, we would go out and get a load. They include Rick Drutchas of Worcester, Mike Palmer of St. Albans, Ed Hazen of Highgate, Franklin Heyburn of Waterville, and myself from Fair Haven.[4]

Following his time in Florida, Genier moved back to Vermont for several years. He then relocated to Hawaii, where he now lives.

---

4 Interview with Peter Genier, May 2015.

# OLDEST APIARY SITE IN VERMONT?

FIGURE 4: **This apiary location, about 3 miles west of Middlebury, is believed to be one of the oldest consistently maintained apiary sites in the state dating back to the 1860s.**

DESPITE THE GROWING INTEREST in migratory beekeeping, a lot of bees in Vermont still stay in Vermont year around. On the top of a rocky ledge about three miles west of the town of Middlebury, Ross Conrad maintains a bee yard that is reported to be a location where, according to Bill Mraz, bees have been kept for as long as anyone can remember going back to at least the American Civil War. This information came to Bill from his father, Charles Mraz who had worked for Philip Crane from 1928–1931 before buying Mr. Crane out. The location of this particular apiary site was just the right distance where a beekeeper could ride out from town with a horse and wagon, get the beekeeping work done, and get back to town in time for the evening meal. While the exact location of the apiary was probably modified slightly when Vermont Route 125 was built through the area, this is one location where bees have been kept longer and more consistently than most any other bee yard in the state.

FIGURE 5: **Adult small hive beetles exposed on the wooden top bars of frames of comb in a hive.** PHOTO CREDIT: STEVE PARISE

## SMALL HIVE BEETLES ARRIVE

The small hive beetle (SHB) is native to Africa and was first discovered in the United States during the second half of the 1990s. The beetles quickly spread to Vermont, undoubtedly with help from some of the migratory beekeepers that move their bees in and out of the state. The adult beetles can survive Vermont winters in the cluster of wintering bees. It is the beetle larvae that hatch from the eggs that the adult beetles lay, however, that can cause severe damage by causing the honey in the combs to ferment and become ruined. This latest pest can also attack and kill honey bee larvae and eat the pollen stored in hives housing colonies of bees that are too weak to defend themselves.

In his turn-of-the-century biennial report, Parise noted:

Another significant event during this biennium was the arrival of the small hive beetle (SHB), or the *Aethina tumida*. The SHB came to Florida in 1998, from southern Africa where it was considered a secondary bee pest. During the first year of infestation, several thousand colonies were destroyed by SHB. Adults and larvae cause damage in hives by feeding on empty comb, combs with honey and pollen and even brood combs. Honey leaks from damaged combs and is often spoiled by beetle feces . . . [However] It is believed that the SHB will be no more of a pest than wax moths are now. Inspections will continue through 2000 and 2001 to monitor this new pest . . . (Parise 2000, pp. 31-32)

Parise further observed:

> With the continued drop in honey prices, the increased fuel costs, and the exposure to new pests, such as small hive beetle, the wear and tear on bees, beekeepers and equipment, the number of beekeepers moving south leveled off and may start to decline. (Parise 2000)

## TREATMENT-FREE BEEKEEPING

A long, non-descript driveway off a main road in New Haven, Vermont, leads to the home of Kirk Webster and his business, Champlain Valley Bees and Queens. Each year Webster maintains about 300 colonies that he uses for honey production, around 400 baby nucs for catching queens that he either uses himself or offers for sale, and he tries to provide for sale an additional 400-500 treatment-free nucs of Russian heritage that have been tested by overwintering them in Vermont. The bees and queens he

FIGURE 6: **Kirk Webster**

produces are highly sought after and prized for their enhanced ability to survive both varroa and the weather extremes we have here in the Northeast.

Webster was born in Baltimore, Maryland. It was during the winter of 1970 as a high school junior that he injured his knee while tobogganing in Vermont. To help him pass his days while being laid up from the accident a friend gave Webster a book to read, a book on beekeeping that he "found fascinating." This was Webster's initial introduction into the world of honey bees.

His first beekeeping mentor was a Ukrainian immigrant named Myron Surmach, who kept about thirty colonies in New Jersey near his parent's home. In 1972, Webster moved to Middlebury and got his first beekeeping job working for Charles Mraz

FIGURE 7: **Kirk Webster inspecting a frame of comb drawn from his home-made foundation.** PHOTO COURTESY OF KIRK WEBSTER

at Champlain Valley Apiaries for about a year. From there, he went to run the farm program at the Mountain School in Vershire, Vermont for three seasons, after which he enrolled in the Environmental Studies program at Evergreen State College in Olympia, Washington. After 3 years, he moved to the Concord and Wenham, Massachusetts areas, where he started his first apiary with four colonies.

In 1986, Webster decided to move back to Vermont, to Addison County, and in 1989 bought out Ken Manchester's bee operation. A couple years later he started renting out Ken's old honey house in Cornwall to use as a base of operations. He eventually moved to Bridport, where in 2001 he built his honey-extracting wagon: a trailer that he outfitted with a custom-made extracting room. The trailer is built to accommodate his extracting equipment and it allows him to extract his honey anywhere he needs to, which can amount to 30,000-40,000 pounds in some years.

FIGURE 8: **Kirk's honey house and mobile honey extracting trailer (to the left).**

FIGURE 9 : **One of Kirk Webster's winter projects is making foundation, which he says is "the hardest thing I have ever had to do in beekeeping." Here Kirk pulls a sheet of home-made wax foundation through milled rollers that embosses the hexagon cell shape of the comb into a sheet of beeswax.** PHOTO COURTESY OF KIRK WEBSTER, CHAMPLAIN VALLEY BEES AND QUEENS

Webster's winter losses since the year 2000 have ranged from 10 to 50 percent...not any worse than most beekeepers who use mite treatments. One of his biggest beekeeping challenges, which most beekeepers can identify with, has been trying to help the bees deal with varroa mites. These days Webster does not treat for mites or worry about them since his yearly hive management approach also helps to address any mite issues he may have. Agricultural pesticides, pollutants, and loss of habitat and forage are his big worries these days, along with the relatively recent unpredictable and challenging weather conditions and patterns that have been less favorable for bees in the Champlain Valley of Vermont.

The biggest challenge Webster has faced in beekeeping has been making foundation from his own beeswax. It has taken a lot of trial and error for him to develop the most efficient methods by finding, building, or modifying his equipment and trying to figure out the ideal temperature for the beeswax during each stage of the foundation making process.

Champlain Valley Bees and Queens is run exclusively on Langstroth-style equipment, though Webster has modified his nuc equipment so that he can over-winter four nucleus colonies in one deep hive body. Webster has become known for overwintering nucleus colonies, but the first time he overwintered nucs in 1986, it was by accident. He would typically combine his small nucs with each other to get them through the winter, but one year he forgot a couple. When he discovered them the following spring, alive and healthy, he got curious. The next year he let several more baby nucs overwinter on purpose and they all survived again. He's been overwintering large numbers of small nucs each winter ever since.

Webster eventually settled in the town of New Haven, Vermont, where he was given a lifetime lease on property owned by environmental author and activist Bill McKibben. He endeavors to lead a simple lifestyle, close to nature and his bees. He does not have a Facebook page, does not twitter, does not own a cell phone, and does not even have an email address. Despite this he survives quite well and lives very comfortably at his home in Vermont. Webster is also a writer and has written many articles and essays, many of which can be viewed on a website that friends have set up for him at kirkwebster.com. Webster uses this website (and the help of some IT-oriented friends) to share his beekeeping knowledge and experiences, explore the issues he thinks are most important—"without interference, editing or censorship"—and allow him to pull together into one place all the things he has written since 2005.

Webster's website seems to sum up his beekeeping journey this way: "If I have made a small success with honey bees, it was achieved by working steadily and ignoring the advice and perspective of all kinds of modern, certified experts and well established beekeepers. I was guided instead by the bees themselves, by the old-time beekeepers—through their books and by using the same tools and equipment they used—and by studying the work of outstanding farmers who guided the energy of Nature into a harmonious outcome, instead of fighting against it."

## FOLLOWING WEBSTER'S LEAD

One result of the massive increase in honey bee losses nation-wide that occurred following the varroa invasion was a movement by many backyard and sideline beekeepers to abandon the use of treatments for mites and/or disease altogether. This movement away from chemical treatments and antibiotics is often fueled by a desire to create apiaries made up of colonies that have developed some level of tolerance to Varroa mites and honey bee pathogens. The primary basis for this treatment-free movement—to what is often termed a more "natural" approach to beekeeping—is the growing evidence that chemical-mite treatments, and the use of antibiotics to control diseases, have sub-lethal effects on honey bee colonies. Although treatments can help to control pests and disease, they can also weaken a colony's overall health and vitality at the same time.

The treatment-free movement in Vermont, spearheaded by Kirk Webster, was taken up by numerous other beekeepers several of which are outlined below:

Andrew Munkres of Lemon Fair Honey Works located in Cornwall, Vermont, keeps 120-150 colonies for honey production and building queen cells. He also maintains 200-300 nucleus colonies that he overwinters each year to offer for sale, or to replace his winter losses. Andrew's apiary was built with bees that he bartered for from Kirk Webster in exchange for labor. His entire operation grew from that first hive along with breeder queens that he brought in from the U.S. Russian Honeybee Breeders Association. He sells queens, nucleus colonies, and produces comb and bottled honey each year.

Tim McFarline founded McFarline Apiaries in Benson, Vermont, and credits Kirk Webster as one of his primary mentors. He maintains around 200 honey producing colonies, as well as, about 300 nucleus colonies and sells as many as 100 nucs a year, along with queens, honey and value-added hive products. Tim does not use treatments and reports that, like Kirk, his honey production colonies tend to sustain much higher losses than his nucleus colonies each year.

Joshua White of Northwoods Apiaries in Westfield, Vermont holds the distinction of being the only beekeeper to ever manage a certified organic apiary in the state. Joshua's operation was first certified by the Northeast Organic Farmers Association (NOFA-VT) in 2002 and remained certified organic until 2011. As a certified organic beekeeper, Josh was not permitted to use synthetic chemicals or antibiotics to control pests and diseases in his hives.

Ross Conrad who runs Dancing Bee Gardens in Middlebury, Vermont maintains about 100 treatment-free hives primarily for honey and nucleus colony production. He also wrote the first book on organic beekeeping to be published in the U.S: *Natural Beekeeping: Organic Approaches to Modern Apiculture*, promoting beekeeping without the use of pesticides, antibiotics and artificial feeding on a regular basis. The book outlines a theory that consists of five management techniques, that, when combined in one manner or another, allows a beekeeper to keep colonies alive and healthy without needing to treat for mites or disease. The five management techniques are: use bees with genetics proven to have some level of resistance to mites and diseases; use screened bottom boards to remove mites from hives that fall off the bees; make regular splits or nucleus colonies in order to interrupt the brood cycle of the mites, slowing their population growth; rotate out the old combs in colonies on a regular basis to reduce wax contamination by pathogens and pesticide residues; and trap mites or cull and destroy the capped drone brood within which varroa mites are reproducing.

According to Conrad, all beekeepers that are treatment-free and successful at it seem to be doing some combination of these five management techniques.[5] Sometimes the beekeeper is doing these things consciously and sometimes they are accomplishing them as a by-product of other actions (such as making up nucleus colonies for sale that at the same time interrupts the brood cycle and causes old comb within the brood nest to be replaced).

Although none of the five techniques tend to be successful on their own over the long run, when combined, Conrad maintains that they can allow an apiary to keep the majority of hives alive year after year without the need for treatments.

In 2015, Conrad applied for and received a $15,000 USDA Sustainable Agriculture Research and Education (SARE) Farmers Grant to test his theory that he had described in detail in the 2nd edition of *Natural Beekeeping* (2013): that treatment-free management techniques could help control varroa mites in colonies as effectively as a commercially available treatment. The three-year trial looked at the differences between mite populations, colony survival, and honey production between the various mite control approaches.

His SARE project (FNE16-840) progress report summary describes it this way: "This project is testing the ability to prevent Varroa mite populations from reaching damaging proportions in honey bee colonies solely through the beekeeper's use of physical management techniques including the use of screened bottom boards, a break in the brood cycle, the culling of older comb, and the

---

5 Unless they are keeping bees in an area where colonies have had the opportunity to build up significant natural resistance to the mite, such as some beekeeping in Africanized honey bee territory.

removal and destruction of capped drone brood that contains reproducing mites. If such techniques, when combined, can be shown to sustain the lives of colonies without the use of chemical treatments, it will reduce pesticide use, while increasing bee health and help reduce the costs and labor associated with yearly colony losses."

Conrad was assisted by UVM's Samantha Alger and Alex Burnham with the statistical analysis of the preliminary data and the preparation of data graphs, while Cornell's Tom Seeley acted as the Technical Advisor for the study.

## MIKE PALMER

Meanwhile, there were beekeepers in the state that used Webster's example not necessarily to be treatment-free but as a springboard to other beekeeping approaches. Mike Palmer, of French Hill Apiaries in St. Albans, Vermont tells his story this way:

I started with a couple of packages I bought from F.W. Jones in Canada in 1974. I took an extension class with Enoch Tompkins. I made a couple supers of honey and got Kermit Mayo to extract it for me. I took all their honey and lost them in the winter. But I was hooked. The next year I got 10 packages.

There wasn't much teaching then. Most people were 'bee havers', not 'bee keepers.' They might as well have had skeps, for the number of times they looked inside hives. Most of beekeeping boiled down to this: pick up dead colonies in the spring; feed the survivors, dose them with powdered sugar and Terramycin™, [an antibiotic—Ed.] put supers on; catch swarms and put them in hives; take off supers; dose them again with powdered sugar and Terramycin and wrap them for winter. You never re-queened. If a colony died, you put a swarm in it the next summer. There was nothing scientific.

The first VBA meeting I went to, I was elected secretary. I began hanging out with a group of guys who were a sort of new breed. They included Franklin Heyburn, Rick Drutchas, Peter Genier, Ed Hazen. In 1979 I applied for the state inspector job too, but Rick Drutchas got it because he had commercial experience in Alabama. That was the best job I never got!

By 1982 I had 200 hives, and I began to take them into the apple orchards for pollination. Then I bought 500 hives from Chazy Orchards in New York. I got up to 1,000 hives but that was too many for the number and quality of workers I had. So I dropped back to about 800 colonies, which was comfortable.

In 2001, I quit pollinating entirely. It was one of the best moves I've ever made. I do way better selling queens and nucs, and the work is more fun and rewarding. Pollination beats up the bees, the beekeeper and the equipment. The bees that pollinated lost a super of honey production, and wintered with higher losses when compared to colonies that weren't moved. That lost production was more valuable than the pollination fee. So, why bother?

I began installing Buckfast queens from Roy Weaver in Texas and they saved me when the tracheal mites hit. You could go down rows and see that all the Italians were dead and the Buckfasts were alive. I never had the 50 percent losses that other guys had, because Brother Adam of Buckfast Abbey had bred those bees to withstand tracheal mites.

FIGURE 10: **Mike Palmer at work with a queen.** PHOTO COURTESY OF MIKE PALMER

As for beekeeping education, there was next to none. Except at the bi-annual VBA meetings. There were no workshops, no certification program, no mentors, no best practices. There were no local clubs and when UVM did away with extension work, there was nothing except the bi-annual VBA meetings. That's why I do the teaching I do, because I remember when there was no framework for teaching; everyone was on their own.

In 2001, Palmer, in answer to a student's question, reflected on the challenges he faced as a professional Vermont beekeeper who sells his honey in bulk 50-gallon drums:

For a while I made some good crops on alfalfa bloom. Well, things have changed . . . The price of corn went up a few years ago. Farmers began planting more of it. Many of my Champlain Valley yards are surrounded by nothing but corn. No crop rotation, *no* clover or alfalfa. Nothing but corn for miles. No honey crop either.

Pests, parasites and diseases are also a major problem. First, the tracheal mite invaded our bees. Lots of beekeepers lost 50 percent or more of their colonies. Anything not resistant to it died. The key was resistance. Some colonies *were* resistant. Breeding from these colonies yield colonies able to stand up to the pressure. We rebuilt our apiaries with these strains of bee.

Then came the second mite, Varroa destructor, which was much more severe. No resistance among our bees. A chemical pest strip was developed using a synthetic pyrethroid. Pricey though. Cost about $3.00 per colony to use it. No choice though.

Then there's the development around Vermont. There used to be lots of places to locate bees. Now, with all the new houses going up, lots of prime locations are being lost. Houses, houses, everywhere.

And the worst problem? Low prices. When I started in 1974, bulk honey (in the 55 gal. barrel) sold for $.55-60/lb. At that time, we received a $.17 subsidy from the government. The National Honey Board was formed to promote honey and increase consumption. We were charged $.01/lb which came out of the subsidy. Trouble was, they didn't promote US honey. Where would General Foods get their honey? The cheapest place they could. China was that place. The Chinese shipped honey to the US for $.35/lb, below their production costs.[6]

But while suffering from low honey prices, Palmer began building up a side-business in queen-rearing and over-wintering nucleus colonies. Palmer says the origins of this practice go back to Dr. C.C. Miller[7] and Brother Adam[8] of Buckfast Abbey in England and that Kirk Webster was the first to practice this in Vermont:

Sometime in the '90s, one April before pollination began, Kirk asked me to come down to his yard. He wanted to show me some nucs.

And he had nuc colonies on top of hives and they have little bee beards sticking off them. This is three weeks before apple bloom! And I say, 'What

---

6 Mike Palmer personal correspondence May 2001.
7 Charles C. Miller (1831–1920) was a trained physician who gave up medicine to become a commercial beekeeper specializing in comb honey. C. C. Miller wrote a popular advice column in the *American Bee Journal* and authored several books on beekeeping including, *Fifty Years Among The Bees,* and *A Thousand Answers to Beekeeping Questions.*
8 Brother Adam (1898–1996) was a Benedictine monk and beekeeper renowned for breeding bees resistant to tracheal mites known as Buckfast bees at Buckfast Abbey in Devonshire, England.

is this!?' I was still buying bees to get my numbers back up after winter losses, and he had these nuc colonies which had come through the winter, pretty as you please.

That's when I started following his example, and changed my techniques to go up rather than out.

Most important to my apiary, have become nucleus colonies made in mid-summer. These will be over wintered in their four or five frame nuc boxes, and be my increase or replacement bees for the following year. They are made not from the strongest of my production colonies, but rather from the weakest.

Every apiary has one or more slow colonies. These slow colonies are allowed to build up until mid-summer . . . July in my area of the north. They are broken up into four or five frame nucs, each being given approximately one and one half frames of brood, a frame of honey/pollen, an empty comb, and just enough bees to cover the brood. I find I get an average of four or five nucs per colony sacrificed. When transferred to ten frame equipment the following spring with an essentially new, young queen, they build quickly into good honey producers.

## VERMONT BEEKEEPING IMPROVES
In his 2002 report, inspector Steve Parise saw some encouraging progress in the economic and biological threats facing beekeepers.

Spurred by the effects of U.S. anti-dumping actions [tariffs] against Argentina and China, a short supply of honey worldwide, and the removal of Chinese honey from major worldwide markets due to antibiotic contamination, the bulk price of U.S. honey rose steadily. At the end of the biennium, prices were more than $1.00/lb, and still headed upwards. With this considerable increase, commercial beekeepers were able to pay down some debt and make some much needed reinvestment in equipment.

Varroa mites were generally under control during the biennium with the availability of CheckMite™ and other pest control strips. Most of the commercial colonies were treated with this material as varroa resistant to Apistan™ continued to spread throughout the bee population. Several other varroa control products are in various stages of production or permitting. (Parise 2002)

During the biennium of 2001-2002, Parise counted 1,500 registered beekeepers with 10,200 hives. He did 4,400 hive inspections, finding varroa in 70

FIGURE 11: **Ross Conrad leads a beginner beekeeping class.**
PHOTO CREDIT: GILLIAN COMSTOCK

percent and tracheal mites in 44 percent of inspected colonies. The varroa rate was the same as two years before and the tracheal rate was down 30 percent from the previous biennium, continuing a trend. He found SHB in 53 percent of the 2,300 colonies inspected for that pest but observed that they did not seem to be reproducing in Vermont's climate and soil.

The AFB infection rate was 2.2 percent, which was close to that of last biennium. Several samples showed a worrying trend toward resistance to the only approved antibiotic, Oxytetracycline, sold under the tradename Terramycin™. Parise advised beekeepers to be vigilant in their inspection routines and not to move infected combs between colonies or harvest honey from infected hives.

## IN-HIVE CLASSES & WORKSHOPS

By 2002, the VBA had developed its own series of workshops at Yankee Kingdom Orchard in Addison, led by Bill Mraz and Jack Eckels. Topics included: unpacking and spring inspections, reversing, disease inspections, making nucleus colonies, supering, extraction, winter packing, and feeding. In 2004, those northern

VBA workshops were moved from Addison to Burlington's Intervale Center to be more centrally located in northwestern Vermont. In 2015, Jeff Hamelman of Hartland and Bill Taft of Windsor established a similar set of summer workshops in the Hartland area.

Some local clubs such as Bennington, Upper Valley, and Central Vermont have set up their own classes. Beekeepers affiliated with the clubs volunteer their bee yards and invite fellow beekeepers to weekend classes that presented information based on the time of year. Kirk Webster hosts open house and field day events at his apiary. Ross Conrad has been teaching organic beekeeping classes annually in Addison County for over a decade.

Another very successful educational undertaking occurs each spring within the evening ACCESS program at Champlain Valley Union High School in Hinesburg. From 2006 to 2018, over 700 people attended the four-class evening sessions taught by Bill Mares, Mike Willard, Scott Wilson, Russ Aceto, Rick Stoner and Kate Blofson.

Of the workshops generally, then state inspector Parise wrote:

> I think the workshops are very valuable to new beekeepers as it gives them a chance to observe a wide variety of colony conditions, and manipulations. Experienced beekeepers can ask questions and get ideas on other 'advanced' beekeeping techniques such as comb honey production, nuc[leus] making, queen rearing, etc. The smaller groups allow for a free flowing discussion and an open atmosphere for sharing questions and answers.[9]

## THE DARKER SIDE OF VERMONT BEEKEEPING

We'd like to think that all beekeeping in Vermont was of the highest quality, but that is not always the case, as inspector Steve Parise wrote:

> Over the 24+ years I was the inspector, I observed on occasion, a commercial operation that routinely sold nucs that had one frame of foundation and often one or more junk combs (moth or mouse eaten). I worked with them for years to improve their product with only limited success. Since I was just inspecting the nucs specifically for disease/mite issues, there was really nothing I could do to prevent them from being sold. There were often great differences between nucs in regards to numbers of bees, amount of honey and even queen quality.

---

9  Interview with Steve Parise, October 2016.

There was an instance many years ago of a commercial beekeeper from PA that was bringing in bees to southern VT for apple pollination. They did not notify me of their presence in VT or provide any proof of inspection. The bees were palletized, each with six. They were two story deep colonies, but most only had bees in the lower box, and almost all of the interior (middle) hives were basically weak nucs, hardly strong enough to fly let alone providing adequate pollination. I sent them a warning after inspecting the hives and they never came back. There was also a case of a NH beekeeper bringing in bees to pollinate pumpkins along the CT river. His hives did not have any paperwork, and were found to have AFB. After inspecting the hives and finding the AFB the owner was notified to remove the hives from VT immediately, and when not done, was fined for failure to comply with VT bee laws and the AFB was burned.

Every year there were also a few beekeepers that brought in nucs from out of state without proper documentation, or beekeepers in VT that sold nucs (or hives) that didn't notify me before the sale for inspection. Fortunately most of these turned out to be AFB free after I tracked them down.

I also had reports of a few stolen hives, but there was not much I could do except look for any unique identifying marks/brands that were on the hives in my travels. I never did find any. There were also a few cases of illegal mite chemicals in hives from time to time. Most of these were oversights by the owners (missed a pallet, group of hives, etc.) although there were 2 cases that were handled at the Agency as official violations.[10]

## THE VBA GOES RECRUITING

During the 1990s, many beekeepers (mostly part-timers) gave up beekeeping after losing all their colonies to mites. In response to the new challenges facing beekeepers, the VBA expanded its mission to both provide better information for its members and recruit public support and participation.

Board members Lynn Lang and Bill Mares spearheaded a Honey Promotion Board-funded project to print and distribute 40,000 brochures across the state. The *VBA Cookbook* continued to sell about 1,000 copies annually. Several beekeepers gave numerous lectures to school and civic groups around the state.

In 2001, the VBA launched a new kind of newsletter. Aided by the editors of the monthly *Agriview* at the then Department of Agriculture [*later to be the Vermont Agency of Agriculture, Food, and Markets(VAAFM)—Ed.*], the Association began publishing *The Flight Path* with news of, about and for

10 Letter to authors, March, 2018.

Vermont beekeepers twelve times a year. Although the primary audience was beekeepers of Vermont, editors hoped to reach others in the Vermont agricultural community with its mixture of quarterly reports by the state inspector, interviews with VBA members, and reports on meetings and workshops for the VBA, and even some humor:

> When a newbee beekeeper exclaimed to the state inspector that there were too many things to think about tending bees, the inspector replied, 'That's what you have to do to keep the bees alive. If you want to just sit there and watch something fly, get a flock of pigeons!'

This effort was short lived and ended in 2005 as no other VBA members stepped up to help with the newsletter and the primary point person for *The Flight Path*, Bill Mares, eventually burned out.

## STATE PROMOTIONS

Starting in 1975, the Vermont Legislature authorized the Secretary of Agriculture to establish a Vermont Seal of Quality (VSQ) for agricultural products produced in the state if they met standards of quality equal to or exceeding federal requirements. The state also encouraged individual commodity boards, including honey, to create labels. Through 1999, maple sugar makers represented about two-thirds of program participants, while the dairy industry dominated the program in sales.

During its first twenty-five years, the VSQ was a regulatory-based program, serving primarily as a means of identifying Vermont farm products that met or exceeded federal standards. It was not until 2003 that other more permanent changes were made to the system. A Buy Local initiative was instituted to promote

FIGURE 12: **Vermont Seal of Quality Logo.**

the purchase and promotion of Vermont farm products. However, there has never been enough money to support the program. For decades value-added products have struggled with erratic marketing support. Those involved report it has been like trying to keep the old tractor running with wire and old parts.[11]

---

11 Associated Press story, April 1, 2010.

By the mid-1980s, as more VSQ products poured onto the market, VAAFM was limited in the number of inspections it could perform and the program suffered from a merry go round of agency homes. Meanwhile, debate grew over what percentage of ingredients in these products had to be local in order to be called "Vermont." One of the state's biggest and oldest honey producers, Mraz's Champlain Valley Apiaries, was prevented from using the seal because it could not produce enough honey from its Vermont hives and had to import honey from other states and Canada to meet customer demand.[12]

In 2002, the Honey Promotion Board supported the VBA in designing and printing 40,000 brochures to distribute to members and hence to the public for promotion. Unfortunately by the mid-2000s, the state shut down several of the commodity promotion boards, including that of honey, for budgetary and manpower reasons.

Also in the early 2000s, using some of the money from the Vermont Honey Promotion Board, the VBA began building a website with help of Sharon Zechinelli of Enosburg Falls, Mark McClary of S. Burlington, Randy and Penny Potvin of Georgia, Greg Smela, Pam Tingiris, and Mike Willard. This site would eventually become a lively, useful compendium of local beekeeping news and programs.

Assuming that members could get answers to broad beekeeping questions from national magazines like *Bee Culture* and *American Bee Journal* and online, the VBA website focuses on Vermont with a marketplace, calendar, and lively discussion pages. Mike Palmer and Scott Wilson field questions and provide colorful answers. The listing service, which includes information such as sellers of bees, is one of the website's most visited areas. There is also a newsfeed for bee-related articles, and the VBA website has became a gateway for the public to stumble into Vermont beekeeping.[13]

Frequently, non-beekeepers came to the site looking for help with swarms. The Vermont beekeepers that answered their calls for help found that many of these frightening creatures were yellow jackets, wasps, hornets, or even bumble bees. But the opportunity to show people the difference between those creatures and honey bees provided teachable moments in the field, which were later supplemented by a feature on the VBA website. As the first person on the list, Bill Mares of Burlington often fielded 5-10 calls through the

---

12 The Buy Local program was shut down in 2010.

13 Visit the VBA home page at: https://www.vermontbeekeepers.org/

summer and fall from people in varying degrees of stress and upset who had "a ton of bees" in trees, eaves, and under porches and decks. Mares' most unusual swarm retrieval was from behind a statue of Jesus Christ at a local church in Burlington.

Figure 13: **Bill Mares cuts down a swarm in downtown Burlington.**
Photo credit: Julie Richards

## BUZZING THE FAIRS

Another way Vermont beekeepers sought to publicize their work and products is at several agricultural fairs. The biggest (and most distant) was the Eastern States Exposition ("Big E") in Springfield, Massachusetts. For many years the "Big E" was a prime location for VBA members to promote and sell Vermont honey. James Gabriel, a beekeeper with Champlain Valley Apiaries in Middlebury who eventually established his own operation (Lapham Bay Apiaries in Bridport) wrote this account:

Well, the Big E, or Eastern States Agricultural Exposition in Springfield, MA was certainly all it was billed to be. Fellow VBA member Jack Eckels and I drove down Thursday in preparation for an all-day presentation on Friday. Thanks to the generous hospitality of Jack's sister, we were treated to a warm welcome in Enfield, CT, a scant twelve miles from the Big E. Friday morning dawned cool and clear. We were situated in an excellent traffic spot in front of the Vermont building. Set up was completed by 9:00 a.m. We brought VBA honey in 1 lb. Queenline and 2.5 lb. jars. We also included Jack's cut comb honey as well as Champlain Valley Apiaries signature Crystallized Honey. It was Vermont Day and the crowd was great. The observation hive was a real attention-getter. We explained the story of the honey bee's lifecycle innumerable times to folks fascinated and proud at their first sight of a real queen bee.

One of the highlights of the entire day was that a number of local schools were given the day off to make a field trip to the Exposition. All these groups were interested and we gave out lots of honey samples. The kids asked fascinating questions. In addition, a number of special needs kids also visited the booth and got a real charge out of the exhibit.

Kudos go to club member Lynn Lang, who was working the Maple Products booth. He was kind enough to give us a break to take a lunch break. Our Vermont Department of Agriculture liaison was very enthused at the great crowd response.

For a couple of years, Ross Conrad gathered enough Vermont volunteers to represent the VBA for all ten days of the Big E, but it was a lot of work, and no one else took up the banner. Even when the state effort was limited to "Vermont Day," it was still difficult. For several years, there was a VBA presence at the Champlain Valley Fair and Exposition in Chittenden County and an attempt to have a booth at the Addison County Farm and Field Days, but it was hit or miss depending upon the number of volunteers. There, again, the booth had to be staffed throughout the entire length of each fair and that was too much for the club.

It was the Tunbridge World's Fair that became the principal showcase for Vermont beekeepers and honey. Over the years, the honey booth grew to be a VBA fixture for many visitors and VBA volunteers led by Bob Eastman of Fairlee, Doug Ouellette of Tunbridge, Bill Mares, the Mraz family, and dozens of others. Each year, the VBA cleared between $1,200 and $1,800 in honey sales.

FIGURE 14: **The popular Vermont Beekeepers Association booth at the Tunbridge Fair. From left to right: Peter Hadeka, Don Gilbert, Jean Conde.**

In a Vermont Public Radio commentary in September 2011 Mares waxed poetic about serving at the fair:

> For a number of years I have volunteered to sell honey and talk bees at the Vermont Beekeepers Association booth at the Tunbridge World's Fair. Country fairs like this one evolved to offer end-of-summer sensory overload, with music, food, rides, competition, and merchandise. But sorting out my thoughts about this year's Fair was like trying to untangle debris along a flood-ravaged river from Hurricane Irene.
>
> It began as I drove the mere five miles from Bethel to South Royalton. After its rampage the White River was back within its banks, its color a sullen gray. The river had chewed new channels. Fields were scoured, scraped and scooped and covered with silt. Rows of corn showed the high water marks. Two bridges looked as if they'd been bombed.
>
> Tunbridge, however, lay in a valley of relative tranquility. The cattle barns had been cleaned of silt. The bridges were secure and the fields were dry.

Scores of polite Norwich University cadets in green and blue sweatshirts directed the parking.

On the way in I chatted with Euclid Farnham, a long-time president of the fair. He said they knew that attendance would be down, but they never thought of canceling. Nor had they cancelled ten years ago in the week after the 9/11 attacks. Instead, I remembered, they had the 10 minutes of silence which was broken only by the occasional lowing of a cow.

I ambled along the midway, moving through ranks of kiosks with the usual heart-stopping foods, including sausages, burgers, onion, and French fries, past robotic carnival workers at pitch and toss and shooting galleries and through a forest of rides. Politicians hawked their promises and dreams; the National Guard sold patriotic adventure; others sold tractors, insurance, T-shirts and fudge.

Iside the Dodge-Gilman building, we beekeepers shared space with Cabot cheese, the Christmas tree growers association, The Grange, or Patrons of Husbandry, and racks upon racks, of prized vegetables and fruits and pump-kins as big as all-terrain vehicles.

Our six-hour shift went non-stop. The world came to us, the thin and round, the young and old, the fleet and lame. We had three irresistible attrac-tions: One was great local Vermont honey to taste and buy. We sold plastic honey sticks by the thousands. Secondly, we could answer anxious questions that despite poor weather this year, Vermont bees were in relatively good health.

But the biggest draw was our observation hive with 3,000 bees crawling around beneath glass, safe from human harm. Everyone from toddlers to totterers with canes could play the beekeeper's version of 'Where's Waldo?' as they searched for the queen bee.

We were a little short on help when one volunteer bowed out with a bro-ken foot, another with a broken leg, and Del Cloud, the town manager of flood-stricken Bethel, asked for a rain check. In the end, however, we had enough volunteers. What's more, we were named the best booth in the entire Fair, a prize which gets us in free next year!

Vermont's beekeepers showed that they had the tenacity to bounce back from two types of mites and a small hive beetle, but yet another challenge was about to make its presence known.

FIGURE 15: **Vermont high school students in a beekeeping class.**
PHOTO CREDIT: HUGH GIBSON

FIGURE 16: **Central Vermont bee yard.** PHOTO CREDIT: RICK DRUTCHAS

CHAPTER 6

# *Bees and Beyond*

*Vermont did not have a single confirmed case of CCD during the height of its occurrence. However we continue to experience a tremendous increase in winter colony loss due to varroa and the viruses they transmit. I see that people are starting to call this increasingly worsening situation with mites and viruses CCD. And that may be the truth. I saw a higher amount of sick bees and brood this year. And so many mite bombs . . . many reports of hives collapsing in late fall and early winter—much earlier than normally reported. Because there is no definitive test for CCD—I cannot call any-thing CCD. Despite the lack of an agreed upon label—we are in a crisis.*

—David Tremblay (December 2018)

## COLONY COLLAPSE DISORDER (CCD)

In the fall of 2006, the nation's beekeepers were shocked by the widespread death of billions of honey bees, starting in Florida. Some beekeepers reported 50-90 percent hive loss, far above the customary yearly rate of 10-20 percent. The heaviest losses appeared to be among the professional migratory beekeepers that trucked their bees thousands of miles annually to fulfill pollination contracts on large farms and orchards. Unable to find a single cause, researchers named the affliction Colony Collapse Disorder.

While traditional hive deaths are often marked by a pile of dead bees inside or just outside the hive, in these cases, beekeepers open their hives and find them empty. Worker bees are gone, and if any bees are left in the hive it is only the queen, and a few of her attendants, all of whom are infected with disease. Hives are often found with plenty of food, as the usual scavenging activities of insects feeding on these dead and dying colonies is delayed. The usual scavengers stay away, as if the neighboring bees, hornets, wasps, wax moths and small hive beetles all know there is something wrong with the hive.

Theories abound. First it was the accumulated depredations of varroa and tracheal mites that impaired the already taxed immune system of honey bees. Then it was a new fungi, or viruses that had been around bees but gained strength as the colonies were weakened from overwork, diseases and pests like the varroa mite. Others blamed poor bee nutrition and weak queens. Some pointed to the stress of migratory transit around the country, to what are in effect, infection wards where massive numbers of bees are brought together for pollination in orchards and on farms in California, Florida, Maine, etc. Even cell phones came under suspicion for supposedly disrupting the bees navigation systems, giving a flashy headline, if not compelling evidence. As time has passed evidence has mounted however, and more and more blame is falling on chemicals, especially a new pervasive class of neonicitinoid pesticides that can harm the bees' navigation systems, lower hive fertility, (Tirado 2013, Williams 2015, Wu-Smart and Spivak 2016, Chaimanee 2016, Dussaubat 2016) reduce foraging effectiveness, negatively impact the insect's immune system, (Alaux 2010, Pettis 2012, De Prisco 2013) and shorten life expectancy, among other things. (Friol 2017)

The honey bee crisis has gone viral on the now muscular and nearly ubiquitous world-wide web and social media. Titles and ledes on mainstream media have appeared that included "Silence of the Bees," "Declining Honey Bees May Affect Nation's Diet," "Declining Bee Populations Pose a Threat to Global Agriculture," and "What is Killing All the Bees?"[1]

Bees and beekeepers have been embraced by the public. At potluck dinners, cocktail parties, and around town we are the uncomfortable stars of the moment. As conversations revolve around the news of the plight of the bees, beekeepers admit that they keep bees to friends who had no idea. Immediately upon discovering their friend's heretofore secret activity, the conversation turns to what is causing all the beekeepers around the world to lose their bees, a question fanned by crisis headlines.

---

[1] A decade after its dramatic entrance onto the national consciousness, CCD would fade and use of the term has gone into decline. While annual colony losses in Vermont and around the U.S. remain near peak CCD levels, a lack of a clear definition and test for CCD has resulted in fewer hive deaths attributed to the disorder over time.

Beekeepers, accustomed to being viewed politely as "characters who get stung on purpose" moved from the comfortable shadows of mainstream society and are thrust under a hot, bright spotlight with questions coming from a rightly concerned, but largely uninformed public. Overnight, beekeepers went from being viewed as quirky and weird to being heroes of environmental (and honey bee) protection. This growing esteem for beekeepers, and farmers in general, as stewards of the land led to thousands of people wanted to be part of "saving" the bees. To their surprise and delight they found that one of the ways they could help is by taking up beekeeping.

## VERMONT BEEKEEPERS BENEFIT
## FROM NATIONAL CONCERN

Even though there had not been a confirmed CCD case in the state,[2] Vermont benefited from this ubiquitous and urgent need to help. With the aid of public and social media, membership in the Vermont Beekeepers Association (VBA) surged.

Beekeepers generally can be classified into three functional groups: full-time, side-line, and backyard beekeepers. In 2014 for example, approximately fifteen Vermont beekeepers produced 40-50 percent of the state's honey crop and about 1600 beekeepers produced the rest. Historically, Vermont, like the rest of the country, has always had a much larger number of backyard beekeepers than full-time or side-liners, a reality that continues to this day.

Vermont has seen a couple surges of beekeeping in all three functional groups, the first in the 1880s coinciding with the national development of the nascent beekeeping industry, and another in the late 1960s and 1970s as the back-to-the-land movement came to Vermont. Now, the huge losses seen around the country and in Vermont led to a new wave of newbee backyard beekeepers and the accompanied publicity, legislative testimony and media coverage. And most importantly, a state-wide desire to save the bees.

Many of the new beekeepers joining the ranks of beekeeping were women and young people, a welcome chronological and gender equalization of membership at association and club meetings. What they lacked in knowledge, they made up for in enthusiasm and hope. They also came with new ideas and

---

2 Although Vermont beekeepers have reported colonies collapsing and exhibiting CCD-like symptoms, no confirmed case of CCD has been identified in Vermont "officially."

FIGURE 1: **Prof. Kristin Wolf shows a frame of bees to Alex Binkhorst and students of Edmonds Elementary School.**
PHOTO CREDIT: STEPHEN MEASE

attitudes. For example, rather than use the time-tested and proven Langstroth technology, many preferred to keep bees in other types of hives including Top-Bar and Warrè Hives. Many of these new beekeeping converts, both in the state and around the country, associated this new bee crisis with large commercial-scale beekeeping practices. Similar to the back-to-the-landers that had come to Vermont 40-50 years earlier, many of these new beekeepers rejected industrial agricultural practices as they applied to honey bees, a belief that helped to propel Conrad's Natural Beekeeping book that was published just as CCD was becoming a house-hold word in beekeeping circles.

For these new and inexperienced beekeepers, the Vermont Beekeepers Association was there to help them meet their needs in many different areas. For many decades VBA has always had two major meetings a year — one in conjunction with the Vermont Farm Show in January and one held in rotating locations around the state during the summer, when travel conditions are less problematic.

In 1992, VBA had the usual 20-30 people present at its winter meeting. The Vermont Farm Show was held at the Barre Auditorium back then, and the VBA met in the basement of the nearby First Presbyterian Church at the foot of the hill leading to the Memorial Auditorium. These smaller meetings were famous for the potluck spread arranged for many years by the wives of VBA beekeepers led by Mrs. Whitcomb.

Future VBA president Kim Greenwood recalled her first VBA winter meeting in 2005: "I don't remember another young woman in the audience. I went into the kitchen where the women were, looking to find my sister beekeepers. There were none, just helpful women getting the coffee and doughnuts out and arranging crockpots for lunch. Finding myself there, I offered to help. It wasn't long before I realized that if I didn't get out of the kitchen, quite literally, I'd miss the whole meeting. My first impression, which would hold true for almost the next two decades, was that beekeeping in Vermont was rather male-oriented."

By 2011, VBA's winter meeting had grown to 110 attendees. The following year, after VBA had moved

FIGURE 2: **VBA President Chas Mraz and Vice President Kim Greenwood (2011).** PHOTO CREDIT: IAN ORMON

its winter meeting location to the larger Mutuo Club in Barre, the Vermont Farm Show moved from its Barre location to the Champlain Valley Fairgrounds and the VBA winter meeting went with it. By 2017, VBA's winter meeting had 160 beekeepers present. Women beekeepers still represented a small proportion of the membership, but their numbers were growing as young women especially, started showing up, to add beekeeping to their skill sets in small-scale agriculture.

These meetings evolved to meet the needs and interests of the growing membership and saw a rock-star line up of speakers including MacArthur Fellowship "Genius Grant" winner Dr. Marla Spivak, author and researcher Dr. Tom Seeley, professor and author Dewey Caron, Maine State Apiarist and Author Tony Jadczak, Bee Culture Magazine Editor Kim Flottum, Researcher and Provincial Apiculturist for Alberta Canada, Dr. Medhat Nasr, and Professor Jim Frazier of Pennsylvania State University. Just as popular as the national experts were Vermont's own Mike Palmer and Kirk Webster, who had become nationally known and revered beekeepers.

To this tsunami of interest, the VBA and beekeeping leaders around Vermont responded. They offered a variety of programs, including classes, mentoring, and a certification program. Attendance at these meetings surged as VBA saw its bi-annual meetings overflow their traditional meeting spaces more than once. VBA membership grew to almost 500 members in 2011, an estimated one quarter of the total number of beekeepers in the state at the time. Through the decade membership numbers rose to over 500, and then settled back to about 450 or so, roughly a third of the beekeepers in the state.[3]

## GROWTH OF REGIONAL BEE CLUBS

As VBA membership and new backyard beekeeper numbers grew, so did the need to support these new and inexperienced beekeepers, many of whom hadn't considered what beekeeping involved before jumping in heart first.

The VBA is the sole *state-wide* association for Vermont's beekeepers. Regionally, individual members of VBA have been inspired to start local clubs to provide hands-on trainings, mentoring, and bring information to their beekeeper-neighbors. Many host their meetings at members' homes and in their apiaries, providing new beekeepers with valuable instruction and guidance. From around 1980 to the present, clubs came and went, or stayed the same, always dependent upon the extraordinary (and often unsustainable) work of their founders. Social media however made it easier than ever to join one of these nearby clubs and to bring beekeepers together in person as well as virtually.

Vermont's longest-running local beekeeping club is in Bennington County. It draws members from the southwestern corner of Vermont, and even western Massachusetts and eastern New York. Jacob Esh, a bookseller in Bennington who was president of the club for many years, gave this account:

> The Bennington County Beekeepers Club (BCBC) was founded in 1977. BCBC by-laws called for two meetings each year in the northern part of county and two meetings each year in the south. Speakers included several state inspectors, Mike Palmer, Charlie Mraz, Dewey Caron, Ross Conrad and Bill Mares, among others.
>
> One of the founders was Bill Damour of Bennington who had worked as a part-time Vermont bee inspector and became a dealer of equipment for the A.I. Root Company. He was an important source of information for the members.
>
> By 1980 there were about 40 member-beekeepers with a few newbees joining every year. Damour and John Page seemed to know who and where all the beekeepers were in the county. When Damour moved to Virginia, Art Carmon of Shaftsbury, took over the Root dealership. When Art

---

3 By the end of the summer of 2018, State Inspector Tremblay estimated that there were about 1200 beekeepers keeping around 12,000 colonies in Vermont.

retired, I became the local dealer, until Root discontinued all dealerships. That's when Bob Stevens started his Betterbee operation in Greenwich, New York, a company which continues today, under different management.

Esh reflects further on the BCBC:

Rene Nolet of Dorset and Rita Vilmer of Shaftsbury, served as president and secretary-treasurer, from 1977–1979. The Merck Foundation's Forest and Farmland in West Rupert had honey bees. Hal Coolidge Jr., a Dorset policeman, had once put honey bees in Terry's Orchard, on Harwood Hill, in Bennington. Those hives were stolen and never recovered. Fred Lombard in Sandgate wintered his hives in his house cellar and claimed they helped heat his house! In the spring he moved them to his south porch before moving them again to his bee yard near the garden!

The beekeeping support provided by the BCBC in Bennington County has been augmented in recent years by the Brattleboro Area Beekeepers Guild.

Other beekeeping associations around the state were formed largely in response to the public's response to the CCD crisis. They all experienced similar rates of growth and interest from new beekeeepers.

The Southern Vermont Beekeepers Club started by Maddie Sobel in 2002 went into eclipse when she left the state, but was reinvigorated under new leadership in 2013 and is still active in 2018. Her account follows:

I started keeping bees two years prior in Connecticut in 2000 as a member of the Backyard Beekeepers Association (BYBA). Ed Weiss, author of 'The Queen and I' was the founder of the club and had a following that was growing steadily . . . When I moved to Vermont, I so wanted to be a part of a beekeepers club like BYBA but there was none close by. That's when I decided that I would start my own. I had befriended Scout Profit, an East Dorset neighbor and she said she would help me get the ball rolling and co-chair the club with me - two women, perhaps the first two to start a club from the ground up. We were fortunate enough to get The Vermont Country Store corporate headquarters in Manchester to donate some space to us for meetings. We sent out fliers to anyone we could think of and were surprised when twelve people came to our first meeting.

We surveyed the group to see what everyone was looking for. The consensus of our survey desired education, speakers, and a general gathering to share

FIGURE 3: **Maddie Sobel.**
PHOTO CREDIT: JANE SOBEL KLONSK

ideas and experiences. The Southern Vermont Beekeepers Association was born. As our group grew, led by great speakers, and publicity became easier (better internet capability) we moved our monthly meetings to the generously donated space of Northshire Bookstore. We started a monthly newsletter and opened all of our meetings to the public. This was a win-win for the bookstore when we brought in authors to speak. We had a mead making workshop with author Howland Blackiston[4], a fun game show, also hosted by Howland. Other speakers included Mike Palmer, Bill Mares, Ross Conrad, and Shane Gebauer from Betterbee.[5]

When we hosted the VBA summer meeting at the Long Trail School in Dorset, I felt as if our club was on the map and brought some state beekeeping interest to Southern Vermont.

Jack Rath (*currently a co-owner of Betterbee and president of the VBA 2017-2020—Ed*) lived in Pawlet. He and his wife Sarah were regular members. Jack gave a few presentations to the club in the early days and when he retired from his veterinary practice, he was able to give us more time. He took over the spring series on "Getting Started with Bees" and held workshops in the summer at his apiary in Pawlet. He was an amazing resource and it was so terrific to have his years of beekeeping experience to guide us. . . . Before I left, I turned the reins over to Susan Marmer. She and Jack continued to run the club after I left.

Meanwhile, closer to the Canadian border, the Northeast Kingdom Bee Club also held its first meeting in 2011, with twenty-three attendees, ranging in age of experience from 0-48 years (one attendee brought a newborn baby). It was led by Heidi Meyer-Bothling with help from fellow St. Johnsbury residents Lauren Jarvi, Gordon Oakes, Steve Slayton, and John Fitch, as well as Paul Berlejung of Groton.

The Central Vermont Beekeepers Association was started by Kim Greenwood and was active from 2008 to 2013. As evidence of the level of interest in beekeeping, the Club grew to over a hundred members in its first year, and topped at

---

4 Author of "Beekeeping for Dummies." (Hoboken: Wiley Publishing 2009).

5 Gebauer would eventually move on to help run Brushy Mountain Bee Farm in North Carolina.

FIGURE 4: **Gib Geiger (far right) teaches a workshop for Central Vermont Beekeepers, June 2013.** PHOTO CREDIT: KIM GREENWOOD

almost 200 members by the second year. It quickly outgrew its meeting space at the Vermont Natural Resources Council in downtown Montpelier, where Kim worked and kept bees on the roof, so the North Branch Nature Center agreed to let the Club meet in their space to accommodate the larger crowds. In-hive meetings were hosted at the apiaries of Gib Geiger in Waitsfield and were very well attended. When the reigns of the Club were turned over to Jon Creighton, in-hive workshops were added at Jeffrey Allen's apiary in Montpelier.

The Upper Valley Bee Club founded by mechanic Bob Eastman of Fairlee lasted five to seven years in early 2000s, until Bob retired to Florida.

The Franklin County Beekeeping Club was started by three individuals from the St. Albans office of the UVM Extension Service. One of those individuals, Elaine Burnor, was the club's first organizer, the champion who got the club off the ground and running. As Elaine recalls:

> Our first club meeting was on Thursday March 17th, 2011. This meeting coincided with St. Patrick's Day and we kicked off in high style with a corned beef boiled dinner, and pints of Ben and Jerry's Ice Cream. That

meeting was tough to beat. The presenter was Lynn Lang, of Essex Junction who talked of beekeeping in general.

The first few club meetings were held at the UVM Extension Service offices. As the club membership grew, we out grew the Extension space and moved club meetings to the Fairfield Town Library. . .

Shortly after the club started, in June of 2011, Janice Girard offered to help organize the club and plan for future club meeting topics and presentations.

Other presenters besides Lang were: Mike Palmer, Michael Willard, Bill Mares, Chaz Mraz, Steve Parise, David Tremblay, and others.

In the early days of the club, our members were primarily Franklin County residents. This changed as word spread about our club and we had Mike Palmer stepping forward to provide presentations and hands-on workshops. This star power and an organized club format started to draw beekeepers from outside Franklin County. Our club email list grew by leaps and bounds, with monthly club meetings becoming standing room only. There was a clear thirst for beekeeping knowledge and the Franklin County Club was helping to fill that void.[6]

The Lamoille County Beekeepers Club was started in March 2014 by Michelle Rauch of Stowe. Typical attendance at monthly club meetings is usually about 20-25 people. The club invites speakers to present on beekeeping tasks as well as related topics such as pollinator habitat, products from the hive, and various methods of beekeeping, with lots of time for questions and discussion. Winter meetings take place at the Stowe Free Library on weekday evenings. Summer meetings are held on weekends during the day to allow for in-hive workshops. There is no fee to join the club and all are welcome. The club aims to sponsor either a full-day or half-day beekeeping seminar each season. LCBC hosted the VBA summer meeting in Stowe during July, 2015. Rauch has since moved to Williston and has tried to recruit another person to take charge of the club, but no one has stepped up to the plate yet.[7]

Recognizing the growth in the number of new beekeepers seeking help in Addison County coupled with the challenges of traveling to Burlington for workshops, the Addison County Beekeepers Association (ACBA) held its

---

6 Notes on FCBC furnished by Mike Willard.
7 Notes from Michelle Rausch.

first meeting in late 2015, organized by Daphne Diego of Addison and Howard Hall of Panton with assistance from Scott Wilson of Monkton.[8] There are currently 190 members in the email chain and Facebook group. ACBA hold four indoor meetings and six outdoor workshops each year having between 35-50 attendees. According to Hall, "One reason we started ACBA was because of the number of notable beekeepers at work in Addison County: Chas Mraz, Andrew Munkres, Ross Conrad and Kirk Webster. We had hoped they would be willing to mentor or give advice to new beekeepers. That's exactly what happened."

The Island Beekeepers (Grand Isle County) held their first meeting in 2009 at Blue Heron Farm owned by Adam Farris & Christine Bourque but alas its membership dwindled and those remaining ended up merging with the Franklin County Club.

We've come so far in 450 years.

Please join your fellow beekeepers for the inaugural meeting of the Addison County Beekeepers Association, for an evening of casual conversation. Whether you're a seasoned veteran, a beginner or just interested in the art of beekeeping, we welcome you to join us.

Thursday, October 15, 2015
6:30 - 8:00 pm

Ilsley Public Library
75 Main Street
Middlebury

Steve Parise, Vermont State Apiculturist
Featured Speaker

Please RSVP to acbavt@gmail.com

For more information contact Howard Hall ████ or Daphne Jones 759-2646

FIGURE 5: **Flyer publicizing the first meeting of a reconstituted Addison County Beekeepers' Association meeting 135 years after its initial formation.**

In 2008, Gregory Soll and Corey Paradis began the University of Vermont Beekeeping Club. As Environmental Studies students at the University (and at the height of colony collapse) they had become concerned with the fragile nature of our food system. They were pointed towards the Vermont Beekeepers Association. There they found the support of Bill Mares, Mike Palmer, and other members. Greg and Corey were able to educate themselves and set up a class to help educate others. The amount of student interest was very high. They set up two hives at the UVM Horticulture Farm where the hives sat in an apple orchard. Other students were mentored through their efforts and went on to manage their own hives. Corey and Greg went through the initial stages of becoming a recognized club at UVM, which waned when they left,

---

8 Wilson would eventually take the reins after Hall and Diego stepped down.

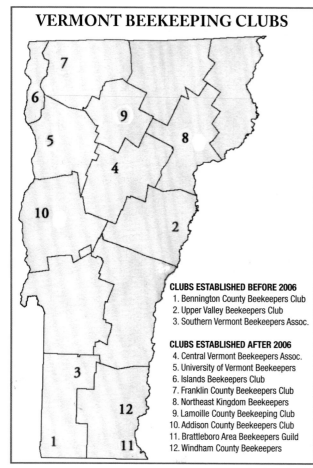

## VERMONT BEEKEEPING CLUBS

**CLUBS ESTABLISHED BEFORE 2006**
1. Bennington County Beekeepers Club
2. Upper Valley Beekeepers Club
3. Southern Vermont Beekeepers Assoc.

**CLUBS ESTABLISHED AFTER 2006**
4. Central Vermont Beekeepers Assoc.
5. University of Vermont Beekeepers
6. Islands Beekeepers Club
7. Franklin County Beekeepers Club
8. Northeast Kingdom Beekeepers
9. Lamoille County Beekeeping Club
10. Addison County Beekeepers Club
11. Brattleboro Area Beekeepers Guild
12. Windham County Beekeepers

FIGURE 6: **The number of active beekeeping clubs in Vermont grew 300 percent following the outbreak of CCD in 2006.**

but was resuscitated by Faculty member Mark Starrett and still exists today. Corey went on to get a 'PhD in beekeeping' with Mike Palmer, and Greg continued to maintain the hives until passing them on to a mentee of his. According to Starrett, the club educates and informs the UVM and Burlington communities on the ecological importance of honey bees. Hives are kept on campus in the newly established apiary located in the meadow across from University Heights Greenhouse, as well as the Horticulture Farm off Shelburne Road.

Curiously, other than UVM's efforts and despite several attempts, a bee club never took hold in Chittenden County, the most populous county in the State. Like CCD, it was a mystery with multiple theories of causation—people too busy, no strong personality to act as a driving force, no convenient meeting place, no critical mass of members, take your pick. Chittenden's more active beekeepers sought to join or start other clubs in Franklin or Addison Counties, or put their energies into the VBA.

All across the state significant numbers of men, women and even a few children continue to join the beekeeping ranks. So much so, that as this book was being written, a Windham County Beekeeping Club is being formed in the Southeast corner of the state. VBA and its various local affiliated clubs are clearly benefiting from the public's interest in personally responding to the plight of the bees.

## BEEKEEPING CERTIFICATIONS

The rapid growth in beekeeping following the outbreak of CCD nationally in 2006 was both a heartbreaking and an exciting time for beekeepers in Vermont and around the world. Despite record colony losses, beekeeping was growing in ways it hadn't in decades. Equipment suppliers were backordered, clubs were growing out of their original spaces and the all-volunteer VBA worked to communicate with and support its growing membership.

Getting bees is easy, keeping them alive is hard. While studies vary, anecdotally beekeepers estimate that 80 percent of new beekeepers fail within the first two years, never to continue beekeeping. There are many reasons for this.

First, it takes an investment of time to learn about bee biology, diseases, pests, and honey bee health to ensure their well-being. Many new beekeepers who started keeping bees during the "save the bees" period of the mid-late 2000s, purchased bees without the necessary commitment to learning about how to keep them alive.

Second, many beekeepers (novice and experienced) lose their bees in late spring due to lack of honey stores. At that point, it is often too late to find a supplier who has nucleus or package bees for sale; many sell out early in the year. Beekeepers then miss out on a season and never start up again the following year.

Third, keeping bees alive and healthy has never been harder. Bees need attention and monitoring and you need to know how to provide a new queen when needed and have a source for queens. While many experienced beekeepers raise their own nucleus colonies for this purpose, new beekeepers often find themselves without a queen source and watch their hive dwindle and die.

Lastly, many new beekeepers, motivated by environmental or bee health concerns, decide to raise their bees "naturally" without using treatments of any kind to take care of their hives. A solid understanding of bee biology, health, and intervention techniques is necessary to keep treatment-free bees this way. New beekeepers often lack a basic understanding of these necessary elements and because of this their bees succumb to varroa mites and die. In the words of one beekeeper "You can't keep bees naturally if they're dead." Many new beekeepers underestimate the skill required to maintain hives naturally, and eventually lose all of their bees to varroa mites or other stressors, leaving them with good intentions but no bees.

FIGURE 7: **Vermont Certified Beekeeper patch.**

Anxious to improve the quality of beekeeping in the state, and to provide new initiates with additional support as well as some formal stamp of approval, state inspector Steve Parise, along with Ross Conrad and Bill Mares put together a "Vermont Certified Beekeeper" program in 2006. The certification program is composed of four components: a written test; a field test; community service on behalf of beekeeping in the State; and a written report describing the beekeeper's experience and lessons learned negotiating the two-year certification process. Graduates of the program receive a certificate suitable for framing, a sew-on patch and the confidence that they are competent in the basics of beekeeping in Vermont. By 2016, VBA had over 20 Certified Vermont beekeepers.

Meanwhile, Scott Wilson of Monkton, became Vermont's first Master Beekeeper with a certificate from the University of Montana Master-Level Course. The 2016 citation read: "Earning this certificate will distinguish you as a beekeeper grounded in science and versed in the latest discoveries in honey bee health."

## MENTORING

A flagship offering of VBA are the mentoring services that connect new bee-keepers with more experienced beekeepers. Sometimes it's as simple as a phone call, or it could be help and hands-on experience in the bee yard. "Remember," Mike Palmer says: "We all had mentors when we began beekeeping!" In 2018 VBA vice-president, Andrew Munkres, and Secretary Scott Wilson, spear-headed a project to hook up every desirous new VBA member with a willing mentor for a projected period of two years. Andrew and Scott hope that by the end of such period newbees will be proficient enough to pass the required tests and become certified Vermont beekeepers.

While we tend to think of beekeeping as uniform throughout the State, Jeff Cunningham, a Windham County beekeeper and newbee mentor of over forty years, corrects that view:

> By the late 1990s, my bee yards had reached a peak of fifty colonies and I was working full time. Even though this was a small operation by Addison

County standards, it was large for Windham county, especially in the forested hills relatively well removed from farm pesticides, but also with a short season and little forage. As Charles Mraz told me based on his significant knowledge of beekeeping geography 'you can't keep bees down there.' In Windham county hobbyists can do well in many favorable micro habitats, and the lower Connecticut River valley offers areas of good forage with longer seasons but perhaps a bit too much human activity in most areas for large beekeeping operations.

FIGURE 8: **Andrew Munkres of Lemon Fair Apiaries fascinates students from the Cornwall school in his honey house.** PHOTO CREDIT: JEN KRAVITZ

We tend to focus as beekeepers on bee culture as a branch of agriculture, but what about the culture of beekeepers? Based on my familiarity with beekeeping in Windham County, in contrast to the Champlain Valley and several beekeeping countries I have visited, beekeeping in this corner of our state faces a peculiar poverty of the popular cultural knowledge of beekeeping that would provide new beekeeper's with a cultural context you might take for granted in Middlebury or Burlington. This thinness of an informed under-current of beekeeping wisdom seems to leave hobbyists more than usually vulnerable to unscrupulous salesmanship and predatory pseudo tutelage. Use of the internet for apicultural edification has both improved and exacerbated the challenges faced by novice beekeepers in Windham County.

Like many of our peers throughout the state, I responded to local public curiosity by bringing the observation hive to markets and schools, fielding questions by phone, and opening my bee yards to newspaper photo-shoots. In addition to conducting apiculture workshops, I have also included novice and beginner beekeepers in research and stock improvement projects, and continue to provide occasional consulting services. The responsibility of disseminating accurate information to mentees and peers makes us better beekeepers. And while I am active in VBA's mentoring programs, I also believe many recent novices with a fresh appreciation of beginner challenges often make the best teachers for the newest beekeepers.[9]

## STUDIES AND GRANTS

With its growth in membership, the Vermont Beekeepers Association became able to consider expanding its reach into several research projects, given that the problems facing Vermont beekeepers are national in origin. The membership gave unanimous support to such investigations. Accordingly, VBA was able to secure a number of grants including several U.S. Department of Agriculture (USDA) Specialty Crop Block Grants from the Vermont Agency of Agriculture, Food and Markets (VAAFM) to help support new beekeepers.

## NEW BEEKEEPER GRANT

VAAFM offers USDA Specialty Crop Block Grants, in part to combat the decline in the numbers of wild honey bees. Maintaining the population of feral bees in turn assists farmers and fruit and vegetable growers with pollination. VBA partnered with the Agency to offer a total of $8,000 to establish a 50/50 cost share program aimed at assisting new beekeepers to purchase hive equipment and honey bees ($200 for one or $400 for two colonies), coupled with technical assistance and educational support. VBA stated in its application, "With the decline in wild honey bee colonies and continued problems of established beekeepers with parasitic mites and diseases, it is important that honey bee populations be maintained on a local level to meet pollination needs. It is equally as important for new beekeepers to have mentoring support and knowledge in beekeeping."

A total of 152 applications were received. In total, thirty-three people were told they were eligible and that they should plan to meet the requirements for the grant. After the initial notification, sixteen of the original thirty-three people on either the initial list or the "back up" list dropped out or were disqualified, citing that they were no longer interested, forgot to order bees, or gave various other reasons. Several simply did not respond to any emails or phone calls.

---

9 Personal correspondence.

In the end, seventeen new beekeepers started up twenty-nine new hives in Vermont as a result of this program and VBA was forced to return money to the grantee due to this lack of follow-through by new beekeepers.

The results of the grant highlighted the difficulty of working with enthusiastic but inexperienced beekeepers who liked the idea of keeping bees more than the act of keeping bees.

VBA grant administrator Kim Greenwood stated in the final report for the project, "The number of people who did not follow through with the basic requirements was surprising. Perhaps some level of commitment to beekeeping should be established before an application can be submitted. This is also indicative of the level of commitment required to start keeping bees—again proving that beekeeping is much more than just setting up a hive of bees in ones backyard."

## GROWING BETTER BEEKEEPERS GRANT

This $5,000 grant in 2011 was awarded by the USDA Specialty Crop Block Grant via the Agency of Agriculture, Food and Markets. VBA cited the threat of CCD as a cause of the new interest in beekeeping. Via this grant, VBA wanted to ensure the success of these new beekeepers by providing classroom and in-hive education via two primary mechanisms. First, by covering a portion of Eastern Apicultural Society (EAS) tuition costs allowing VBA members to attend the 2012 EAS meeting in Vermont. This would allow new beekeepers to be exposed to some of the nation's smartest and most innovative beekeeping minds and their research, ensuring a quality and diversity of ideas they couldn't normally get in Vermont. Second, VBA provided funding to develop Mobile Mentors around the State to help new beekeepers with hive inspections. The grant was used to train five experts around the State, under the guidance of State Apiculturist Steve Parise. By having the Mobile Mentors

FIGURE 9: **Marking a queen during a queen rearing workshop.** PHOTO CREDIT: CHERYL DORSCHNER

FIGURE 10: **Jack Rath inspects a frame of queen cells. Reported Jack: "That class was really helpful for me. It gave me the confidence to start raising queens and to eventually teach queen rearing classes at Betterbee each year. One of my queen class students is now producing several hundred Vermont queens annually. So the benefits have been passed on which is the way it should work."**
PHOTO CREDIT: JEANETTE DUNN

help Steve inspect hives around the State, a much greater capacity to perform hive inspections was added to Steve's efforts. The Mobile Mentors provided training in disease detection and prevention, good beekeeping practices and ensured that new beekeepers had the knowledge and confidence to be successful at raising bees and producing honey.

## QUEEN REARING GRANT

The original goal of this program (awarded in 2010) was to introduce ten Vermont beekeepers to the process of queen rearing, with the intention of increasing the number of locally produced queen bees available to Vermont beekeepers. Because southern-raised stocks don't necessarily winter well here in the North, it was hoped that raising northern-raised queens selected for their ability to carry their colonies through our Vermont winters, would improve the beekeepers' chances of success. In recent years, wintering bees in the North, using the available southern stocks, has become a real challenge.

A total of nine Vermonters took part in the program that was taught by Mike Palmer. They were:

Jennings Berger, Brookline
Rick Drutchas, Middlesex
James Gabriel, Bridport
Gib Geiger, Waitsfield
Bob Hedges, Hinesburg

John Mailloux, Williamstown
John McNeil, Orange
Jack Rath, Pawlet
Mike Willard, Fairfax

In the two years of the grant, a total of 602 mated queens were harvested. Of these, 238 were used in colonies owned by Vermont beekeepers. The queens used for VBA's nuc-making workshop in 2011 were provided by Mike Palmer and members of the grant program. (Willard 2011)

## VBA BECOMES A NON-PROFIT

On the state level, in 2009, VBA re-constituted itself as a non-profit corporation and by 2011 became a tax-exempt 501(c)(3) organization under IRS rules. This allowed the Association to accept donations both conventional and on-line. It also buttressed VBA's case for hosting its third Eastern Apicultural Society Conference, which came to fruition at the University of Vermont campus in 2012.

## BEES AND BEYOND: EASTERN APICULTURAL SOCIETY CONFERENCE (EAS) 2012

They came from 25+ states and two Canadian provinces. Over 750 beekeepers flooded the University of Vermont campus to learn, practice and share information about honey bees. For the first time in thirty-two years, the Eastern Apicultural Society was holding its annual conference in Vermont. At the last Vermont EAS in 1980, beekeeping was a lot simpler. There was really only one disease (AFB), wax moths and bears to worry about. Honey production was the core topic. Today, globalization has brought a host of pests, parasites and pathogens. And the big money in beekeeping is in pollination for hire. Most of the beekeepers attending EAS were serious amateurs, but there was a sprinkling of professionals and part-timers, known in the industry as sideliners. Common to all was a dedication to these fascinating and productive creatures that live on the cusp between the domestic and the wild.

The conference theme was "Bees and Beyond" with lectures and workshops on how bees fit in with other areas of agriculture. One group toured the Intervale with its 350 acres of manifold and lush agricultural enterprises. Others attended workshops on honey and chocolate, and honey and cheese, the latter led by a master chef and world expert on honey tasting from Northern Ireland.

A host team of seventy-five VBA members, led by Bill Mares and Diane Meyerhoff and others brought beekeepers and vendors together for a most educational and upbeat event. Among those VBA stalwarts were Mike Willard, Scott and Valarie Wilson, Bill Smith, Chas Mraz, Kim Greenwood and Heidi

FIGURE 11: **Diane Meyerhoff and her collection of sewing machines.**
PHOTO CREDIT: DON WELCH

Meyer-Bothling.[10] And, a special thanks to Dewey Caron for planning an extensive and thorough Short Course. The Honey Show was guided by Mike Palmer who energized the competition, soliciting donations, and providing winners with trophies. Once again, the Bee Olympics provided a fun-filled late afternoon with events, as well as trips to Burlington's world-renowned Intervale with its 350 acres of various community food systems, to explore in celebration of food and farming. Many in attendance dined at Shelburne Farms—a 1400-acre working farm and National Historic Landmark, on the shores of Lake Champlain. Organizers placed twenty beehives on the UVM campus green between Howe Library and the Fleming Museum. On loan from Champlain Valley Apiaries in Middlebury, the bees were used in workshops throughout the week. The keynote speaker was Vermont writer Rowan Jacobsen, author of a best-selling book about the bee crisis. His catchy title was *It's Terroir, Not Terror.* And then he explained the vital link in food between place and taste. With missionary zeal he urged the attendees to "make honey the next wine." Dr.

---

10 EAS officers who also gave generous help were Kim Flottum and Kathy Summers (Ohio), Jim Bobb (Pennsylvania), and John Tulloch (Tennesee).

Marla Spivak presented her research on how propolis helps colonies build tolerance to the pathogens associated with the ubiquitous and predatory varroa mite. Other topics covered included Dr. Tom Seeley describing his work that reveals clues to how feral honey bees are able to mitigate the impacts of varroa, and Vermont's own Ross Conrad on natural beekeeping.

VBA and 2012 EAS President Bill Mares was presented with the annual Charles and Evelyn Divelbiss Education Award, for "reaching out to the non-beekeeping public to explain the value of honey bees in our lives." [11]

Besides helping Bill Mares with some of the initial organization for the EAS conference, Diane Meyerhoff volunteered for the Mother of all Sewing Marathons. Her account follows:

FIGURE 12: **EAS Conference bag designed to double as smoker fuel.** PHOTO CREDIT: DON WELCH

About three years ago, while kicking around ideas for EAS 2012, Bill Mares and I talked about how much we dislike inexpensive conference bags. From there, an idea was born—why not make them out of used burlap coffee bags and then beekeepers can burn them as smoker fuel? Who knew that the next 2 ½ years would be filled with old sewing machines, thousands of yards of thread, a hundred bobbins, and incredible dust bunnies?

Some have said the bags are too nice to burn. I disagree. Please, go ahead and burn your bag with gusto as a final tribute to EAS 2012.

And, of course, the thank yous: to Green Mountain Coffee Roasters and Speeder & Earl's coffee shop for donating the coffee bags free of charge; to Mike Willard and Bill Mares for coffee bag hauling—and a long future of burlap dust in their vehicles; to Marty and Oscar at our local re-use store, ReSource, for keeping an eagle eye out for old working sewing machines; to Valarie Wilson for a night's worth of sewing; and, to the person who really made this possible—with tremendous encouragement and many days of sewing—the best friend a girl could have, Cecilia Plum . . . THANKS!

---

[11] Other Vermont winners include Charlie Mraz (1990), Dewey Caron (1999), and Mike Palmer (2018).

## THE WORLD WIDE WEB AND SOCIAL MEDIA

FIGURE 13: **Bee yard near Richford, VT in the early 1980s.** PHOTO CREDIT: RICK DRUTCHAS

The year 2012 marked the third time that Vermont would host the Annual EAS conference. It was also the beginning of VBA's greater social media involvement on top of the already well-developed website. Social media as communication tools during 2012 were still in a nascent phase and the early platforms like Facebook, Twitter and Instagram were not immediately accepted by VBA members. That began changing in 2015 and 2016 as Facebook became the tool it is for many of the approximately 850 people now using the VBA Facebook page.

During this early life of the VBA Facebook page, a number of local Vermont bee clubs started their own pages. These include Franklin County, Lamoille County, Northeast Kingdom Beekeepers, Brattleboro Area Beekeepers Guild, The Southern Vermont Beekeepers Association, The Windham County Beekeepers, and The Addison County Beekeepers Association. These social media platforms supplanted what had become a rather stagnant VBA web site. Local clubs spurred more local engagement. As beekeeping interest and numbers grew, local clubs emerged to support the needed demand, often through innovative use of social media.

While social media provided more of a quick time response, the web page continues to provide a deeper and broader repository of information and data. Many

VBA members realized this, and thus responding to membership demands, the new 2017 Board of directors contracted in February of 2018 with Greg Smela to redesign the VBA website. The new version of the website offered links to scientific articles, forums for beekeeping discussion, online membership registration, calendars, tools for those new to beekeeping to learn how to get started, and mentoring advice. Other key players in the development of the new site were VBA Secretary, Scott Wilson, and Vice President, Andrew Munkres.

Part of the integrated function is to have links directly to Facebook and Twitter so that whatever is added to the webpage is then transmitted to these social media platforms connecting even more folk's with information. The result provides a world-class communication tool that helps to meet the needs of the beekeeping community

## CHANGES IN VERMONT APIARY LAW

Through the years, apiary law in Vermont remained fairly unchanged, with only two major updates.

The original law passed in 1910 set up a state apiary inspection program. The law, *An Act for the Suppression of Contagious Diseases Among Bees* spelled out the consequences of allowing hives to become infected with disease, complete with fines and possible jail time for scofflaws.

The first major amendment in 1983 added provisions that required beekeepers register their hives with the state and banned another beekeeper from putting an apiary within two miles of an existing apiary registered to a different person unless it was on their own property. It further stipulated that such apiary placement would only be allowed if the neighboring beekeeper had ten or fewer hives, or the beekeeper got written permission to place the hives within the two mile exclusion zone. This was in response to outbreaks of American foulbrood and was aimed at keeping commercial beekeepers from spreading this disease to other beekeepers.

Then in 2013-2014, more changes were proposed to Vermont's law. The largest change was that registrations of apiaries would now also come with a requirement to submit payment for registration and imposed fines for failing to register apiaries. VBA quickly formed a legislative committee, led by VBA President Kim Greenwood, Mike Palmer, and former legislator Bill Mares.

At the time, all other livestock that required Vermont registration had a registration fee associated with it. Hive registrations did not, so the Vermont Agency of Agriculture, Food and Markets (VAAFM) thought it made sense to be consistent and add a fee to recoup some of the costs to administer the registration as it does for other programs. The proposed revenue generated (approximately $9,000) was not proposed to add capacity for the State Apiculturist, but rather to offset some of the current costs of that program.

The position of the Vermont Beekeepers Association was:

a) VBA members are not necessarily opposed to the fee if it directly supports the state's sole bee inspector. In other words, there should be no siphoning of the moneys collected to the general fund.

b) Current inspector, Steve Parise, is the only paid, non-volunteer person in the state of Vermont for beekeepers to turn to. He is invaluable, respected and plays a critical role in not only protecting bees but also protecting our crops. There is universal support and appreciation for the work that he does and we want more of his time.

c) Steve is retiring in four years and VBA wanted to see a solution set up before he goes so that we are not fighting for his position to not be eliminated.

After a unanimous vote of support from VBA at its summer 2013 meeting, VBA testified in support of the change during the 2014 legislative session, but the proposal was voted down in committee as legislators thought that Vermonters as a whole should be supporting the services of the apiculturist, not just placing that costs on registered beekeepers.

It wasn't until 2015, after much discussion between the VBA and VAAFM, that the law was updated. Ultimately, the law ended up requiring an annual $10 fee per apiary be paid by each beekeeper. Initially it was estimated that it would raise $20,000 per year. The original proposal required that $9,000 would go to the Agency to support Steve Parise's apiculture work, specifically to manage the registration program and expenses of the state apiculturist who by that time was devoting only 35 percent of his time to the beekeeping industry each year. The remainder (estimated at $11,000) would be granted to VBA to hire a supplemental inspector or two, for the summer months, to work under Steve's guidance and to support a mentoring program for backyard beekeepers in Vermont.

FIGURE 14: **David Tremblay inspects Ross Conrad's nucleus colonies prior to sale.**
PHOTO CREDIT: RACHEL FLOYD

## A NEW BEE INSPECTOR

At the 2016 VBA Winter Meeting, Agency of Agriculture, Food and Markets (VAAFM) Secretary Chuck Ross introduced Vermont's new state bee inspector, David Tremblay, who was to replace retiring inspector, Steve Parise.

David Tremblay studied entomology at the University of Massachusetts in Amherst where he received a BS in Plant and Soil Science in 1987. Prior to taking on the role of State Apiarist in 2016, David worked with the VAAFM and US EPA in pesticide law enforcement for twenty-seven years. His bio continues: "David is a Justice of the Peace, a volunteer EMT and long-time beekeeper. He is an ultra-endurance athlete and has competed in Paris-Brest-Paris, The Canadian Ski Marathon, and The Tour Divide but now spends his time in search of Vermont's last rusty patched bumble bee."

Secretary Ross also announced the state's Apiary Inspection Program will continue to have seasonal, part-time inspectors who assist Tremblay throughout the beekeeping season.

By 2016, the duty of the apiary inspector had evolved back into a full-time position that emphasized technical assistance and education as well as the regulatory component. Among the activities performed by the inspector were: Providing technical assistance to beekeepers to maintain healthy, productive hives; inspecting bee hives for the presence of diseases and pests; Coordinating sellers and buyers of honey, bees wax, bees and other hive products; Assisting Vermont beekeepers in getting State and Federal approval of new mite control materials; Providing judging for honey and honey products at Fairs and Field Days; Assisting fruit and vegetable growers with securing honey bees to pollinate crops; Working with apiculture officials in other states and at the Federal level on honey bee related issues; Issuing Health Certificates to beekeepers who are selling bees or moving bees out of state; and Presenting educational talks to beekeepers, schools, and civic groups about honey bees and pollination.

While this on-going and enhanced state assistance will be critical in helping Vermont beekeepers to weather the growing challenges they face, let's look at the clues Vermont's collective beekeeping history provides for what fate may hold as apiculturists in Vermont journey into the future.

FIGURE 15: **Salisbury Vermont nuc yard with upper deeps packed with insulation for winter.**
PHOTO CREDIT: ANDREW MUNKRES

FIGURE 12: **Honey bee working seaholly in Lincoln, Vermont.**
PHOTO CREDIT: KATHRYN WYATT

CHAPTER 7

# One Small State—One Big Impact

*The old beekeeping is dying, and a new one is struggling to be born. Are you going to the funeral, or assisting with the birth?*
—Kirk Webster

When reviewing the history of beekeeping in Vermont it is clear that the number of challenges confronting Vermont's apiculturists has grown tremendously. Today, beekeeping is more challenging in Vermont than it has ever been, just as it is for the rest of the United States and much of the world. Thankfully compared to previous centuries, information and the educational infrastructure and resources available to Vermont's beekeepers are unparalleled. From bee clubs, to classes, workshops, websites, mentor programs, books and publications, and the ubiquitous internet and accompanying social media; this embarrassment of edifying riches is likely to play a crucial role in helping beekeepers in the state rise to meet the future challenges they will face.

Since the time when the first swarms of bees settled into the landscape that would become known as Vermont, the honey bee has become an integral part of the state. Studying the history of beekeeping in Vermont can prepare the state's beekeepers to better meet future challenges by helping us understand the forces and events that shaped what we know as Vermont beekeeping today. This

FIGURE 1: **Farm field in the Champlain Valley full of dandelions in bloom.**

history can also allow us to learn from the past so we can manage similar circumstances better in the future, and potentially anticipate a future course of events.

## ADDISON COUNTY AS EPICENTER OF VERMONT BEEKEEPING

In the heart of the Champlain Valley along the eastern shore of Lake Champlain lies the county of Addison, which is nestled in-between Burlington's Chittenden County to the north, and Rutland County to the south. Addison County has consistently produced nationally recognized and influential beekeepers, beginning with John M. Weeks during the mid-1800s. Then emerged A.E. Manum and the Cranes, in the later part of the 19th century. The Crane family went on to assist Charlie Mraz in forming Champlain Valley Apiaries, an operation that has seen two more generations of Mraz's take the helm of the business. Over the years the Mraz family took on numerous hired hands, many would end up keeping bees in their backyards, and some went on to run their own beekeeping businesses. This later group includes, Kirk Webster, Ross Conrad, James Gabriel and Shawn Comar, all of whom not only have established operations of their own, but also teach and mentor others. Thus, today we see a direct lineage of extraordinary, often, nationally recognized beekeepers, with one beekeeper directly sharing information and teaching another in an unbroken chain tracing all the way back to the 1830s. Few areas of the country can claim such a feat.

## PEOPLE AND THE LAND

Addison County became the center of beekeeping in the state of Vermont for a number of reasons, including the fact that it got an early boost in beekeeping. This was due to the fact that Addison County's shire town, Middlebury, boasted the state's largest population in Vermont from 1820 through the 1830s followed by Burlington. (McGrory Klyza 2015) It wasn't until 1840, that Burlington became the states most populous city, followed by Rutland. Ironically, the likely reason for the early focus of beekeeping in Addison County, a larger population compared to much of the rest of the state, would be the same liability preventing the faster growing counties of Chittenden and Rutland from usurping Addison County's role due to the significant development and urbanization of much of their landscapes. Vermonters who moved into the cities were simply less likely to farm and keep bees and if they did, they would keep fewer colonies than those residing on farms in the countryside. The establishment in Middlebury of the very first beekeeping association in the state is likely a direct result of having the majority of the state's bees and beekeepers in Addison County.

Geography also helped Addison County's ascension as the state-wide leader in beekeeping. The Champlain Valley is full of glacial, lake, and in-land sea deposits forming a mixture of silt, loam, limestone and heavy clay soils that tend to be highly fertile, if sometimes difficult to work. The large expanse of relatively flat valley floor located in the Champlain Valley is the state's largest, dwarfing that found in the Connecticut River Valley. These physical properties combined with the normally favorable weather and temperature patterns found in the low-lying valley expanses, make the Champlain Valley the foremost place to farm in Vermont. As a result, Addison County hosts more farms and acres of land in agricultural production than any other county in the state. (USDA 2012)

There was a time when the Champlain Valley was the bread basket of the colonies. Then the majority of farmland in Vermont was used for grazing sheep until the conversion to dairy cows in the late 19th and early 20th centuries. The raising of livestock meant that farmers also created lots of pastures full of legumes such as clover, vetch, trefoil, and alfalfa that would not only feed their livestock, but offer honey bees a bounty of forage for much of the year. This rich, agricultural sector, close to the local markets of Burlington and Rutland, and railroad access that brought the large regional markets of Montreal, Boston and New York City within reach, did much to help thrust Addison County into the premier place to keep bees, and maintain that designation over time.

## FUTURE CHALLENGES: INVASIVE PESTS

The collective history of Vermont's beekeepers can not only show us why beekeeping is the way it is today, but it can provide clues to what we can expect down the road. From the earliest days of beekeeping in the original colonies, bears and the wax moth were the only real pests that were of serious concern.

FIGURE 2: **European honey bee larvae parasitized by *Tropilaelaps* mites.**

The same was true for Vermont. That all changed dramatically beginning about thirty-five years ago when first tracheal mites, then Varroa mites, and then small hive beetles, all made their way into the state. Given the nature of today's global economy, we can expect additional pests to sail onto our shores, be driven into our mountain ranges, or be flown to our ports of entry.

One invasive threat that has been predicted to arrive at some point is the mite, *Tropilaelaps clareae*. Native to tropical and sub-tropical portions of Asia, *Tropilaelaps* has the potential to be just as damaging, if not more so, than its cousin *varroa destructor* has been.

## DISEASES

Traditional disease threats, such as American Foulbrood, continue to keep American beekeepers in general and Green Mountain apiarists in particular, on their toes. As has been the case with honey bee pests, a host of new pathogens have been popping up throughout Vermont and the rest of the country. From the digestive disease caused by the parasite *Nosema ceranae*, to a host of honey bee viruses, Vermont bees are under constant threat. The emergence of migratory beekeepers in Vermont during the late 20th century, undoubtedly aggravated this trend that can be expected to continue for the foreseeable future.

## HABITAT LOSS

Generally speaking, the condition of Vermont's honey bees is a microcosm of the condition of bees nationally. This is particularly evident when it comes to the issue of habitat loss. Not only is urban sprawl, housing, and business development eating up valuable and productive farm land, the farms themselves are changing. In the early days as settlers needed more land, they began to clear the forests. The cutting and "improving" of the land continued to the point where Vermont was about 70 percent open fields by 1870. Today, with the decline in farming, the state is about 70 percent forested.

In recent decades since the advent and wide adoption of genetically engineered crops, many farm fields are growing corn instead of hay crops to feed their cows. This reduced pollinator forage availability, combined with the adoption of high tech modern equipment that allows farmers to quickly mow large tracts of land, greatly reduces pollinator access and has done much to reduce the productivity of honey bees in the Vermont landscape.

Due largely to oversupply and low prices, dairy farmers in Vermont have been going out of business at alarming rates, a trend that spawned numerous legislative remedies, all of which have, so far, only served to prolong dairy's deterioration rather than reverse it. Meanwhile the parallel decline of pollinators in the state, both wild and managed, is creating growing alarm. This concern, related to world-wide environmental worries, tends to view bees as a canary in a coal mine; providing advanced notice to humanity that the ecosystem that supports us is seriously degraded.

## CLIMATE DESTABILIZATION

Scientific observation and data inform us that carbon dioxide levels in the Earth's atmosphere are over 40 percent higher than they were in the beginning of the industrial revolution. While such high $CO_2$ levels have been documented on Earth in the past, this appears to be the first time that is has occurred in such a short time-frame geologically speaking; in less than 300 years.

The destabilization of the climate impacts honey bees directly through an increase in extreme weather events that bring high winds, heavy flooding, severe droughts, and out-of-control fires; all of which can threaten the safety and viability of colonies. Scientists have also established that the high $CO_2$ atmosphere is causing plants on our planet to produce less protein and more sugars and starches. For example, researchers have confirmed that the overall pollen protein content of goldenrod has declined by approximately one-third since the latter half of the 20th century. (Ziska 2016) Since the protein content of pollen is a critical nutrition source for developing bee and other insect larvae, this raises grave concerns for the long-term well-being of our pollinators.

## PESTICIDES

Since their inception, agricultural and ornamental pesticide use has been a challenge for beekeepers and a problem for honey bees, going back at least into the 1800s in Vermont. Modern farming methods have grown to rely more and more on the use of chemicals to control pests and diseases and today, more pesticides are sold and used world-wide than at any other time in history. This is also likely to be the story in Vermont, although hard data is difficult to come by. While the state collects data on the use of pesticides within Vermont, there is to date no working database that will allow officials to manage the data effectively and produce reports on Vermont's pesticide use. Until the state is able to actually organize and make use of the reams of pesticide data it collects, effectively addressing issues of non-target chemical exposure is likely to remain elusive.

## VERMONT RESPONDS

Despite the daunting challenges Vermont beekeepers strive to forge a viable future for their industry and their colonies. Utilizing both commonplace and novel approaches, beekeepers throughout the state continue to exhibit their creativity and perseverance.

## NATIONAL HONEY BEE SURVEY (NHBS)

In 2009, a comprehensive examination of colony health in apiaries throughout the United States was organized to address the emerging concern about the diminishing health of honey bee colonies. The Vermont Beekeepers Association supported Vermont's first involvement with this National Honey Bee Survey in 2015, led by then University of Vermont PhD Candidate, Samantha Alger. Dr. Alger has managed the survey since then along with UVM PhD candidate Alex Burnham.

Alger recalls her journey:

> In 2014, I was working on my dissertation research and began looking for research related to viruses in Vermont bees. No one had studied viruses in Vermont, bumble bees or honey bees! However, I learned that many states were involved in a national effort funded by The Farm Bill through the National Honey Bee Survey. This is a nation-wide effort to gather baseline data on bee pests and disease. It is run by the U.S. Animal Plant Health Inspection Service (APHIS) and Bee Informed Partnership (BIP). I called BIP and asked if I could get Vermont involved. The answer was 'yes, as long as you have the support from the state. Support from the bee clubs would also help.' A few weeks later, I learned that VT would receive funding through The Farm Bill . . . The Farm Bill has funded the survey every year since.
>
> For the survey, 24 apiaries are sampled every year. Bees are analyzed at the Beltsville Lab in MD and the University of MD for apiary-level disease data for Nosema, Varroa, and RNA viruses. In 2016, we tested wax for pesticide residues. In 2017, we tested pollen for pesticide residues.

The NHBS is Vermont's first and only standardized survey of honey bee pests and disease and could not have arrived at a better time. Continued participation in this important program is likely to play a pivotal role in successfully negotiating the challenges old and new diseases and pests will pose for Vermont beekeepers in the years ahead.

FIGURE 3: **Samantha Alger and Alex Burnham prepare their sampling equipment.**
PHOTO CREDIT: MICHAEL WILLARD

## APIARY CENSUS

Meanwhile, as Samantha Alger explains, a newly developed apiary registration census program has the potential to be a powerful tool for Vermont's beekeeping industry: "I am working with David Tremblay to collect data on Vermont beekeeping management practices and hive losses. In 2017, we developed a census form that was distributed with the apiary registration forms to Vermont beekeepers. These data were entered by the UVM beekeeping club and I am currently working to compile and analyze the data. Results will be presented at the VBA summer meeting. Data will help both research and outreach efforts to improve bee health in Vermont."

## LAROUA FOODS

An example of Vermonters capitalizing on the threat posed by a pest is Laroua Foods. The brainchild of University of Vermont graduates, Kitty Foster, and Julia (Jules) Lees, Laroua seeks to establish a market for honey bee larvae that is supported by top chefs who are advocates for sustainable, nutrient-dense food sources. They pay Vermont beekeepers for drone brood collected when culling mite-infested brood combs from hives. From Jules and Kitty's perspective, drone brood removal, as part of a treatment-free varroa control program, adds to the branding of drone brood as human food, and can potentially help sustain the beekeeping industry by providing a new source of revenue for beekeepers. "I think a lot of people don't do anything to control their varroa mites so I feel like there's a huge niche for us to come in and say, 'you need to control your mites, your bees are dying because of the mites and, we'll pay you to do it,'" says Jules. She goes on to explain that it was their common background in sustainable agriculture that led the duo to start the business. "... What has really been good about this business for us is that it is at the nexus of our mutual interests in food systems, nutrition, and environmentalism. It's an opportunity to encourage beekeepers to organically control their varroa mites while at the same time creating an additional food stream from something that would otherwise be a waste product. And it's good for you! It feels like it takes all of our interests and brings them into one." Laroua's company slogan is "Save the bees. Eat them!"

## BEE THE CHANGE

One opportunity to reverse the trend in decreased and degraded pollinator forage and habitat is taking place in Vermont fields where solar panels have been installed. Rather than leave solar farms covered in turf grass or gravel, Middlebury's Mike Kiernan and his family founded Bee the Change. The organization works to install arrays of plantings in and around solar fields with the goal of supporting a diverse array of pollinators.

The Bee the Change website explains:

> Our first field, was installed in May 2016, and several more fields are under construction at this moment. A survey of the pollinator population in our first year at the South Ridge field in Middlebury demonstrated 34 unique pollinator encounters in a 15 minute period. One year later, surveying the same plots, we encountered 174 unique pollinators in 15 minutes. That impact will increase the productivity of plants beyond the boundaries of the solar field and support downstream species who rely on that productivity-birds, fish, other wildlife and, of course, human beings.

Bee the Change sells honey from the bees they place in solar fields along with beeswax candles, and other bee related products.

FIGURE 4: **Bee the Change founders Tawnya and Mike Kiernan.** PHOTO COURTESY OF MIKE KEIRNAN

## POLLINATION CONFERENCE 2016

In response to growing concern about loss of pollinators generally, President Obama issued a memorandum creating a Pollinator Health Task Force in June 2014. Co-chaired by the USDA and the Environmental Protection Agency (EPA) it was charged with creating a national pollinator health strategy to promote the health of pollinators, including honey bees.

In the beginning of 2016 Vermont held its first ever conference on beetles, bees and butterflies, to consider the threats these pollinators face in Vermont. The conference was a response to President Obama's directive to create a national strategy to promote the health of honey bees and pollinators.

Conference speakers described a smorgasbord of stresses. While honey bees, wild bees and other pollinators are all threatened by the globalization of parasitic mites and diseases, global climate destabilization, nutritional deficiencies, and pesticide exposure, the honey bee also must contend with the hazards of intensive management and transport for crop pollination.

Common threats identified for all pollinators include the loss of habitat through edge-to-edge cultivation for farm corn, the early cutting of forage crops, and homeowners' obsession with uniformly green lawns. Global climate destabilization is affecting species survival, forage areas and reducing growing periods for many crops.

Numerous speakers pleaded for an end to prophylactic (or automatic) application of pesticides to crops and lawns. One speaker urged the audience to accept more "messy" gardens which would be richer in nutrients and less toxic to pollinators. And "to stop treating dandelions as horticultural terrorists."

Working together isn't always easy, but the conference atmosphere was resolute, reminding one attendee of Ben Franklin and his revolutionary words that: "We must hang together, or assuredly, we shall all hang separately."

Around the same time in Montpelier, a bill proposing to ban certain pesticides was amended to regulate what are called "treated articles." This is the term the EPA uses to denote products treated with pesticides, such as utility poles, commercial crop seeds, nursery plants and lumber. That bill passed 123-16.

Another outcome of the Pollinator Health task force's work at the national level was the implementation of a policy by the EPA that among other things, recommended that states and tribes in the U.S. establish Pollinator Protection Plans.

## VERMONT'S POLLINATOR PROTECTION COMMITTEE

In 2016, the Vermont legislature responded to the EPA by passing Act 83, a bill creating a Pollinator Protection Committee. The Committee, made up of beekeepers, ecologists, government officials, UVM researchers and members of the farming community, came together to develop a plan that would conserve and improve pollinator health in Vermont. Ross Conrad and Mike Palmer represented Vermont's beekeepers on the ten-member committee that released its report in February 2017.

The report contains over 50 specific committee recommendations that were approved by unanimous vote. The recommendations cover the areas of: Education criteria and additional topics for pesticide applicators; Changes to the state pesticide regulations; data gaps and statewide goals; Neonicotinoid products; State land management and outreach; Agricultural practices and incentives; and Beekeeper education and pest/pathogen reduction.

Although the Pollinator Protection Committee officially disbanded following the release of the report, members volunteered to reconvene unofficially during the winter of 2018-2019, and work on drafting Best Management Practices as part of an eventual Pollinator Protection Plan for the state of Vermont.

## LEGISLATIVE ACTION

Vermont took a small step in taking on the pesticide industry with the 2019 passage of *An Act Relating To The Regulation Of Neonicotinoid Pesticides H.205* (Act 35). The bill removes the ability of homeowners and consumers who are not certified applicators, to use neonicotinoid pesticides legally in Vermont. It also developed resources to fund a pollination specialist and pesticide enforcement specialist by increasing the registration fee chemical companies pay to register pesticides in Vermont.

The Vermont Beekeepers Association welcomed the effort to protect the 40-million-dollar Vermont beekeeping industry, as well as the state's wild and endangered pollinators. However, the VBA Board of Directors felt that the bill as initially proposed was too weak in some areas and too over-bearing in others. For example, the bill exempted treated agricultural seeds and pet products, which constitute the two of the largest economic uses of neonicotinoids.

H.205 also proposed a large state program to educate and certify the roughly 1000 beekeepers in the state, when much of this kind of activity is already provided by the VBA. Association members testified before the house and senate agriculture committees and as the bill moved through the legislature, it improved, including a provision for the state to collaborate with VBA on educating Vermont's beekeepers.

VBA members also testified in favor of not just retaining a bee inspector in the state, but making the position full-time if possible. Without an inspector, good beekeepers are at the mercy of bad beekeepers—because there are, after all, no good fences in beekeeping.

## VERMONT BEEKEEPERS WORK ABROAD

A number of Vermont beekeepers have carried their skills to other lands to both share and learn from fellow beekeepers around the globe. The first and most prominent was Charlie Mraz of Middlebury. According to his grandson Chas Mraz, Charlie worked all over the world, but most notably in Mexico.

Charlie first worked for the Mexican honey producer Miel Carlotta in the 1950s. They were having major problems with queen breeding and

I remember Charlie telling me that the queens down there were almost totally inbred and useless. He brought some of his queens down and taught the beekeepers how to make 'walk away nucs.' The Mraz queens apparently did very well down there and the walk away nucs eventually did so well that the workers refused to use the bred queens that the same operation was producing.

A number of people credited Charlie with saving the Mexican beekeeping industry! At one of the numerous speeches he gave, he was once introduced with three questions to the audience: 'Do you know who the President of Mexico is?' 40 percent raised their hands. 'And who is the Pope?' 60 percent got that right. 'And who is Charlie Mraz?' Everyone raised their hands!

Decades after Charles Mraz's foray into Mexico, other Vermont beekeepers would follow suit.

While writing a book with Rick Peyser, head of social responsibility for Green Mountain Coffee Roasters, Bill Mares of Burlington got intrigued with the idea that honey might provide some supplemental income to the coffee farmers to fight seasonal hunger, and, could bees help with coffee pollination? To both questions the answer was yes.

With Dewey Caron, and the non-profit Food4Farmers, they found that farmers needn't own land. The bees produced multiple products besides honey— pollen, wax, propolis, royal jelly, etc. One Mexican beekeeper calls a beehive, the "local pharmacy" for traditional medicine.

Honey prices have proved to be more stable than those of coffee and there are local, national and international markets. The bees are good pollinators of coffee, while promoting plant diversity generally, and at the same time beekeeping offers a range of jobs, including working with stingless bees.

While he has presented on beekeeping topics in Europe, another Mexican connection was made by Mike Palmer in December of 2017, when he was honored to meet with beekeepers in Teocelo, Veracruz, Mexico. The four-day seminar, organized by Union Ganadera Apicola Nacional (UGAN), was held at a small resort/coffee plantation. The first two days were spent addressing a group of queen breeders. Palmer showed them how he use nucleus colonies to boost the strength of his cell builders. Explained Palmer, "I believe the presentation was well received. I'm pretty sure those that received them were excited about their new Vermont Beekeepers Association caps." On Friday and Saturday, the general meeting was held at the honey processing facility of Santa Rosa.

FIGURE 5: **Visit to the Maya Vinic Coffee Cooperative in Acteal, Chiapas, Mexico. From left to right: Jose Arias, beekeeper, coffee grower and President of the board of the 500 Asociados of Mayo Vinic, Antonio Ruiz, Manager of the cooperative, Bill Mares, Dewey Caron, and manager of the plant.** PHOTO CREDIT: LUIS ALVAREZ

While its proximity to the U.S. makes it relatively easy and attractive for cross-cultural beekeeping expeditions, Mexico has not been the focus of all Vermont beekeeping activity abroad.

In 1993, Jeff T. Cunningham of Putney, Vermont, traveled to Uzbekistan working on cultural exchange.

Reports Cunningham:

In my papers I carried the name of a Russian Uzbek beekeeper provided by Kirk Webster, a key mentor. They had corresponded about a Heat Therapy used for years in the USSR to treat colonies for Varroa mites, after temporarily removing the bees from the long box, large frame, Russian style hives. I carefully documented the method, and, back in Putney, conducted tests in my bee yard followed by dozens of hours of experimental design and planning that incorporated the insights of apiculturists and researchers

FIGURE 6: **Bees being inserted into a heat treatment unit that removes varroa mites from bees.** PHOTO CREDIT: JEFF CUNNINGHAM

including Maryann Frasier, John Harbo, Mike Palmer, Steve Parise, and Jennifer Ramstetter. As senior investigator and coordinator for "Evaluating a heat-therapeutic control of the honey bee mite Varroa destructor" (NESARE LNE96-066), I established and maintained eight bee research yards around Windham County for eighteen months.

Exposure to beekeepers and bees in overseas environments stimulates ideas and generates understanding on multiple levels as reported by many beekeepers. Other illuminating international experiences included working with beekeepers in Jordan, where they, their bees, and medicinal honey receive great public appreciation. Although they used primarily the latest Langstroth equipment, I encountered some traditional clay cylinder colonies in the 1990s. More recently, I met the tiny *Apis florea*, [dwarf honey bee] a charming native of the Persian Gulf that resembles early honey bees from which *Apis mellifera* evolved.

In 2012, Dr. Kristin Wolf of Champlain College traveled to Peru for the first time to help with a new beekeeping project initiated by her mentor, Germán Perilla. He was working with the Maijuna communities, located a day's journey north on the Amazon River from Iquitos. Dr. Wolf reports:

FIGURE 7: **Germán Perilla explaining to residents of the Diamante community (Northern Peru) how to transfer a stingless bee colony from a tree hollow to a vertical hive.** PHOTO CREDIT: KRISTIN WOLF

During our time there, we assembled equipment, trained beekeepers, and built out an Africanized honey bee program in collaboration with community leaders, as we were warmly hosted by the Sucusari and Nueva Vida villages. The experience was remarkable and we have traveled back many times in the years since to continue this work with other communities and with students from Champlain College. Our work has developed into a form of sustainable development that focuses its efforts at the local level and understands the necessity of community collaboration to ensure the lasting success of its projects.

We recognize that beekeeping has been used as a tool for sustainable development long before it was ever categorized as such. The production of bee products and rendering of pollination services can be an excellent form of supplemental income, in addition to the former's widespread use in traditional medicine. And while honey bees have demonstrated success in agricultural settings in the developing world, the immense diversity of stingless bees has expanded opportunities for the management of native bee varieties in forested landscapes. Furthermore, because stingless bees are generally more successful in undisturbed environments, the keeping of these bees encourages sustainable use of the land in which they are housed. Native bees require native forage.

In recent years, we have worked closely with the Chino community, a few hours south of Iquitos on the Amazon. Here we collaborate with beekeepers on sustainable management techniques of four species of *Melipona* bees—*M. eburnea*, *M. elota*, *M. favosa*, and *M. compressipes*—with the goal of transferring wild colonies to vertical hives. Traditional beekeeping techniques required the felling of bee trees and kept bees in their original tree hollow, which made manipulation of the hive difficult and destructive.

The vertical hive structure, which positions the brood chamber in lower boxes and honey and pollen pots in shallow trays above, has numerous benefits, including a less invasive entry to the hive for harvest and allowing for splits to be made for further colony propagation. After a couple years of experimentation to identify species-specific preferences for wood varieties and tray depths, there are many successful colonies in the community and an ever-increasing interest in keeping bees. Community members report a vast array of medicinal uses for their honey (treating cataracts, respiratory illness, intestinal parasites, and infertility to name a few) and can sell and trade the higher quality honey harvested from vertical hives for an increased value.

It has been highly rewarding to the see the success of these beekeeping projects over the years and to help optimize their use and value in the communities that they serve. Furthermore, graduate and undergraduate students who visit are often inspired to create their own projects in consultation with community members and benefit greatly from an experience that expands their perspectives and forges their own sense of a global environmental ethic.

Ross Conrad of Middlebury has taught several beekeeping classes and offered presentations to beekeepers north of the border in Canada over the years, but in March of 2015, he spent time on the much warmer island of Bermuda sharing ways to control varroa mites in hives without the use of pesticides. The varroa mite was first discovered on the island in 2009. Having learned from the experience of other countries, Bermuda's beekeepers want to avoid the synthetic pesticide chemicals that have led to resistant mites and contaminated combs.

Many of the island's beekeepers initially turned to the Mite Away Quick Strip (MAQS) formic acid treatment to control varroa. The application of the treatment unfortunately occurred during a time of high temperatures and humidity which caused many of the bees to abandon their combs and beard up on the outside of some of the hives. This treatment just happened to also coincide with the arrival of a hurricane, and the accompanying rains that saturated the ground caused the Argentine ants to come up out of their underground nests. Since the strong winds of the hurricane had stripped much of the island's vegetation bare of fruits, flowers, and leaves, there was little food available for the ants so they ended up moving into the hives that the bees had been forced out of. This caused the bees to abandon their hives altogether, absconding and increasing beekeeper's losses even more. As a result, many of the beekeepers on the island became understandably apprehensive about the use of mite treatments and prefer not to treat their bees with anything at all to control varroa. This prompted the Bermuda Environmental Sustainability Taskforce (BEST) to bring Conrad in to work with the island's beekeepers.

During the Spring of 2016, Samantha Alger of Shelburne traveled to Cuba to study the island's ecosystems, farms and beekeeping practices. She found that despite hosting the same bee parasites and diseases as in the US, such as *Varroa* and Foul Brood, reported colony losses were much lower. On the trip, she got to interview several Cuban beekeepers and look in their hives. "I made some really good connections," she says, and became deeply interested in a Cuban bee mystery: "They have a lot of the bee diseases that we have here in the U.S., like chalkbrood and varroa mites," she says, "but they don't lose nearly as many hives." She suspects that honey bee genetics as well as the limited use of agricultural chemicals on the island may play a role in Cuba's low colony losses. Samantha hopes to pursue research in Cuba to understand this topic as well as aid in the transfer of beekeeper knowledge between Vermont, Cuba, and Puerto Rico.

## HONING SKILLS

Due to its rough terrain, severe climate and short growing season, Vermont's beekeepers have been forced to evolve and innovate simply to survive. The continued sharing through workshops, classes, presentations, and mentoring will continue to be critical in disseminating and improving beekeeping skills and techniques. Bee clubs and associations will continue to play an important role in bringing in experienced beekeepers to share both practical and technical information and we can expect new clubs to continue to proliferate as demand for information continues to grow among new beekeepers.

Often bee clubs don't have to look too far for expert speakers. There are two primary areas of beekeeping that have emerged in which beekeepers in Vermont excel and are recognized as leaders the nation: Northern Queen Production and Overwintering. Among the largest and most successful beekeepers that shine in these areas are Kirk Webster and Mike Palmer.

Kirk Webster's entire operation revolves around overwintering nucleus colonies and not using treatments to prop up the health of his colonies. Webster makes late season nucs in June and July using queen cells or mated queens that he raises. He makes sure all are well fed by the middle of October and then overwinters the nucs either on top of well-established honey producing hives which are packed in cardboard packing cases and foam placed underneath the outer cover, or clustered together in groups of four nucs per pallet, with foam insulation on top and bottom and wrapped together with tar paper. These nucs tend to be small with two or four nucs per single hive body.[1] This allows for the testing of a large number of queens with a minimal amount of equipment. Nucleus colonies wintered on either four or eight combs are typically sold the following season, while the overwintered baby nucs are used for producing queens either for sale or for use in his operation. This means that his baby nucs live on the equivalent of two deep frames—four little half-frame combs—all winter. His primary motivation in keeping bees this way is not only so he can overwinter large numbers of queens easily, but also so he can find the queens quickly and easily as compared to keeping full-size 5- or 10-frame nucs, for instance. According to Webster, "finding the queen is the biggest bottleneck in queen rearing."

Webster's queens are all tested prior to use as breeders for his nucs. He describes the process he believes screens the bees for most of the beneficial traits that beekeepers need and look for in successful hives: "Their first winter was spent in nucleus colonies and then. . . they headed honey production colonies that made a good crop. To be considered as a breeder, a queen must pass all of these tests and still be heading a healthy, vigorous colony after her second winter."

Mike Palmer makes nucs for a variety of tasks, and has imitated Kirk by overwintering nucs but with a twist. About his approach, he wrote:

> In 1999, I visited Kirk Webster, just before apple bloom. We drove out to one of his apiaries where he showed me some of his over-wintering nucleus colonies. These nuclei were wintering on top of production hives and there were bee beards hanging from the entrances of the nucleus boxes.
>
> When I tried this technique I thought of them as stocks for replacing Winter losses and as stocks for making increase. But why wait? Why just give a weak colony valuable brood resources only to discover a failing queen later in the Summer? Why not just kill that old queen and give the colony an over-wintered nucleus?
>
> The results were quick and lasting. The larger cluster created by adding combs of emerging brood not only boosted the colony population in the

---

1 Two nucs in a hive body live on four frames, each while four nucs in a single hive body live on the equivalent of two frames of comb (four mini frames).

FIGURE 8: **A frame from a baby nuc. The Reduction in comb size in each nuc makes finding the queen much quicker and easier.** PHOTO CREDIT: KIRK WEBSTER

short term, that increased cluster size lasted through the Winter and come Spring, those colonies were among the strongest in the apiary. It was as if I had dropped a bomb on each colony and I jokingly referred to them as 'Bee Bombs' in an article I wrote for *Bee Culture Magazine* . . . And that is the difference. My bees are healthier and more productive. I have the resource in my nucleus colonies to build up my honey producers so they have a chance to make a good crop.

By 2006, Palmer felt comfortable enough with this technique to accept an invitation to address the Massachusetts Beekeepers Association. He remembers how the old-timers shook their heads in disbelief when he described his system. But two years later, when he came again those same skeptics had become believers.

Kirk Webster sums up what has become the reality of beekeeping in Vermont today:

. . . really healthy apiaries cannot be bought or sold, borrowed, stolen, or connived by any means. They can't even be owned by anyone—they have to be recreated constantly, one apiary at a time, by steady, careful, creative work. I know now that each generation of bees doesn't have to be weaker than the one before. . . no one can tell me anymore about the inevitable demise of honey bees and beekeeping. With a change of attitude, the answers are close by and there's plenty of inspiration and guidance. The work might be hard, but only because we are not used to it. If we care about future generations, and the other beings who share the Earth with us, we have to stop expecting other people to solve our problems; to learn from others instead of taking from them, and do our share of the work. This work is more satisfying and meaningful than just about anything else you can do at this point. The old beekeeping is dying, and a new one is struggling to be born. Are you going to the funeral, or assisting with the birth? They are both occurring at the same time, so you have to choose.

FIGURE 9: **Honey bees on a Cosmos blossom in Lincoln, Vermont.**
PHOTO CREDIT: KATHRYN WYATT

CHAPTER 8

# *A Cluster of Beekeepers*

*I first started beekeeping by collecting bees in empty milk bottles and wait-*
*ing for them to make some honey for me. They never made any honey, and*
*soon died in the bottles from starvation.*
—CHARLES MRAZ[1]

## TO BEE OR NOT TO BEE

At one time, a large green and white traffic sign on the side of Route 7 heading
south from Burlington read: WELCOME TO ADDISON COUNTY THE LAND OF
MILK AND HONEY. As if to foretell the fate of Vermont's dairy and beekeeping
industries, the sign was removed in the mid-1980s.

Both national honey bee surveys (BIP) and anecdotal evidence from the
majority of Vermont's beekeepers indicate that annual honey bee colony losses
have hit an all-time high during the first two decades of the twenty-first century. Despite this, as the decades pass, the number of colonies in Vermont has
remained relatively stable, even as average honey yield per colony and beekeeper
numbers have declined from historic highs...yet all is not lost.

In 1929, President Calvin Coolidge gave his famous "Brave Little State of
Vermont" speech. He ended it this way:

> I love Vermont because of her hills and valleys, her scenery and invigorating
> climate, but most of all because of her indomitable people. They are a race of

---

1 *Health and the Honeybee* by Charles Mraz, p. 1

pioneers who have almost beggared themselves to serve others. If the spirit of liberty should vanish in other parts of the Union, and support of our institutions should languish, it could all be replenished from the generous store held by the people of this brave little state of Vermont.[2]

Now imagine that Coolidge was a beekeeper, just like his fellow Governor Lee Emerson who governed Vermont from 1951–1955. Coolidge could have written the speech in this manner:

I love Vermont, because tucked away in the hollows, hills and valleys amongst her scenery and invigorating climate, Vermont's indomitable group of beekeepers share an apicultural heritage that dates to the pioneering days of beekeeping in North America. This hardy race almost beggared themselves as they convey the skills of this ancient, and yet ever evolving craft to others. If their common history is any indication, the declining fortunes of the honey bee may well be reinvigorated and restored from the generous and inventive spirit held by the beekeepers from the brave little state of Vermont.

*Allow us to introduce you to a sampling of these beekeepers.*

~ ~ ~

## KATE BLOFSON, JERICHO
**When did you start keeping bees?**
In 2009, I was living in Philadelphia. I started helping a friend with their bees at the Mill Creek Farm, which along with a community garden occupies a city block and runs education and training programs for kids and a weekly market selling their incredible fresh produce at fruit truck prices. People from the neighborhood were always stopping in to enjoy the beautiful bit of green, and they were always very interested in the bees - particularly the honey. I remember picking what seemed like a dozen virgin queens out of a swarm that landed on the roof of the cob shed with my sister, a group of schoolchildren running over to watch and carry on. I took over care of the Mill Creek hives, and also kept bees at Bartram's Gardens in Southwest Philadelphia. But I also had a seasonal

---

2 Delivered by Vermont native and 30th President of the United States (1923–1929), Calvin Coolidge, in Bennington September 21, 1928.

FIGURE 1: **Jeremy Grenon, Mike Palmer and Kate Blofson at the queen marking table.**
PHOTO COURTESY OF KATE BLOFSON.

job working on a sailboat at the time, and didn't really start learning about bee-keeping until I moved to Vermont in 2011.

### How did you learn? With mentors? Alone?
I've learned beekeeping from working with friends and mentors, although I've read a lot and dabbled with all sorts of hives. Five seasons with Mike Palmer at French Hill Apiaries imparted most of my practical beekeeping skills and knowledge. I also worked a bit with Sam Comfort of Anarchy Apiaries [New York], including some semi-harrowing bee hauls from Florida to the Hudson Valley.

### Where are your bee yards located?
I have bee yards in Jericho, Burlington, and Richmond. I produce small amounts of honey to share and barter. My sights are set on producing queens and nucleus colonies, and turning cornfields into flowers.

**What are your biggest beekeeping challenges?**
I think the biggest challenge to beekeeping is/will be adapting to climate change and wierd weather. For now it's mites, and figuring out how to keep mite levels and chemical treatments down. Of perhaps even more concern to me is the threat that mites pose to our native bees.

**What was your greatest beekeeping success?**
A few supers full of perfect goldenrod comb honey a few seasons back. Divine. And it's always great to witness all of Mike's successes through the seasons with his bees and queen breeding program at French Hill.

**What type(s) of hives/equipment do you use?**
Langstroth usually, also Warre & Top Bar. I would use anything, like the bees.

**What have you done to help other beekeepers and beekeeping in Vermont?**
Relieve some of Mike Palmer's workload! I do help a few friends with their hives, and am always ready to chat with interested people and advocate for the bees.

**Why do you keep bees?**
I really enjoy living close to the weather, flowers, and nature, rolling with their cycles. I beekeep every day during the season, and I find that I love being outside all day, tuned in to every new bloom, temperature drop, and weather front coming in. I also appreciate following the flow of tasks throughout the season, which are linked to our honey flows. In the apiary I feel as if I've really grown to know this one small corner of nature, the bees' world, that includes all sorts of pheromones and smells and different kinds of buzzes that are now familiar and easily understood - and yet I learn something new every day. There's something really satisfying in that. Bottom line, the bees and working outdoors keep me interested, inspired, and in nature - and those things make me happy.

# JON T. CREIGHTON, EDEN

**How did I start?**
I started beekeeping in 2009, solely as an effort to increase the pollination of a half dozen apple trees. Through contact with the VBA, I was directed to the

FIGURE 2: **Jon Creighton in the dead of winter.** PHOTO COURTESY OF JON CREIGHTON

Central Vermont Beekeepers Club, at the time facilitated by Kim Greenwood, and was mentored by Gib Geiger. As both Kim and Gib mentored me through the initial ups and downs of learning beekeeping, the craft became more of an addiction rather than just improving the pollination of my apples.

My apiary is located in Eden, shadowed by Belvidere Mountain and surrounded by state forest and farmers hay fields. My honey crop consists primarily of liquid raw honey, though occasionally I produce cut comb honey. I'm also listed on the VBA's website for swarm capture in the northern Lamoille County area.

**Biggest challenges?** The most challenging aspects of beekeeping for me are getting my hives to overwinter in Eden's harsh conditions, treating for mites, and maintaining sufficient charge in my electric fence to ward off the occasional bear visits.

**Greatest success?** I define beekeeping success as getting through the winter with a high survival percentage and producing 120-150 lbs of honey from 3 to 4 hives while leaving sufficient stores heading into the next winter.

Upon request, I try to give assistance to new beekeepers, just as Kim and Gib helped me. I also really enjoy talking bees to the many folks visiting the VBA booth at the Tunbridge Fair. Additionally, at every opportunity, I speak about the importance of maintaining and preserving forage for pollinators.

**Why do I keep bees?** I started beekeeping as a means to improve the pollination of my apple trees. I continue because of my addiction to and love of beekeeping, no matter the success or the failures—and sometimes the hefty expense.

## JEFFREY T. CUNNINGHAM, PUTNEY

**How did I start?**

In the winter of 1972, at age ten, I prepared for the purchase of my first colony by reading *Beekeeping: The Gentle Craft* by John Adams and Dadant's *First Lessons in Beekeeping*. The timing was likely my father's idea of a healthy focus—a kind of family apitherapy while my mother underwent cancer treatment. My grandfather, Leslie Gallup, was a UVM-trained pomologist and beekeeper in West Brattleboro and Berlin, Vermont who gave us his 1940s-era hive components

FIGURE 3: **Jeff Cunningham works a hive.**
PHOTO COURTESY OF JEFF CUNNINGHAM

and equipment. One June day at dusk, my father and I drove to pick up the colony from an egg farmer/ beekeeper named Oscar, who secured the hive entrance with window screen and tufts of grass and provided all the practical advice needed that first year. Although my parents had lived, met, and married in West Brattleboro, we were living at the time on a suburban remnant of a nineteenth-century orchard in Connecticut, where we placed the colony on a neat stack of flagstones to pollinate apple, plum, peach, cherry, and mulberry trees. The bees contributed knowledge of natural history and morsels of honeycomb to myself and childhood friends.

Years later, in Brattleboro, I joined the VBA and the farmers' market, eventually developing two dozen organic products including herb-infused honeys, propolis tincture, and salves. In 1990, a horticulturist asked me to pollinate melons in Westminster West near where I later settled with my wife and built a small diversified farm. I trained in organic inspection and was active in the development of organic honey standards. My apiary eventually reached fifty full-sized colonies, but forage was often insufficient due to local mowing and farm management practices (a continuing issue).

## SHERI ENGLERT, VERMONT BEEKEEPING SUPPLY, WILLIAMSTOWN

**How did I start?**

My dad was a beekeeper. I never paid too much attention to that; my father had many, many interests and I had other things to do. Then one day, I found myself up a very tall pine tree trying to catch a swarm

FIGURE 4: **Sheri Englert.** PHOTO COURTESY OF SHERI ENGLERT

from his hive. He had suffered a heart attack and he looked pretty defeated as he watched his last hive fly out. I managed to get them into a box and down the tree, but they didn't stay. That was my first experience with honey bees.

The next year, my father passed. Shortly after, I cleaned out the hive that had swarmed but left it set up. I liked having it in the yard. One day, I noticed a few bees flying in and out and a few days after that, I lifted the lid and found seven rows of perfect, white comb with capped brood, nectar, and pollen, although I had no idea that's what I was looking at! I was hooked.

I don't know that I was ever a hobbyist. I never took beekeeping that casually. I've tried to be more of a steward. I guess I became a sideliner when I began sharing my passion with other people. In fifteen years of keeping bees and the last five years mentoring new beekeepers and selling bees and supplies, my objective has always been to provide people with the supplies they needed. In addition, I thought it my duty to pick up the phone at 9 P.M. on a Saturday night to answer questions and calm fears. My store hours are "if I'm home, I'm open"! I think it's been the passion for beekeeping that has fueled our business growth and success.

I am blessed to have helped over 500 folks start their beekeeping journeys. Some have dropped away in frustration, but most have continued in spite of all the hurdles, because they understand the importance of the continuing battle.

FIGURE 5: **Gib Geiger.**
PHOTO CREDIT: MOLLY GEIGER DOODY

## GIB GEIGER, WAITSFIELD
**How did you start?**
When we bought this farm almost saeven years ago, the land came with bee hives that a man named Bob Tracy down the road owned and kept here. He has taught me everything I know, plus I've gotten into reading-up on bees through books and magazines. I seemed to love how interesting the life of a bee really is. As Mike Palmer once said, "Ask three beekeepers one question, and you'll get six different answers!" So I ask a lot of questions, and listen, and see what works for me.

**Do you sell your honey?**
Yes, we sell one-pound bottles and jars of raw honey right here at our small "help yourself" stand, within the front room of our big barn, that is right on the road. We often have people come to take a carriage or sleigh ride, and to see our animals, so once they are here, they get the whole story of how we hay all of our fields to fill our barn for the seven draft horses, how we press cider from our 200 apple trees to freeze and then thaw later to use for hot cider with the sleigh rides. We tell them how we make maple syrup with all of our neighbors and sell that too. Finally we talk about the bee hives and how all of that works. People are fascinated. Most people don't know one thing about honey bees.

With any luck, by the time the ride is over, they want to buy syrup and honey to take back home!

**Do you pollinate?**
Yes, I have 250 apple and pear trees and also sunflowers and pumpkins.

**What are the most satisfying things about keeping bees?**
It's watching how well they work as a society, and how each year something different happens within the hives. It's also teaching about bees. Bob Tracy and I put together a couple workshops every spring here in Waitsfield, and I help him with that. I also have spare veils here on the farm for anyone who is interested. I also love getting out and meeting new beekeepers.

**What's the most frustrating thing?**
Mites, diseases, and bears!

## HUGH GIBSON, ESSEX JUNCTION

Hugh Gibson taught beekeeping as part of the Agriculture program at the Essex Technical Center beginning in 1979 and continued that endeavor for thirty-two years. During that time period Hugh found that even the most hardened student took interest in the business of bees. He thought that might be because if there is something to have some respect for, it is the tail end of a honey bee.

Hugh also said students found it exciting to produce a product for market entirely on their own, by raising the bees, managing and extracting the honey, processing, learning labeling laws, and developing unique advertising that leadings to sales. He noted that teaching beekeeping in the high school setting was unique

Figure 6: **Hugh Gibson.**
Photo credit: Hugh Gibson

because incoming students in September started their journey by first removing and extracting the honey. Then in the spring these same students would start a hive and acquire managing techniques, setting up a honey crop for the next September class.

Hugh said that removing honey mid to late September also posed the problem of extracting cold honey. In regards to that, he and his students decided to experiment by heating a stack of full honey supers over a hot plate. As Hugh said, "that's when the educator got an education." After the smoke cleared and most of the honey was saved, Hugh wrote an article for *Bee Culture Magazine* (Jan. 1989) titled "Up in Smoke."

Even mistakes can have benefits, he said, because the article resulted in students receiving letters from many places including England. Lessons also included field trips such as ones to the apiary of John Tardie, a local and unique individual who accepted them at anytime. Hugh recalls, on one such trip while in the bee yard a student says to another, "Dude, you got a bee on you." The other student replies, "That's okay I got a veil on." First student: "I know. . . its inside your veil."

Hugh also taught evening beekeeping classes for adults but always insisted the excitement was with kids and what might happen on any particular day. Hugh retired from teaching Agriculture at the tech center in 2011, but the beekeeping class he started lives on today.

## KIM GREENWOOD, DUXBURY

Kim Greenwood explores the Duxbury side of Camel's Hump in the five seasons with her husband, Ian. She has lived there since 2001 with a varying number of rescued pets. She has worked as an advocate, engineer, and regulator of Vermont's natural resources for twenty-five years and currently serves as Director of Environmental Compliance for the State of Vermont Agency of Natural Resources. She reads, rug hooks, gardens, plays piano or takes photographs every day.

### How did I start?
Stupidly! I didn't have a mentor and didn't know another beekeeper except the newbee I was starting with. I had *Beekeeping for Dummies* and a few other books that made no sense until I got my first hive. I still remember how nerve-racking it was driving those bees home from Middlebury. My notes from my first training include "find out what a varroa mite is." That's how little I knew.

I was fortunate that our bees lived the first year, but it was not due to the beekeeper's skills. I had no idea what I was doing. They were Kirk Webster bees that lived for years and years. I credit that I'm still beekeeping now to the fact that Kirk's bees were so healthy and they overwintered while I was learning.

We have two apiaries. One is up on Camel's Hump at our home and another yard at my parent's house in East Randolph to help out my father's apple trees. Those hives border a 10-acre field of vegetables and the farmers are former beekeepers who once even planted some buckwheat for our bees. The two apiaries have completely different beekeeping years: one thrives on the early trees and is quite shaded with early honey

FIGURE 7: **Kim Greenwood.**    PHOTO CREDIT: IAN ORMON

that is light and fragrant; the other has long sunny days and is in a valley of fields with honey that is more traditional. It's neat to compare the two apiaries throughout the year and is a great way to learn to observe.

### Biggest challenges?

Our biggest challenge is producing honey up in the cold of Camel's Hump, and we're on the dark side of the mountain. Our per-hive honey production is lower than the Vermont average but the quality is consistent.

### Greatest success?

Overwintering. Since I've been keeping bees, we've only lost a handful of hives. We keep our hives wide open all winter and treat for mites early. And, as Kim Flottum says, we "take care of the bees that take care of the bees that go into winter."

In addition to honey and wax, the sweetest gifts of the hive have been the beautiful friendships I have formed with other beekeepers. That came in handy after my finger swelled up from a sting I got on my ring finger while teaching a VBA workshop, and I got my engagement ring cut off in the emergency room.

It's been really fun being a part of VBA and being an officer over the years. From the Central Vermont Beekeeping Club that I started and kept running for a few years, I've made some really great friends. Some of the best and most interesting people in the world are beekeepers. As only the second or third female VBA president, one of a handful of VBA vice presidents, and a fairly active mentor, I hope in some way I've encouraged other women to become beekeepers and overcome any worries that they might have about joining a male-dominated beekeeping world.

## Why do I keep bees?

Why wouldn't you?! You can spend as much time learning about bees as you have the capacity for learning and still not know everything. I love that. I also love the heightened awareness of the seasons that beekeeping brings. There's nothing like that first day in spring when they're bringing in the maple pollen and you sigh a little sigh of relief. If I stopped beekeeping today, I bet it would take a long time to break that habit. Lastly: honey. It brings us happiness and does the same to all that we share it with and sell it to.

# PETER W. HADEKA, CASTLETON

## How did I start?

I believe I got my start around 2001–02. Originally, a friend at work had some extra woodenware, frames, etc. and said if I wanted to buy the bees, mail order, he would loan me the hive. I ordered a package from Georgia ($69.00). Two weeks later, after a panicked call from the Rutland Post Office, I picked up my first hive. I brought them home, mixed up some sugar water, and sprayed them down. The next evening my friend came over and we installed the package. Whew!

During the first few years, I was really a floundering beekeeper. It turns out that my friend knew very little about keeping bees. I started attending several VBA workshops, both in Burlington and Ascutney. I also attended a beginner's class at Betterbee and then attended several evening classes that Jack Rath put on at the West Pawlet firehouse. I read several books, watched YouTube videos,

FIGURE 8: **Peter Hadeka at the VBA Tunbridge honey booth.**
PHOTO CREDIT: DEBORAH D. HADEKA

and basically gained as much information as possible from whomever and whatever I could.

When I retired in 2011, my beekeeping accelerated somewhat. I attended VBA summer and winter meetings, as well as the Southern Adirondack Beekeepers seminars.

With the help of my two sons, I built a very nice honey house. I have a powered (15-frame) extractor and various tools and gadgets that go with extracting. Every time I extract honey from my five hives, I count that as a success. My products are honey and a small amount of wax.

**Biggest challenges?**
I believe the varroa mites and overwintering hives are the biggest challenges.

**Greatest success?**
Remembering my own novice period, I've tried to help others get through their first years in beekeeping. I put up a table to answer questions a couple years ago at the Boy Scout camp during their jamboree. I also set up a booth at the Northshire Bookstore in Manchester, again to promote beekeeping. Last fall, I represented the VBA with a booth at the Golden Stage Honey Festival in Proctorsville. The owner had asked the VBA for someone to attend, and I

accepted. I have volunteered at the VBA booth at the Tunbridge Fair. I became a VBA-certified beekeeper as well.

### Why do I keep bees?

First, I like the challenge of having a successful summer (and winter) of producing the honey and getting the bees through tough winters. I enjoy attending the various meetings and getting a wealth of information from Vermont speakers like Mike Palmer and world-renowned experts like Tom Seeley and Dewey Caron (and many more). I also enjoy being able to give honey to family and friends, as well as to sell enough, hopefully, to cover my expenses. I just enjoy working with bees, learning beekeeping, and sharing that information whenever possible.

## JEFFREY HAMELMAN, HARTLAND

### How did I start?

I got my first package in the spring of 1982, while living on Martha's Vineyard. I had read a book several months before getting my first bees—the title was something like *The Charm of Beekeeping*. Not a how-to book, more of a rural-ish rhapsodical sort of thing. I have no idea what induced me to pick it up; something internal must have been gestating. I had no mentors, had never looked inside a beehive, and knew no other beekeepers. But I scrupulously read my 1923 edition of *The ABC and XYZ of Beekeeping* (still a treasured book), subscribed to *Gleanings*, and exchanged some letters with Richard Taylor. His book, *The How-to-Do-It Book of Beekeeping*, had a huge impact on me and still does—for the techniques, and even more, for his philosophy.

I bought new equipment from Walter T. Kelley, because I loved the logo with his head and a bee's body. The frames, of course, were all crimp wired. The good old days. . .

Needless to say, I made every mistake possible that first year, and that was the best learning curve I could have wished for. The next year I got a few more hives and kept them on a couple of nearby farms. That first colony, at my home, made 100 lbs of honey in its second year. If there were any doubt that I would quit bees, it was instantly erased once I had tasted the first teaspoon of that honey. In 1983, I moved to Vermont full time and started a bakery in Brattleboro. I returned to the Vineyard the next year to retrieve my colonies, and we have been in Vermont since then.

Figure 9: **Jeffrey Hamelman.** Photo credit: XChiho Kaneko

All of my bees are at my home in Hartland Four Corners. I have an old metal chair that I keep less than 2 feet from one of the hives, and it's my favorite place to take a nap in summer, carried away by the soft lull of the bees' voices. I have bear fencing, and within it I can hold eight colonies. I used to keep a dozen or more colonies, but now I find that if I have more than eight, it feels too much like work, so I try to stay at eight or fewer. Since I co-teach the VBA classes at the South Yard in Ascutney, I also have nucs, swarms, and/or colonies there as well.

I've never harvested pollen, feeling like the bees should have it all, but I enjoy purifying wax—the aroma of beeswax is unlike anything else on Earth, pure magic. From time to time, I give some to a carpenter or someone making salves or lip balms. I keep most for myself to brush on plastic frames and also to make an incredible old French pastry called Canelé de Bordeaux. These delicious treats are baked in small fluted copper molds, the insides of which are coated with pure beeswax, which you can taste in the finished product.

**Biggest challenges?**

My biggest challenge is devoting enough time to the bees, due to the other activities in my life. Other than that, my challenges are broadly the same as for other beekeepers—managing varroa, minimizing swarming, and learning to smile broadly and sincerely when I see one of my colonies swarm. I just wish I knew how those swarms figured out to cluster 5 feet higher than my tallest ladder!

**Greatest success?**

For my beekeeping public service, I've worked with newbees for a number of years, and for the past 3 or 4 years, I have co-taught the South Yard workshops in Ascutney. I am far, far from being an expert beekeeper, but if I can impart to new beekeepers a sense of wonder, beauty, and rightness about what it means to be a beekeeper, along with some good advice and good technique, then I've done enough.

**Why do I keep bees?**

I don't; they keep me. When I am with them, I feel suffused with a primordial life connection, a profound sense of awe, and a feeling of eternal serenity.

## BOB HEDGES, HINESBURG

FIGURE 10: **Bob Hedges (right), with Bob Haven.**
PHOTO COURTESY OF BOB HEDGES

**How did I start?**

I first took up beekeeping in 1976. Bill Wilson, a friend who worked for the state Agriculture Department, was leaving the state for a job elsewhere. He had some honey bees that he could not take with him and he offered them to me free in a deal I couldn't refuse.

For years, I learned the hard way—[limping] along—until I met Bill Mares and got involved with the VBA and other beekeepers. I have been keeping bees for over 42 years, but I can see the light at the end of the tunnel.

Over the years, all of my hives have been here in Hinesburg. I have bought packages, raised my own nucs, and retrieved swarms from houses, barns, and trees. Besides honey, I have produced wax for candles, lip balm, and hand lotion. I also do some extraction for hire.

### Biggest challenges?
One of the biggest challenges is getting the bees through the winter. If they don't make it, we start over in the spring.

### Greatest success?
My biggest success has been making my own nucs in the spring. It always amazes me how fast they will build up. Over the years, I have mentored a number of beekeepers and also helped some catch swarms.

### Why do I keep bees?
I keep honey bees because I enjoy them. They are one of God's greatest little creatures. Without them we would have no food as they are great pollinators. Love the honey bees!

## LARRY KARP, SWEET PROMISE APIARIES AND CATE HILL ORCHARDS, GREENSBORO AND HARDWICK

Larry Karp is a clinical psychologist who lives, and has a therapy practice, in Hardwick, Vermont. He moved to Greensboro, Vermont in 1969, purchased an old hill farm, raised a family and learned rural arts to provide fresh food for his family and neighbors. He has two grown sons who continue to live on and farm the land in Greensboro

FIGURE 11: **Larry Karp.**
PHOTO CREDIT: LARRY KARP

with their families. Larry continues to be an active beekeeper which he finds therapeutic.

**How did I start?**
I got started beekeeping in 1971 in Greensboro. We had bought an old farm that had an apple orchard on it and it seemed like a good thing to do for pollination. I attended an informational meeting at the local church and quickly became fascinated with the hobby. From a Sears & Roebuck catalogue, I ordered bees and a hive setup with the necessary gear.

I proceeded to subscribe to both *Gleanings in Bee Culture* and *American Bee Journal* and began buying every book on the subject I could find, including *The Hive and the Honey Bee* and *The ABC and XYZ of Beekeeping*. And I still do. I'll talk to any beekeeper I meet and compare notes.

All the local folks I talked to said you can't keep bees here. We've had more success than they suggested, but not as much as we would like. The mites and viruses have made sure of that. It's definitely gotten more challenging over the years.

I stopped beekeeping for a few years (1984), just before the mites came in, to go back to graduate school. My son Josh had taken over our old farm and made it in to an organic apple orchard and wanted to have the bees back. So I got back into it in 2007, when I started teaching him, and we continue to have bees today. We've had as many as forty hives. Raising locally adapted queens is our next goal.

We have bees in Greensboro and in Hardwick now. We produce honey to sell and pollination for our farm and a neighbor who grows berries.

**Biggest challenges?**
The first major challenge was figuring out how to winter bees. Getting some hives through the winter was a major success. Now it's learning how to "live with" mites.We use all Langstroth 10-frame equipment: two deep hive bodies and then medium supers for honey.

**Greatest success?** I have given talks about bees many times over the years and been a mentor to some.

**Why do I keep bees?** I have enjoyed bees and continue to be fascinated by them more than any other farm livestock I've raised. I continue to learn as much as I can even if it's never enough! I enjoy the bees as much today as I did back in 1971. I can't imagine not having bees.

## HEIDI MEYER BOTHLING, ST. JOHNSBURY

**How did I start?** In 2009, I had never seen a hive and I didn't know anyone with hives. Apparently, my grandfather in Austria had kept bees before World War II, but I never met him. I didn't particularly care for honey. But I purchased a nuc from Singing Cedars in southwestern Vermont and drove home with it in my Prius, playing Bach cello suites on the stereo to soothe and entertain them.

Initially I read books, mainly Kim Flottum's *The Backyard Beekeeper*. I joined the VBA and attended the monthly southern yard workshops that were led at that time by Bob Eastman in Thetford. These were tremendously helpful. We would look at and pass around frames, discussing what was happening at that point in the season. Bob would say things like, "you can work your bees in the rain, but they

FIGURE 12: **Heidi Meyer-Bothling.** PHOTO COURTESY OF HEIDI MEYER-BOTHLING

might not be happy about it." I still hear his guidance in my mind. In 2010, I attended a workshop on organic beekeeping led by Ross Conrad, and in 2011, I participated in the EAS' comprehensive short course and annual conference in Rhode Island. I've now completed the VBA's basic beekeeping certification course.

I have one yard at my home in St. Johnsbury. It's near my extensive medicinal herb and vegetable gardens and surrounded by about 10 acres of former pasture land that now hosts mainly native grasses and wildflowers.

My neighbors are delighted with how my bees pollinate their fruit trees and berry bushes. I've experimented minimally with producing comb honey. I aspire to make beeswax candles, and, having tried, have enormous respect for anyone who is able to render beeswax into a pure, fragrant candle. I use raw honey in my herbal medicines and make propolis tincture. I view honey bees as part of the garden ecosystem, and I appreciate the symbiotic relationship that the bees have with their preferred trees and plants.

### Biggest challenges?
I struggle with requeening. I have facilitated a colony raising their own queen, but when a queen is somehow lost or I've made a new split, I've had difficulty introducing a new queen without the colony rejecting her.

### Greatest success?
Successfully collecting a swarm is always exciting. I've climbed a ladder into a tree and sawed off the branch that the colony was hanging on with one hand while holding the branch with the other hand (no hand for the ladder). I then descended the ladder with the football-sized swarm hanging on the branch.

I use eight-frame Langstroth hive equipment. I made that choice early on and I'm very glad I did. I tend to run a few large colonies, and this equipment allows me to lift full supers of honey from a tall stack of hive boxes.

From 2010 to 2013, I coordinated the Northeast Kingdom Beekeeping Club. We had regular meetings and I arranged speakers, mainly through my contacts in the VBA, but also with other established beekeepers in northeastern Vermont. When the VBA hosted the EAS annual conference in Burlington in August 2012, I helped manage the registration function for 700-plus attendees.

### Why do I keep bees?
Originally, I got into it for the pollination. There were fruit trees and berry bushes in my garden, but it seemed like we weren't getting much fruit. Fast forward to 2017, and we got hundreds of pears from our three trees! We also enjoy red and black currants, raspberries, apples, blueberries, and this year for the first time, plums. Beyond that, the bees are an inspiration for how to live consciously and sustainably. They are humble, resourceful, and community-oriented. And there is a sweet and inspiring peacefulness in the way they float out of and back into the hive.

# FRED PUTNAM, JR., BRANDON

## How did I start?

I grew up on a dairy farm, and from the age of nine, I actively participated in all aspects of animal and plant husbandry, as well as maple production. My projects in the 4-H program and my work on the farm greatly helped me understand plant and animal husbandry.

My work on plant and animal husbandry has continued to this date and beekeeping husbandry is an extension of all of this. I have cared for animals and cultivated and tended vegetable, fruit, or berry crops every year since I was very young and now am also immersed in the care of honey bee colonies.

FIGURE 13: **Fred Putnam, Jr.**
PHOTO COURTESY OF FRED PUTNAM, JR.

Beekeeping is another type of husbandry that requires considerable effort to learn enough to do it well. It is a fascinating technical endeavor that requires as much specialized knowledge as does raising dairy animals or vegetable and fruit crops. It also entails a very steep learning curve, but I feel such a great responsibility to the living things that I tend, to care for them properly. I don't like doing things half-baked. I've been to many educational sessions and am happy to be able to help lead some of them now.

I've also served on boards of directors for a number of not-for-profit organizations. Some were small and some quite large. In every volunteer organization in which I've served, my first concern is the success of the volunteers in the organization. The frequent thought in my mind is: "What can this organization do to ensure not only the success of our mission, but also the volunteers who make up the organization?"

I'm a fan of long-range thinking and planning to deal with the more challenging issues and to build consistency over the years. I am also a fan of working by consensus rather than dictate—work with people to resolve differences to come up with the best plan of action.

I am also happy for the chance to help the VBA on the many issues facing us in the beekeeping world.

## PEDRO SALAS, BEE HAPPY VERMONT, STARKSBORO

My interest in beekeeping began in 1997 when I was touched on the shoulder by the parent of a violin student whom my sister-in-law, Pam Reit, was teaching. This person was Michael Palmer, who needed help to smoke the many pallets of beehives he was putting on a truck to be moved to Florida.

For me it was the most scary time because I was afraid of bees, and seeing a dark cloud of them covering the sunlight was a nightmare.

In my native Peru I had a career as a fisheries biologist, but circumstances changed and now here I was in the state of Vermont, and needed to find new work. Michael Palmer's professional experience and willingness to share, drew me into this job: there was contact whith nature, bees, birds, mammals and weather, working in his many apiaries and in the warehouse where we processed the honey. I spent some years working and learning with Michael and grew to love it. I am also an artist and realized that the beeswax was a wonderful material to work with; so I took a class on how to create my own molds.

In the year 2000, I began to make candles and process my own honey, a wonderful natural product with no need to add preservatives. I eventualy quit my part-time jobs and began my own full-time business as a beekeeper and vendor in the local farmers markets.

I built my workshop where I create my candles and process the honey, make cream honey, honey mead and also paint and produce art cards to sell at the farmer's markets.

FIGURE 14: **Pedro Salas.** PHOTO CREDIT: JOSE SALAS

My wife Susan also helped by planting new flowers for the bees and developing other value-added products to sell like honey baklava, lip balms, toasted nuts in honey, and a special recipe from a friend K.K. Wilder that her Greek father use to make called "Pistoli." This is a honey bar made with nuts, seeds, and honey.

Today I am a member of the Burlington, Richmond, Fletcher Allen Hospital, and Winooski Farmer's Markets and have a quite comfortable life. I even do my own bee sting therapy for my sciatica pain. I am so happy with my work with the bees that I called my business "Bee Happy Vermont."

## LARRY SOLT, BURLINGTON

Larry Solt, musician, music educator and conductor for over five decades continues research on a "History of Vermont Town Bands." He and his wife, Stephanie, love to travel. Currently, Larry conducts the Vermont Wind Ensemble at UVM as well as the Burlington Concert Band at Battery Park during the summer months.

### When did you start beekeeping?
I started keeping bees in 1978 in Elmore, VT. There were four of us who together made our own bee keeping equipment at a local school. We had a large vegetable garden and the three hives of honey bees helped pollinate the plants. Our neighbors told us after we installed bee hives, their garden had never produced so many vegetables before. To enrich the soil, I asked the local dairy farmer if he would spread manure on the garden. I would then take him honey from our hives for payment. He would tell everyone that he really got the sweet end of the deal. Moving to Burlington years later, it was a challenge to find a place for the hives, so there were a couple of years I had no active hives. Then I had an offer to start up two hives at the Rock Point School where they had just built a barn for both honey and maple syrup production. After a few years I then moved the two hives to a local community garden.

FIGURE 15: **Larry Solt with U.S. Representative Peter Welch at the Tunbridge Fair.**
PHOTO COURTESY OF LARRY SOLT

**How did you learn? Did you have mentors or were you self-taught?**
I learned the basics from Frank Kellog in Stowe, Vermont, and from the *ABC and XYZ of Bee Culture*, 1975 edition, A.I. Root Bee Library. Much was learned from trial and error. At least back then, I did not have to deal with varroa mites. Joining VBA certainly helped in learning more about better beekeeping practices. The workshops at the "Northern Yard" in the Intervale really assisted in learning better practices in beekeeping.

**Where are your bee yards located?**
As a hobbyist, I have the hives at my home in Burlington.

**What are your biggest beekeeping challenges?**
Keeping up with mites, the changing climate with such fluctuations in temperature, and keeping productive queen bees.

**What are your greatest beekeeping successes?**
A rewarding success was to introduce many gardeners at the community garden to the pollination benefits of honey bees on their plants in the gardens. Some gardeners even started keeping bees after seeing the hives at the garden. The local summer program for school students got to see the hives and learn more about honey bees. As a retired educator, this warmed my heart seeing young people learning about honey bees.

**What type of equipment do you use?**
I use Langstroth ten-frame hives, two deeps, with shallow honey supers.

**Why do you keep bees?**
The pure joy of learning and working with honey bees, their importance to the environment, making mead and enjoying the flavors of honey. Whenever we travel to other countries, I love to talk with beekeepers and bring back honey from those countries.

**When did you start beekeeping?** 1978

**How did you learn? Did you have mentors or were you self-taught?**
Self-taught

**Where are your bee yards located?**
Home back yard

**What are your biggest beekeeping challenges?**
Wintering over

**What are your greatest beekeeping successes?**
Being able to make mead using my own honey; building most of my own equipment.

**Why do you keep bees?**
The pure joy of learning about honey bees and their importance to the environment.

# RICK STONER, SHELBURNE

**How did I start?**
I began keeping bees in 1998 because I wanted the bees to help enhance the natural world around my property in Shelburne.

Enoch Tompkins was helpful in installing my first packages of bees, but after that, it was seat of the pants for two years. Joining the VBA and networking with other beekeepers got me to a point where I felt comfortable mentoring others so they wouldn't repeat my mistakes!

Besides honey, I have provided wax to the Education Program at Shelburne Farms.

**Biggest challenges?**
My biggest challenges are mites and the weather. I try to intervene as little as possible and have treated using different medications. The weather . . . well, we are all farmers as far as the weather is concerned, and you roll with the punches.

**Greatest success?**
Being able to excite new beekeepers and keep them engaged with their hives and the lessons they have to teach us. Mentoring has been rewarding, as has helping with the beekeeping classes at Champlain Valley Union high school.

**Why do I keep bees?**

The colonies continue to amaze and stimulate me. Working them can also be a great form of meditation for me. It's an honor to be an observer of their lives.

## MERRIL TITTEMORE, ST. ALBANS

**How did I start?**

When I was 12 years old, a swarm of bees entered a knot hole in the milk house wall, then swarmed into the apple trees in the orchard. We were able to retrieve the swarm and put it into one of my grandfather's old hives. After retrieving the swarm, I developed an interest in beekeeping and learned hands-on with guidance from my father. He had gained knowledge from his father-in-law, who

lived in West Berkshire. That's when I had my best production year for honey, ever.

With my father's help, we cared for them for two or three years. I started working at sixteen-years-old in a factory and then after several years, I started my career driving as a teamster. When I retired in 1981, I immediately started keeping bees again in Orwell. I use Langstroth with beeswax wired foundation.

My hives now are located on the Hudack Farm in St. Albans. I make hives in my garage over the winter as a hobby. In the spring and summer, I also produce queens and make nucs for myself and a few for sale. I also sell my beeswax in bulk.

**Biggest challenges?**

The biggest beekeeping challenge I have is controlling varroa mites.

**Greatest success?**

As I have worked with the bees, I have gained many new friends and acquaintances. I enjoy helping them with any

FIGURE 16: **Merril Tittemore and his Grandson Finn Howrigan from Fairfield.** PHOTO CREDIT: LOUISE TITTEMORE

issues getting them started and following up with any problems they may have. I also have given two complete hives to my great-grandsons, who market their honey as Nolon's Nectar, Grady's Golden Goodness, and Howrigan. (We sadly lost Grady in 2017 due to a tractor accident.)

### Why do I keep bees?

My wife of 68 years has been asking that same question for years, "Why do you keep bees?" My only explanation is that I enjoy every minute of it and when I am working on bees I forget all my other problems.

### CHERYL AND AMANDA WERNER, WERNER TREE FARM, MIDDLEBURY

The Werner family can trace their roots back to the 4th or 5th ship that came to the new world from Europe and their decedents have been living in Vermont since before the Revolutionary War. They run a Christmas tree farm in Middlebury, supplementing their tree sales by also producing honey, maple syrup and lumber.

The Werner's have not always kept bees as part of their working farm. Cheryl's first exposure to beekeeping was as an agriculture student at Cornell where she took a bee course with Roger Morse. Cheryl got started in bees with

FIGURE 17: **Cheryl Werner works a hive on her farm in Middlebury.** PHOTO CREDIT: DAVID WERNER

help and mentoring from her beekeeping cousin George Hurlburt who lived on a dairy farm in Monkton and had kept bees in the 1960s and 70s. She kept a

**FIGURE 18: Holiday display of Werner family farm honey and maple syrup in their Christmas shop.**
PHOTO CREDIT: AMANDA WERNER FAMILY

couple hives in the early 1980s, but after a couple years they failed to overwinter. That combined with the birth of her son William, caused her to give up beekeeping. In 2008, she started up again after William bought his sister, Amanda, something she had always wanted: a bee hive. Amanda has learned beekeeping mostly from Cheryl, and "by attending beekeeping meetings, reading books, and watching YouTube" videos online. Amanda also helped local cheesemaker Carlton Yoder, with his bees when she was working for him.

Cheryl and Amanda keep up to a half dozen hives on their farm to pollinate their garden and to produce honey. They "manage our northern bees using organic methods. All of our honey is raw and only passed through a coarse filter." The Werners sell their honey and maple products along with their trees, wreaths, and garlands on the farm at Christmas time and out of their house the rest of the year, as well as, through a local farm stand run by Mike Merril on Route 7 south of Middlebury.

## MIKE AND NICOLE WILLARD, GREEN MOUNTAIN BEE FARM, FAIRFAX

### How did I start?

In the spring of 2009, I started keeping bees with two nucs purchased from Betterbee. We first took a beginner beekeeping class at Champlain Valley Union high school in the winter of 2008. Our beekeeping education was continued by attending valuable hands-on workshops offered by the VBA at the Intervale on Saturdays throughout the summer.

FIGURE 19: **Mike Willard.** PHOTO CREDIT: NICOLE WILLARD

To continue our beekeeping knowledge, we subscribed to the magazine *Bee Culture* and were avid readers of the online blog "Bee Source." The online venue offered valuable insight on the various opinions on beekeeping methodology and approaches to different situations. Our earliest mentor was Mike Palmer, who is incredibly generous with his beekeeping knowledge and experiences. He is still our mentor. Most of my bee yards are located in Franklin County.

The decision to start Green Mountain Bee Farm, LLC was a natural progression with how quickly we were expanding the number of managed hives we had and the resulting increase in honey production. We were realistic about this proposition, recognizing beekeeping is much like any agricultural endeavor, unpredictable and at the whim of Mother Nature. Understanding honey production can vary each season, we diversified our business also to offer bee-related products like all-natural lip balm and lotion bars made from our beeswax.

**Biggest challenges?**

Every year beekeeping seems to offer a new challenge. Our biggest beekeeping challenge of late is managing varroa mite levels in our colonies. Varroa mites are one of the greatest threats beekeepers face and [they affect] the eventual overwintering success of honey bee colonies.

**Greatest success?**

Our greatest beekeeping success was learning to raise our own queens and keeping track of our honey bee genetics. Learning about queen rearing elevated our knowledge about honey bee biology and their life cycle. The immersion into queen rearing was a pivotal moment in our beekeeping success. We can now select for genetics that we want in our own bees; overwintering, gentleness and honey production. Our queen rearing method is the model explained by Brother Adam in *Beekeeping at Buckfast Abbey*.

We believe that it's important in life to pay it forward. Other beekeepers were very generous to us as we got started, and we feel compelled be the same way to the next generation of beekeepers. We help teach a beginner beekeeping class at Champlain Valley Union high school three times a year, along with offering free presentations at local schools, libraries, and community centers.

**Why do I keep bees?**

For us, beekeeping started out at a casual interest, then a hobby, and now a full-blown sickness. Over the years, we developed a love and incredible respect for honey bees. They are an incredible species that exhibit social and cooperative behaviors. If honey bees had a motto, it might be the famous Three Musketeers saying of "All for one and one for all." With every passing beekeeping season, we are always amazed and delighted to have the ability to work with these amazing creatures. I always reflect on how the world might be different if humans exhibited the same social values as honey bees.

## SCOTT AND VALARIE WILSON, HEAVENLY HONEY APIARY, MONKTON

Scott Wilson, originally from Nutley, New Jersey, has enjoyed a career within the semiconductor, mechanical manufacturing, office environmental management, and aerospace industries. He has a Bachelor's of Science in Business Management, is a Vermont Certified Beekeeper, and holds a Certificate of Master Beekeeping from the University of Montana. He has the distinction of being the first Vermont beekeeper to achieve Master Beekeeper status. He has been married to Valarie for twenty-nine years and has one son, Christian, currently active duty in the Air Force.

**How did we start?**

Our interest was piqued in 2007 when we both took a course in beekeeping at Depot Hardware in Essex Junction. We spent the day with seasoned beekeeper Lynn Lang, learning until our brains were about to explode. Lynn was using words like "brood box," "supers," and "nucs."

As the season progressed, we read our bee books, inspected our new hive, and spotted our queen. We joined the VBA and went to their summer meeting. During this meeting, Valarie was voted in as their new librarian. We attended all of the rest of the North Yard workshops for the season and continued to gain knowledge about our newest hobby.

FIGURE 20: **Valarie and Scott Wilson.** PHOTO COURTESY OF VALARIE AND SCOTT WILSON

Our honey bees produced forty-five pounds of honey for us our first season. We couldn't have been more thrilled.

Our first few years were spent trying to figure out if we had the commitment to stick with it once the novelty wore off. After about three years, we gained confidence in our beekeeping skills such that we started thinking about whether the hobby could grow to the point of providing enough money for a vacation. That was the initial financial goal.

We also took a look at the skill sets that we had and realized that we could run a business. Scott has a BS in business management; he spent nearly twenty-five years in semiconductor sales and marketing. Valarie has an accounting background, is skilled in web content, social media, and search engine optimization (SEO), and has quite an eye for packaging and production.

So, we took the step and began to seek out niche areas to begin providing product. We wanted to avoid traditional routes like local supermarkets and sought out specialty stores in an effort to keep revenue and margins up. Once we obtained a few customers and started working a local farmers market, we began to gain revenue, allowing us to continue the expansion. We moved on to helping teach at workshops and at Champlain Valley Union high school and then Scott took the Master Beekeeper Course at the University of Montana.

Since joining the VBA, Valarie has served as the librarian and membership secretary. Scott has served as recording secretary, membership secretary, and vice president. Both have worked to manage the Addison County Beekeepers Association.

Our thirty to forty hives are located in Hinesburg, Monkton, and New Haven. Besides honey, we produce and sell pollen, propolis, and beeswax candles. We offer mentoring and perform extractions for other beekeepers.

In five years, we hope to be raising queens, providing overwintered nucleus colonies, and writing two children's books about beekeeping.

**Biggest challenges?**
Our biggest challenges are adapting to what seem to be later spring starts and longer fall periods.

**Greatest success?**
- A 2017 honey crop of 2,500 pounds.
- Being able to stop doing farmers markets.
- Successfully overwintering nucleus colonies.
- Holding several positions with the VBA.
- Managing the 2017 VBA summer meeting.
- Writing the foreword to Dede Cummings' book, *The Good Living Guide to Beekeeping*.
- Being profiled in the *American Bee Journal* in 2013.

**Why do I keep bees?**
It's something that we had never done, it has a unique aspect to it, and it provides a challenge. Plus, it's just plain fun.

## DR. KRISTIN WOLF, WATERBURY

I was introduced to beekeeping during my doctoral work in 2005 by my dear friend and mentor, German Perilla. After many years of bee work in Colombia, German started an educational apiary in northern Virginia and we spent many happy afternoons in the bees in the years that followed. German was ever patient with me and other newbees and never missed an opportunity to *show* you the answer to your question. When an inquiry about brood development could have been easily answered verbally, he would take the time and effort to remove heavy supers, dig into the brood chamber, and show you what you were asking about—hence the educational api-

FIGURE 21: **Dr. Kristin Wolf.** PHOTO COURTESY OF KRISTIN WOLF

ary. These experiences gave me the confidence and experience to start my own apiary on the campus of Champlain College, where I am a faculty member, which has had thousands of visitors who I now delight in showing the answers to their questions.

The Champlain College Apiary has become a living laboratory for students of all majors to use and develop their professional skills. Over the years, students have optimized our honey operation, developed new products, written grants and articles, landscaped for bee-friendly habitat, made video games, advocated for pollinator protection, created pollinator curriculum for young visitors, and bottled and sold over a thousand pounds of honey. In addition to the on-campus opportunities that the apiary has provided, it has also been the stimulus for beekeeping endeavors abroad. Since 2014, German and I have brought students from Champlain College and George Mason University to work with rainforest communities on beekeeping projects in the Peruvian Amazon.

As an urban beekeeper with Langstroth hives, my biggest concern is swarm prevention. Swarms can be frightening for our campus community (and risk management team!). My strategy has been to create a "feeder hive" that I continually move brood into during the swarm season in order provide space and reduce swarm urges—it basically serves as a simulated swarm and the feeder hive raises its own queen.

My greatest success as beekeeper comes every spring when our educational programming begins. Watching students of all ages standing hive side in complete awe of this vital organism brings me immense satisfaction. It is one of the most illustrative ways to demonstrate the complexity and wonder of the non-*human* world and our responsibility to protect it. Another important moment that sticks in my mind was when we were interviewing members of the Chino community in Peru. A beekeeper described her deep disappointment in losing some of her Melipona hives and said that she treats the one remaining colony like it's one of her children. It made me realize that a love of bees translates across geographies and cultures and that beekeepers, in all their challenges and achievements, have forged a collective spirit through their shared experience.

## PAUL YANUS, UNDERHILL

### How did I start?

I fell in love with honey bees while living in New Jersey in 1976 and purchased my first two bee hives while living in Vermont in 1985. For the first 10 years, I learned pretty much alone from books. Now I have great beekeeper friends like Mike Palmer, Bill Mares, and Michael Willard with whom I can bounce different beekeeping methods back and forth.

I have yards in Underhill Center, Underhill, Jericho, and Westford. Besides honey, I produce wax candles, bees wax, nucs, and queens.

FIGURE 22: **Paul Yanus.**
PHOTO COURTESY OF PAUL YANUS

### Biggest challenges?

My biggest beekeeping challenges are mites and wind.

### Greatest success?

And my greatest success is keeping the girls alive and creating the educational booth at the Farm Show.

I help people who have bee or wasp and hornet problems in their homes. I lecture to groups of people who want to get into beekeeping or who are interested in helping the honey bees. I have mentored numerous new beekeepers and am always ready to answer questions young beekeepers may have.

### Why do I keep bees?

The girls. I love the honey bees and watching them grow. When I am with my bees, nothing else is going on in the world and I am at total peace; no problems and no stress or pressures. Also, when you think you might understand the honey bees, they throw you a curve ball and you are back to the books and/or asking other beekeepers for their thoughts about a solution.

FIGURE 23: **Woodcut Print by Mary Azarian, Plainfield, Vermont.**

# ENDNOTES

## CHAPTER 1

A Keeper of Bees (April 28, 1847) *Green-Mountain Freeman*, Poland, Editor; Montpelier

Al-Waili, Noori S. (2004) Natural Honey Lowers Plasma Glucose, C-Reactive Protein, Homocysteine, and Blood Lipids in Healthy, Diabetic, and Hyperlipidemic Subjects: Comparison with Dextrose and Sucrose, *Journal of Medicinal Food*, Vol. 7, No. 1

*American Bee Journal* (1861) Volume 1, No. 1, January, p.199 published by A.M. Spangler, Book and General Printer, No. 25 N. 6th St., Philadelphia

*American Bee Journal* (1870) The Bee Comb Guide Patent, February 1870, Vol. V, No. 8, pp.167-168.

Anonymous (1860) From Enoch Tompkins files

Child, Hamilton (1882) Child's Addison County Gazetteer, Gazetteer and Business Directory of Addison County Vermont for 1881–1882, Compiled and published by Hamilton Child, Syracuse, New York

Colton, A., and Bennett, J. M. (11 June 1846) *Green-Mountain freeman.* (Montpelier, Vt.), *Chronicling America: Historic American Newspapers.* Lib. of Congress. http://chroniclingamerica.loc.gov/lccn/sn84023209/1846-06-11/ed-1/seq-3/

Crane, Ethel Eva (1999) The World History of Beekeeping and Honey Hunting, Routledge

Cutting, James A. (1844) *Short Treatise on the Care and Management of Bees and the Construction of the Changeable Bee-Hive* (Newbury, Vermont: L. J. McIndoe), p. 12

Engel, S., Michael & Hinojosa, Ismael & Rasnitsyn, Alexandr (2009) *A honeybee from the Miocene of Nevada and the biogeography of Apis (Hymenoptera: Apidae: Apini).* Proceedings of the California Academy of Sciences, p. 60

Flanders, Wooster A. (1867) *Nature's Bee: a practical treatise calculated to assist the bee-keeper in overcoming the difficulties and mysteries of bee-keeping and insure profitable returns for labor and capital invested.* Published by L.D. Myers & Brother, Mansfield, Ohio.

Goodwin, Mary (1956) *Response to request for info on beehives and bee culture,* Williamsburg, VA: Rockefeller, John D. Jr. Library.

Horn, Tammy (2005) *Bees in America: How the Honeybee Shaped a Nation,* Lexington, KY: The University Press of Kentucky

Kellar, B. (n.d.). *Honeybees Across America,* from the Oregon State Beekeepers Association website

Kidder, K. P. (1863) *Secrets of Beekeeping,* Burlington, Vermont

Kingsbury, Susan Myra (1906) *The Records of the Virginia Company of London The Court Book,* From the Manuscript in the Library of Congress 1619—1622 Vol 1 and 2. Washington: Government Printing Office

McGrory Klyza, Christopher and Trombulak, Steven C. (2015) *The Story of Vermont: A Natural and Cultural History,* University Press of New England: Second Edition, p. 52

Mello, Robert A. (2014) *Moses Robinson and the Founding of Vermont,* p. 7, Vermont Historical Society publication.

Oertel, Everett (1980) History of Beekeeping in the United States, Agricultural Handbook Number 335 (Washington D.C.—U .S. Department of Agriculture: Revised)

Otis (1865) The Prairie Farmer, September 16, 1865, p. 118

Commissioner of Patents (1866) Annual Report of the Commissioner of Patents, Government Printing Office, Washington: Part 1, Volume 1, p. 868

Pellett, Frank Chapman (1938) *History of American Beekeeping,* Iowa: Collegiate Press, Inc.

Robinson, D. (2014). *The Bugs that Bugged the Colonists: The weevil wrought evil, but the bee brought sweetness and light*, The Colonial Williamsburg Foundation website: https://www.history.org/foundation/

Samanta, A., Burden, A. C., Jones, A. R. (1985) Plasma Glucose Responses to Glucose, Sucrose, and Honey in Patients with Diabetes Mellitus: An Analysis of Glycaemic and Peak Incremental Indices, *Diabetic Medicine*, Vol. 2, Issue 5, pp. 371-373

Sanborn, J. L. (1860) *Green-Mountain Freeman* Vol. XVIII, No.37, Montpelier, Vermont

Shambaugh, P & Worthington, V & H Herbert, J. (1991). Differential effects of honey, sucrose and fructose on blood sugar levels, *Journal of manipulative and physiological therapeutics*, 13. 322-5.

Snow, M. S. (1891) *American Bee Journal*, Vol. XXVIII, No.1, pp. 655-656

Supreme Court (1832) Reports or Cases Argued and Determined in the Supreme Court of the State of Vermont, Vol. III., St. Albans, Vt., J. Spooner, printer: pp. 421-422

*The Voice of Freedom* of Brandon (1847) J. Holcomb, Editor & Publisher.

Weeks, John M. (1860) *History of Salisbury, Vermont* (Middlebury, Vermont: A.H. Copeland, p. 356

Whitcomb, William (1845) Whitcomb Bee-Hive, *Vermont Pheonix*, March 21, 1845

Whitman, Abial (June 1835) beehive description, *Journal of the Franklin Institute*, p. 391

Williams, Samuel (1794) *The Natural and Civil History of Vermont*, by, LL. D. (1743–1817), member of the Meteorological Society in Germany, of the Philosophical Society in Philadelphia, and of the Academy of Arts and Science in Massachusetts. Vol 1, pp. 156-158; First edition, Rutland, Vermont, July 16, 1794. Second edition, Burlington, Vermont, 1809.

*The Wisconsin Farmer* (1866) Vol. XVIII, No. 5, p. 495, Madison, Published by Walter B. Davis, State Journal Block.

Wisconsin State Journal, (January 8, 1870), Volume XVIII, Number 108, Madison, Wisconsin

CHAPTER 2

Balivet, Robert F. (1965) *The Vermont Sheep Industry:* 1811–1880, Vermont Historical Society, vol. 33, no. 1: pp. 243-249

Beecher, Henry W. (1910) *The Honey Bee in Vermont*, Senior Thesis presented in partial fulfillment of the requirements for the Degree of Bachelor of Science in Agriculture, University of Vermont, Burlington

Burlington Free Press Association (1899) 18th Report of the Vermont State Board of Agriculture, Manufactures and Mining, Vermont Agricultural Report (Burlington)

Carlisle, Lilian Baker and Samuel J. Hatfield (1976) Look Around Chittenden County, Vermont. Chittenden County Historical Society, Burlington p. 320

Child, Hamilton (1882) *Child's Addison County Gazetteer, Gazetteer and Business Directory of Addison County Vermont for* 1881–1882, Compiled and published by Hamilton Child, Syracuse, New York

Crane, J. E. (1929) Building an Industry, Gleanings in Bee Culture, Vol. LIX, No. 7

Crane, J.E. (1874) Vermont State Board of Agriculture, Manufactures and Mining, Second Biennial Report, "Bee Culture" Freeman Steam Printing House and Bindery

Crane, J. E. (1884) Annual Report of Vermont State Board of Agriculture, Manufacturing and Mining, Watchman and Journal Press

Crane, J. E. (1894) 14th Report of the Vermont State Board of Agriculture, Manufactures and Mining, Report of the Vermont Board of Agriculture, Burlington Free Press Association (Burlington)

Dearborn, Reg. (2016) "Tales of the Bristol Beekeeper", Burlington Free Press, Sept. 25, 2016

Holmes, R. H. (1898) 17th Report of the Vermont State Board of Agriculture, Manufactures and Mining, Report of the Vermont Board of Agriculture, Burlington Free Press Association (Burlington)

Holmes, R.H. (1900) "Bees and Honey", Nineteenth Agricultural Report of the Vermont State Board of Agriculture, Manufactures and Mining, Opinion Press (Bradford) pp. 94-97

Kinney, Thaddeus L. (1898) Vermont State Board of Agriculture, Manufactures and Mining, Report of the Vermont Board of Agriculture, Burlington Free Press Association (Burlington)

Larrabee, W. G. (October 3, 1910) Personal Letter to James E. Crane (Files of Vermont Agency of Agriculture)

Lowery, O.J. (1896) Experiments in Bee Keeping, Ninth Annual Report of the Vermont Agricultural Extension Station Argus & Patriot Printing House, Montpelier

Meiners, Danielle (2010) Agricultural History of St. George, Vermont Barn Census, Chittenden County Student Research Project

Oertel, Everett (1980) History of Beekeeping in the United States, Agricultural Handbook Number 335 (Washington, D.C.—U.S. Department of Agriculture: Revised)

Peck, Cassius R. (1898) "Experiments in Bee-Keeping" Eleventh Annual Report of the Vermont Agricultural Experiment Station, pp. 307-309, Vermont Watchman Co. Burlington

Pellett, Frank C. (1938) *History of American Beekeeping*, Iowa: collegiate Press, Inc.

Poland, J. & J.M. (1878) Vermont State Board of Agriculture, Manufactures and Mining, Fifth Report on the Vermont Board of Agriculture (Montpelier: Official State Printers)

Poland, J. & J. M. (1872) Vermont State Board of Agriculture Report: Manufacturing & Mining: Montpelier: J & J. M. Pollard's Steam Printing Establishment

Root (1890) *The ABC of Bee Culture* (Medina, Ohio) A. I. Root Co.

Root (1895) *The ABC of Bee Culture* (Medina, Ohio) A.I. Root Co.

Root (1899) *The ABC of Bee Culture* (Medina, Ohio) A. I. Root Co. pp. 40-41

Root, W. P. (1905) *The ABC of Bee Culture* (Medina, Ohio) A. I. Root Co.

Root, W.P. (1908) The ABC of Bee Culture (Medina, Ohio) A.I. Root Co.

Sammataro, Diana & Avitabile, Alphonse (2011) *The Beekeeper's Handbook, Fourth Edition,* Comstock Publishing Associates, pp. 199-200

Tuttle Company (1895) VSA Chapter 183, Section 4343, Vermont Statutes 1894 (Rutland: The Tuttle Co.)

Vermont General Assembly (1910) *Public Acts of the State of Vermont* No. 18: An Act For The Suppression of Contagious Diseases Among Bees

Watchman and Journal Press (1884) Eighth Biennial Report of Vermont State Board of Agriculture, Manufacturing and Mining (Montpelier) pgs. 136-8

## CHAPTER 3

Carroll, Hanson (1960) "Dr. Jarvis's Great Switchel Revival," *Vermont Life*: pp. 47-51

Crane, J. E. and Rock, J. P. (1913) Vermont State Board of Agriculture, Fifth Annual Vermont Agriculture Report, St. Albans Publishing Co. (St. Albans)

Crane, J. E. and Rock, J. P. (1914) Vermont State Board of Agriculture, Sixth Biennial Vermont Agriculture Report, St. Albans Publishing Co (St. Albans) pgs. 21-23

Crane, J. E. and Rock, J. P. (1916) Vermont State Board of Agriculture, Eighth Biennial Vermont Agriculture Report, St. Albans Publishing Co. (St. Albans) pgs. 8-9

Crane, J. E. and Rock, J. P. (1918) Vermont State Board of Agriculture, Ninth Biennial Vermont Agriculture Report, St. Albans Publishing Co. (St. Albans)

Daley, Yvonne (2018) *Going Up The Country: When the Hippies, Dreamers, Freaks, and Radicals Moved to Vermont*, University Press of New England, p. 21 (Lebanon, New Hampshire)

Dunne, Alan, *The New Yorker*, April 16, 1960 p. 50. Source: Vermont Historical Society

Dwinell, H. A. (1930) Vermont State Board of Agriculture, Fifteenth Biennial Vermont Agriculture Report (St. Albans), p. 19

Jarvis, D. C. (1958) *Folk Medicine*, Fawcett Crest Books (New York)

Khouri, Lance (1979) Bee-Lining, *Vermont Life* (Summer) p. 15

Mayo, Connie (1970) Vermont State Board of Agriculture, 36th Biennial Vermont Agriculture Report, p. 105

Mead, Robert (1958) Vermont State Board of Agriculture, 29th Biennial Vermont Agriculture Report, p. 15

Mead, Robert (1960) Vermont State Board of Agriculture, 30th Biennial Vermont Agriculture Report p. 16

Mead, Robert (1962) Vermont State Board of Agriculture, 31st Biennial Vermont Agriculture Report p. 15

Mead, Robert (1968) Vermont State Board of Agriculture, 34th Biennial Vermont Agriculture Report: p. 84

Mead, Robert (1970) Vermont State Board of Agriculture, 35th Biennial Vermont Agriculture Report, pgs. 74-75

Mead, Robert (1972) Vermont State Board of Agriculture, 36th Biennial Vermont Agriculture Report: p. 81

Mead, Robert (1974) Vermont State Board of Agriculture, 37th Biennial Vermont Agriculture Report: p. 84

Mead, Robert (1976) Vermont State Board of Agriculture, 38th Biennial Vermont Agriculture Report: p. 64

Mraz, Charles, (1940) Vermont State Board of Agriculture, 20th Biennial Vermont Agriculture Report, p. 105

Noonan, Joseph (1967), *Vermont Life*, XXI #3 Spring, p. 2

Ogden, Herbert, (February 2, 1975) Letter to Vermont Agriculture Department.

Root, W.P. (1908) The ABC of *Bee Culture* (Medina, Ohio) A.I. Root Co. p. 60

Stoner, Rick (August 10, 2017) Personal Correspondence, Letter to Authors

State of Vermont (1917) "An Act to Protect Wild Bees and Honey," Vermont Public Acts: No. 221, p. 240

Strickland, Ron (1998) VERMONTERS: ORAL HISTORIES FROM DOWN COUNTRY TO THE NORTHEAST KINGDOM (Hanover University Press of New England) p. 100

Taylor, Laurel (February 27, 2015) Home Front Friday: Waxing the Way to Victory, See & Hear: Museum Blog: The National WWII Museum, www.nww2m. com/2015/02/home-front-friday-waxing-the-way-to-victory

Thoreau, H. D. (1906) *Collected Works*, v. 10 (Boston: Houghton, Mifflin & Co.) pp. 368-375

Tompkins, Enoch H. (1961) *Honey Production and Marketing Bulletin*, Vermont Agricultural Experiment Station, University of Vermont (Burlington)

Towne, Elmer (1956) Vermont State Board of Agriculture, 28th Biennial Vermont Agricultural Report

VBA Newsletter (1954) Vol. V No. 3

VBA Newsletter (January 1960) Vol. XI, No. 1

Weed, Pat Orvis (August 15, 1962) Nun Gets Stung by Hobby, Burlington Free Press (Burlington)

## CHAPTER 4:

*Agriview*, (April 18, 1979) Vermont Agency of Agriculture Food & Markets, Volume XXXVIII, #4

Drutchas, Rick (1979-80) Vermont State Board of Agriculture, 40*th Biennial Vermont Agricultural Report*, pp. 31-32

Drutchas, Rick (1981-82) Vermont State Board of Agriculture, 41*th Biennial Vermont Agricultural Report*, p. 40

Drutchas, Rick (1984) Vermont State Board of Agriculture, 42*th Biennial Vermont Agricultural Report, p.* 22

Drutchas, Rick (1988) Vermont State Board of Agriculture, *44th Biennial Vermont Agricultural Report*

*Drutchas, Rick* Interview with Authors Oct. 2017

*EAS Journal* (1980) Vol. 8 # 5 Fall, pp. 1-5

Hardie, Todd D. (1979) Letter from Department of Agriculture, March 21, 1979

Hill, (1979-80) Vermont State Board of Agriculture, 40*th Biennial Vermont Agricultural Report*, pp. 31-32

Ramsey, Samuel D., Ronald Ochoa, Gary Bauchan, Connor Gulbronson, Joseph D. Mowery, Allen Cohen, David Lim, Judith Joklik, Joseph M. Cicero, James D. Ellis, David Hawthorne, and Dennis vanEngelsdorp (2019) Varroa Destructor feeds primarily on honey bee fat body tissue and not hemolymph, Proceedings of the National Academy of Sciences of the United States of America, PNAS published ahead of print January 15, 2019 https://doi.org/10.1073/pnas.1818371116

Tardie, John (1980) *EAS Journal*, December, Vol. 8, No. 6, pp.1-7

## CHAPTER 5:

Parise, Steve (1992) 46th Biennial Report of the Vermont Department of Agriculture, Food & Markets, (1991-92) pp. 27-28 St. Albans Publications, (St. Albans)

Parise, Steve (1994) 47th Biennial Report of the Vermont Department of Agriculture Food & Markets (1993-94) pp. 23 (Montpelier)

Parise, Steve (1996) 48th Biennial Report of the Vermont Department of Agriculture Food & Markets (1995-96) pp. 23-24 (Montpelier)

Parise, Steve (1998) 49th Biennial Report of the Vermont Department of Agriculture Food & Markets (1997-98) pp. 24-25 (Montpelier)

Parise, Steve (2000) 50th Biennial Report of the Vermont Department of Agriculture Food & Markets (1999-2000) pp. 30-32 (Montpelier)

Parise, Steve (2002) 51th Biennial Report of the Vermont Department of Agriculture Food & Markets (2001-2002) pp. 30-32 (Montpelier)

## CHAPTER 6:

Alaux, C., Brunet, J.L., Dussaubat, C., Mondet, F., Tchamitchan, S., Cousin, M., Brillard, J., Baldy, A., Belzunces, L.P., Le Conte, Y, (2010) Interactions between Nosema microspores and a neonicotinoid weaken honeybees (*Apis mellifera*), *Environmental Microbiology*, 12(3): 774-782

Chaimanee, V., Evans, J.D., Chen, Y., Jackson, C., Pettis, J.S., (2016) Sperm viability and gene expression in honey bee queens (Apis mellifera) following exposure to the neonicotinoid insecticide imidacloprid and the organophosphate arcaricide coumaphos, *Journal of Insect Physiology* 89:1-8 doi: 10.1016/j.jinsphys.2016.03.004

Di Prisco, G., Cavaliere, V., Annoscia, D., Varricchio, P., Caprio, E., Nazzi, F., Gargiulo, G., Pennacchio, F., (2013) Neonicotinoid Clothianidin adversely affects insect immunity and promotes replication of a viral pathogen in honey bees, *Proceedings of the National Academy of Sciences* 110:46 pp 18466-18471

Dussaubat, C., Maisonnasse, A., Crauser, D., Tchamitchian, S., Bonnet, M., Cousin, M., Kretzchmar, A., Brunet, J.L., Le Conte, Y., (2016) Combined neonicotinoid pesticide and parasite stress alter honeybee queens' physiology and survival, *Scientific Reports* 6: Article number 31430 doi:10.1038/srep31430

Friol, P.S., Catae, A.F., Tavares, D.A., Malaspina, O., Roat, T.C., (2017) Can the exposure of Apis mellifera (Hyenoptera: Apidae) larvae to a field concentration of thiamethoxam affect newly emerged bees? *Chemosphere*, 29;185:56-66

Pettis JS, VanEngelsdorp D, Johnson J, Dively G. (2012) Pesticide exposure in honey bees results in increased levels of the gut pathogen *Nosema. Naturwissenschaften.* 99:153–158. doi: 10.1007/s00114-011-0881-1)

Tirado, R., Simon, G., Johnston, P., (2013) Bees in Decline: A review of factors that put pollinators and agriculture in Europe at risk, *Greenpeace Research Laboratories Technical Report,* (Review)

Willard, Michael (2011) VBA Summer Meeting Minutes

Williams, G.R., Troxler, A., Retschnig, G., Roth, K., Yanez, O., Shutler, D., Neumann, P., Gauthier, L., (2015) Neonicotinoid pesticides severely affect honey queen bees, *Scientific Reports* (5)14621: doi:10.1038/srep14621

Wu-Smart, J., Spivak, M., (2016) Sub-lethal effects of dietary neonicotinoid insecticide exposure on honey bee queen fecundity and colony development, *Scientific Reports* 6, Article Number 32108 doi:10.1038/srep32108

## Chapter 7:

McGrory Klyza, Christopher and Trombulak, Steven C. (2015) *The Story of Vermont: A Natural and Cultural History*, University Press of New England: Second Edition: p. 93

USDA (2012) Census of Agriculture—County Data, National Agriculture Statistics Service (NASS)

Ziska, Lewis H., Jeffery S. Pettis, Joan Edwards, Jillian E. Hancock, Martha B. Tomecek, Andrew Clark, Jeffrey S. Dukes, Irakli Loladze, and H. Wayne Polley (2016) Rising atmospheric $CO_2$ is reducing the protein concentration of a floral pollen source essential for North American bees, 283 Proceedings of the Royal Society B: Biological Sciences http://doi.org/10.1098/rspb.2016.0414

# VERMONT BEE BOOKS

IT HAS BEEN CLAIMED that more words have been written about honey bees and beekeeping than any other topic other than mankind itself. According to Philip A. Mason, author of *American Bee Books: An Annotated Bibliography of Books on Bees and Beekeeping 1492-2010* (The Club of Odd Volumes, Boston 2016), the very first American bee book was written in 1792 and attributed to Isaiah Thomas, published in Worcester, Massachusetts.

Early Vermont beekeeping books (throughout the nineteenth century) were written primarily as promotional pieces by beekeepers that had invented and/or patented a novel hive design. Overall however, for a small state that boasts the second lowest population per square mile in the nation, Vermonters have published a surprisingly high number of beekeeping related books. This suggests an educated literate population that harbors a strong desire to share and disseminate beekeeping information in a state hampered by challenging weather and terrain.

At their 2007 meeting in Bridport, the Vermont Beekeepers Association inaugurated a lending library of books, videotapes and DVDs. Valarie Wilson was appointed as the first librarian for the VBA and Ross Conrad donated the first book to the library. The VBA library offers a wide variety of titles to its membership, many of them written by Vermonters.

What follows is a list of all the bee books ever published in Vermont, or written by Vermonters but published elsewhere, up to the year 2018 (Mason 2016).

## Books published by Vermonters in Vermont

John Weeks (1836) – *A Manual: Or An Easy Method of Managing Bees, in the Most Profitable Manner to Their Owner, With Infallible Rules to Prevent Their Destruction by the Moth*, Knapp & Jewett Printers, Middlebury, Vermont – This book was intended to accompany Weeks's Vermont Hive. (Milum 1965, pg. 329) A Manual went through four editions, as well as two editions of the New Edition, Revised and Enlarged.

John Weeks (1840) – *The Bee-Keeper's Guide To Manage Bees in the Vermont Bee-Hive*, Argus Office, Middlebury, Vermont – This is a condensed version of *A Manual*.

James A. Cutting (1849) – *A Short Treatise on the Care and Management of Bees, and the Construction of the Changeable Bee-Hive*, Printed for the inventor, Manchester, Vermont – Cutting received a silver medal for his hive that was exhibited at the 19th Annual Fair of the American Institute in New York 1846.

Wooster A. Flanders (1854) – *The Honey-Bee and Hive*, Woodworth & Gould, Printers, Northfield, Vermont – Pamphlet promoting Flander's hive that featured an adjustable convex lens for observing the bees. Later versions of this hive featured adjustable frames.

*Gilmore's Patent Bee-House and Bee-Hive, Patented June 5, 1849*, Second Edition, Vermont Chronicle Press, Windsor, Vermont (1856) – This pamphlet was rewritten in order to improve upon the "imperfect" information in the first edition published in New York.

K.P. Kidder (1858) – *Kidder's Guide to Apiarian Science, Being a Practical Treatise, in Every Department of Bee Culture and Bee Management. Embracing the Natural History of the Bee, from the Earliest Period of the World, Down to the Present Time; Giving the Anatomy and Physiology of the Different Species of Bees that Constitute a Colony*, Samual B. Nichols; Rufus Blanchard, Burlington, Vermont, Chicago, Illinois – Three other editions of this book were published under the title, *Secrets of Bee-Keeping*, or *Beekeeping*, and primarily promote the bee hive Kidder patented.

K.P. Kidder (1865) – *He That Wishes to Thrive and Make Money with Ease, Should Buy Kidder's Pat. Hives, and Commence Keeping Bees. Send for Kidder's Secrets of Bee-Keeping for 1865*, Burlington, Vermont – Promotes Kidder's book (*Secrets*) and his patented hive.

K.P. Kidder (1867) – *To Bee Keepers Generally. Pure Italian Queens for Sale and also Full Swarms*, Burlington, Vermont – This pamphlet promoted Kidder's Italian bees and includes a price list for bees, swarms and beekeeping equipment.

A.E. Manum (1879) – *Bristol Hive*, Bristol, Vermont – The companion book for Manum's Bristol Hive, which he manufactured and sold as part of his beekeeping supply business. Three Editions.

Henry W. Beecher (1910) – *The honey bee in Vermont,* Vermont Department of Agriculture, Montpelier, Vermont. Booklet, Vermont Agriculture Bulletin No. 6

Alice Cooke Brown, editor (1957) – *Granny's honey and beeswax prescriptions,* Tuttle Publishing Co., Rutland, Vermont – Brown compiled this book after reviewing nine early American books dating from 1808–1869 that mention honey and beeswax use for medical cures and the domestic economy (home remedies).

A.G. Woodman (196_) – *Honey Cookery,* Industrious Honey Bees, Burlington, Vermont – American Honey Institute materials.

Enoch Tompkins (1961) – *Honey Production and Marketing in Vermont,* UVM Vermont Agricultural Experiment Station, Burlington, Vermont – A state survey of Vermont beekeepers from 1956

Beverly Kees (1973) – *Cooking with Honey!* The Stephen Greene Press, Brattleboro, Vermont

Enoch Tompkins and Roger Griffith (1977) – *Practical Beekeeping,* Garden Way Publishing, Charlotte, Vermont – This manual for beginner and intermediate beekeepers was printed in both hard cover and paperback with eighteen printings through 1992.

*Garden Way's Starting Right With Bees:* A beginner's handbook on beekeeping, Storey/ Garden Way Publishing, Pownal, Vermont (1980) – Booklet is part of a series: Garden Way Publishing Country Wisdom Bulletin A-36.

Joanne Barrett (1981) – *Cooking with honey,* Garden Way Publishing, Charlotte, Vermont

L.A. Stephens-Potter (1984) – *The Beekeeper's Manual,* David & Charles, Inc., North Pomfret, Vermont

John Vivian (1986) – *Keeping Bees,* Williamson Publishing, Charlotte, Vermont – Covers the basics of beekeeping

Vermont Beekeepers Association (1985) – *The Vermont Beekeeper's Cookbook,* Vermont Honey Promotion Board Vermont Department of Agriculture, Montpelier, Vermont – This booklet was intended to be sold by members of the VBA and was designed to promote and encourage the use of Vermont honey. A revised edition was published in 1999 by the Vermont Beekeepers Association in cooperation with the Vermont Department of Agriculture, Food, and Markets and the Vermont Honey Promotion Board.

*The New Complete Guide to Beekeeping,* (1994) – The Countryman Press, Woodstock, Vermont – This follow up to *The Complete Guide to Beekeeping* (1972) includes a new chapter on Africanized bees.

Charles Mraz (1995) – *Health and the Honey Bee,* Queen City Publications, Burlington, Vermont – The story of Mraz's work and experiences practicing bee venom therapy.

Ross Conrad (2007) – *Natural Beekeeping: Organic Approaches to Modern Apiculture,* Chelsea Green Publishing, White River Junction, Vermont – The first book on organic beekeeping to be published in the USA. A revised and expanded edition was also published by Chelsea Green, (2013) White River Junction, Vermont.

Nathaniel Altman (2010) – *The Honey Prescription: The amazing power of honey as medicine*, Healing Arts Press, Rochester, Vermont – A review of the healing aspects of honey.

## BOOKS WRITTEN BY VERMONTERS AND PUBLISHED BY NON-VERMONT PUBLISHERS

*Gilmore's Patent Apiary*, C.M. Saxton, New York (1854) – Mr. Gilmore's initial attempt to promote his patented hive.

Murray Hoyt (1965) – *The World of Bees: A Vivid Account of the Remarkable Life of the Bee*, Coward McCann, Inc., New York.

Bill Mares (2005) – *Bees Besieged: One beekeeper's bittersweet journey to understanding*, Root Company, Medina, Ohio – An exploration of the state of beekeeping in the U.S. during the first decade of the twenty-first century.

Rowan Jacobsen (2008) – *Fruitless Fall: The collapse of the honey bee and the coming agricultural crisis*, Bloomsbury, New York – An investigation into the dramatic global decline of the honey bee that began in 2006.

Dede Cummings (2016) – *The Good Living Guide to Beekeeping: Secrets of the Hive, Stories from the Field, and a Practical Guide That Explains It All*, Good Books, Skyhorse Publishing, New York.

## BOOKS WRITTEN BY NON-VERMONTERS PUBLISHED IN VERMONT

Richard E. Bonney (1990) – *Hive management: A seasonal guide for beekeepers*, Storey Communications, Pownal, Vermont – Bonney owned and operated Charlemont Apiaries in Massachusetts, and taught at the University of Massachusetts, Amherst.

Richard E. Bonney (1993) – *Beekeeping: A practical guide*, Storey Communications, Pownal, Vermont

Simon Buxton (2004) – *The Shamanic Way of the Bee: Ancient wisdom and the healing practices of the bee masters*, Destiny Books, Rochester, Vermont – An exploration of an ancient shamanic tradition from Europe.

Les Crowder and Heather Harrell (2012) – *Top-Bar Beekeeping: Organic Practices for Honeybee Health*, Chelsea Green Publishing, White River Junction, Vermont.

# Vermont State Bee Inspectors & Assistant Bee Inspectors

The following people were hired by the state to act as state bee inspectors, or assistant bee inspectors, for Vermont.

James Crane of Bridport
J. P. Rock of Lyndonville
Frank L. Stearns of N. Bennington
C.E. Lewis of East Shoreham
C. H. Carpenter of Enosburg Falls
Roger S. Jones of Johnson
Charles (Charlie) Mraz of Middlebury
Robert Mead of White River Junction
William Damour of Bennington
William Matson of White River Junction
Todd Hardie of Starksboro

Rick Drutchas of Middlesex
Richard (Dick) Brigham of Shrewsbury – Asst.
Charles Andros of Walpole, NH – Asst.
Steve Parise of Orwell
Drew Harding of Barre Town – Asst.
Scott Dolan of Barre Town – Asst.
David Tremblay of Moretown
Anna Smith of Burlington – Asst.
Brooke Decker of Andover
Laura Johnson of Sharon – Asst.

# Vermont Beekeepers Association
## Presidents

James Abair, Waterbury
P.C. Abbey, Essex
Dr. F. Bond, Cornwall
G. Clogston, S. Fairlee
Ross Conrad, Middlebury
J.A. Corey, N. Ferrisburgh
M.F. Cram, Brookfield
James Crane, Bridport
Richard DuBois, Middlesex
Lee Faneuf, Wilder
Charles Ferree, Grand Isle
Kim Greenwood, Duxbury
Franklin Heyburn, Waterville
Grace Hill, Hinesburg
R. H. Holmes, Shoreham
Clifford Hurlburt, Brandon
Walter Larrabee, Shoreham
H. L. Leonard, Duxbury
Fabian Little, Williamstown

O.J. Lowrey, Jericho
Frank Manchester, Cornwall
A.E. Manum, Bristol
Bill Mares, Burlington
Bill Mraz, Middlebury
Charles Mraz, Middlebury
Chas Mraz, Middlebury
Rene Nolet, East Dorset
Mike Palmer, St. Albans
Jack Rath, Pawlet
H. William Scott, Barre
G.C. Skinner
Roland Smith, Orwell
John Tardie, Jericho
Enoch Tompkins, Shelburne
James Warren, Springfield
Mike Willard, Fairfax
Clyde Wood, South Woodstock

# 1979 VERMONT NECTAR AND POLLEN SURVEY

IT APPEARS THAT THIS WAS AN EARLY SPRING and not to be trusted for an average. Dates were sent in from high and low altitudes so we got some one-week variances right in the same town. A lot of dates were not distinguished as beginning, full or enåd of bloom. With these factors in mind, we will approximate the dates, give or take a week depending on altitude, latitude, weather, soil conditions, sun exposure, etc. The important dates to notice are:

| I. Early Pollen Sources | Beginning | End |
|---|---|---|
| 1. QUAKING ASPEN | 4/1 | 4/10 |
| 2. POPLARS | 4/17 | 4/25 |
| 3. WILLOWS | 4/1 | 4/30 |
| 4. SOFT MAPLES | 3/24 | 4/27 |

| II. Spring Nectar and Pollen | Beginning | End |
|---|---|---|
| 1. DANDELION | 4/26 | 5/21 |
| 2. APPLE | 5/15 | 5/25 |
| 3. FLOWERING CRABAPPLE | 5/6 | 5/20 |
| 4. CHOKE CHERRY | 5/8 | 5/15 |
| 5. YELLOW ROCKET | 5/20 | 6/5 |
| 6. SHAD | 5/1 | 5/15 |
| 7. DOGWOOD | 5/30 | 6/10 |

| III.  Main Nectar Flow | Beginning | End |
|---|---|---|
| 1. WHITE CLOVER, DUTCH (NEEDS SWEET SOIL) | 5/25 | Frost |
| 2. BLACKBERRY | 6/1 | 6/13 |
| 3. RASPBERRY | 6/8 | 6/25 |
| 4. ALSIKE CLOVER (NEEDS SWEET SOIL) | 6/5 | 7/10 |
| 5. BLACK LOCUST | 6/1 | 6/18 |
| 6. BIRDSFOOT TREFOIL | 6/4 | 8/1 |
| 7. YELLOW SWEET CLOVER | 6/11 | 7/20 |
| 8. WHITE SWEET CLOVER (NEEDS SWEET SOIL) | 6/18 | 8/1 |
| 9. ALFALFA (NEEDS SWEET SOIL) | 6/13 | 9/15 |
| 10. SUMAC | 6/16 | 6/25 |
| 11. MILKWEED | 6/25 | 7/15 |
| 12. BASSWOOD | 7/1 | 7/15 |
| 13. PURPLE LOOSESTRIFE (DAMP AREAS) | 6/30 | 8/1 |
| 14. FIREWEED (NEEDS SOUR SOIL) | 7/7 | 8/15 |
| 15. THISTLE | 7/29 | 8/8 |
| 16. BURDOCK | 7/29 | 8/8 |
| 17. EARLY GOLDENROD | 8/1 | 8/25 |

| IV.  Fall Flow | Beginning | End |
|---|---|---|
| 1. LATE GOLDENROD | 8/25 | 9/20 |
| 2. ASTERS | 8/22 | 10/1 |

These dates are very around about, but close. With a couple more years of surveys, we should have a good idea of the blooming dates.

# GLOSSARY

**Acaricide**: a pesticide specifically designed to kill mites.

**Agriview:** monthly newsletter of the Vermont Agency of Agriculture, Food and Markets.

**American Bee Journal**: monthly periodical on beekeeping published by Dadant & Sons of Hamilton, Illinois.

**American Foulbrood**: bacterial disease that is highly contagious and usually leads to colony death unless treated with antibiotics, or the removal of all AFB spores from the hive.

**Apiary:** a location where one or more hives of bees are kept.

**Apiary House:** see *Honey House.*

**Apiculture:** of or relating to honey bees.

**Apiculturist:** someone who practices apiculture.

**Apitherapy:** the use of honey bee and hive products (honey, pollen, propolis, royal jelly, honey bee venom) for health and healing.

**Artificial Swarm:** see *nucleus colony.*

**Bee Beard:** the practice of wearing several thousand honey bees on the face, usually as a sideshow-type demonstration at agricultural shows. Hive bees are attracted into position by a queen in a small cage worn under the chin. A bee beard may also refer to a cluster of bees on the outside of a hive.

**Bee Culture:** monthly publication on beekeeping published by the A. I. Root Company of Medina, Ohio; formerly titled *Gleanings in Bee Culture.*

**Bee Escape:** a device that when placed in a hive allows passage of bees in one direction while preventing passage in the opposite direction and typically used to remove bees from honey supers during the honey harvest.

**Bee Hunting:** see *Bee Lining*.

**Bee-Lining:** an ancient art used to locate feral honey bee colonies. It is performed by capturing and marking foraging worker bees, then releasing them from various points to establish (by elementary trigonometry) the direction and distance of the colony's home.

**Bee Space:** the area between objects in a hive that measures between ¼ and ⅜ of an inch and within which the bees tend not to build comb, preferring to leave the space open for ventilation and for use as a passageway within the hive.

**Beeswax:** a substance that is produced by the wax-secreting glands on the underside of the worker bees' abdomen that is molded and shaped by the bees into comb.

**Bottom Board:** the piece of hive equipment that makes up the bottom or the floor of the modern bee hive.

**Box Hive:** a simple hive constructed by assembling four boards into a square and attaching additional boards at the top and bottom.

**Bee Hunting:** see *Bee-Lining*.

**Bee Venom Therapy:** the therapeutic use of honey bee venom, either injected by stings from live bees or injected by needles. BVT is used to treat a variety of ailments, primarily neurological and immunological, including chronic pain, arthritis, and multiple sclerosis.

**Brood:** young honey bee larvae, pupae, and immature bees.

**Brood Chamber:** the body of a hive that typically consists of a box 9-⅝ inches deep and containing frames of comb within which can be found the majority of the brood within the hive; sometimes referred to as a *Hive Body*.

**Cappings:** the thin covering of beeswax that bees build over cells in comb once they are full of ripe honey in order to seal them and store the honey for future use.

**Chalkbrood:** a disease state created by the presence of the fungus *Ascosphaera apis* that affects honey bee larvae and pupae, resulting in their "mummification" and taking on the appearance of little pieces of chalk.

**Cluster:** a formation of honey bees that typically occurs within a hive at temperatures around 57°F (14°C) or below and characteristically consists of a dense ball of bees with the queen and brood at its center.

**Colony:** a family of honey bees occupying a single cavity or hive.

**Colony Collapse Disorder:** a term developed during the winter of 2006-2007 and used to describe the death of a honey bee colony that exhibits the following symptoms: The rapid decline of a hive's population to the point where few or no adult bees are found dead or alive in or around the hive, either on the combs, on the bottom board or in front of the hive entrance. If any living bees are present they are a handful of young worker bees accompanied by a queen. Brood in various stages are present in larger quantities than the remaining cluster is able to maintain. There is a noticeable delay of two to three weeks after the initial collapse before there is any robbing/scavenging activity by other bees, wasps, hornets, wax moths, small hive beetles and other scavengers within the dead hive.

**Comb:** a structure manufactured by honey bees out of beeswax and consisting of hexagon-shaped cells built back to back and used by the bees to raise brood, store honey and pollen, and communicate to each other in the hive.

**Comb Foundation:** a sheet of beeswax foundation that is exceedingly thin and used in the production of comb honey. see *Foundation*.

**Comb Honey:** honey as naturally found prepared by the bees in the comb and minimally processed for human consumption. Sometimes called Honey Sections, or cut comb.

**Cut Comb:** see *Comb Honey*.

**Drone:** the male of the honey bee species characterized by a wider body mass and larger eyes as compared to the female honey bee. The drone is not endowed with a stinger and does not participate in any of the work activities of the colony.

**Drone Brood:** the immature stage of the male honey bee.

**Eastern Apicultural Society:** The Eastern Apicultural Society of North America, Inc. (EAS) is an international nonprofit educational organization founded in 1955 for the promotion of bee culture, education of beekeepers, certification of Master Beekeepers and excellence in bee research.

**European Foulbrood:** a bacterial disease that effects honey bee brood prior to the capped stage of development. Although not as deadly as American Foulbrood, European Foulbrood disease is characterized by dead and dying larvae that can appear curled upwards, brown or yellow in color, and/or dried out and rubbery.

**Foraging:** the gathering activities of the worker bee. Honey bees typically forage for nectar, pollen, tree resins (that they use to produce propolis) and water.

**Foundation:** a thin sheet of beeswax or plastic, that has the outline of the hexagonal-shaped honeycomb cells embossed onto both sides of its surface and used by the bees as the starting infrastructure for building beeswax comb.

**Frame:** a human contraption made of wood or plastic and typically fitted with foundation to encourage bees to build comb within the confines of the frame. Frames contain a top bar, two side bars and a bottom bar and are used to support and enclose combs and allow for easy removal from a hive for inspection and harvesting without damaging the comb so that it may be reused.

**Fume Board:** a contraption that resembles a slightly smaller metal or plastic outer cover, but fitted on the inside with an absorbent material that is soaked with a liquid chemical that gives off a strong odor and repels the bees.

**Gum:** see *Log Gum.*

**Hive:** a home for bees. Hives manufactured by humans typically consist of a bottom board, one or more boxes with frames of comb stacked one on top of the other and covered with an inner cover and an outer cover.

**Hive Body:** the body of a hive that typically consists of a box 9-⅝ inches deep and containing frames of comb within which can be found the majority of the brood within the hive; sometimes referred to as a *Brood Chamber.*

**Hive Tool:** an essential piece of beekeeping equipment consisting of a flattened piece of metal that resembles a mini-crowbar and is used for prying, scraping and manipulating parts of the hive.

**Honey:** the nectar from flowers that has been gathered, processed and concentrated by worker bees into a sweet, viscous solution composed primarily of glucose and fructose, and containing numerous trace minerals and small amounts of vitamins, pollen, and enzymes.

**Honey Comb:** see *comb.*

**Honey Flow:** the period when flowers produce enough nectar to allow significant honey storage in the hive resulting from a concentrated period of nectar foraging by worker bees, usually over a relatively short period of time; sometimes referred to as a *nectar flow.*

**Honey House:** a building often in or near an apiary where beekeeping equipment and supplies are stored, where honey is extracted from the comb and stored, and which serves as the beekeeper's workshop. Sometimes called an *apiary house.*

**Honey Hunting:** see *Bee-Lining.*

**Honey Section:** see *Comb Honey.*

**Honey Super:** a box filled with frames of comb used for honey production that is placed above, or superior to, the brood nest in order to provide room for a colony to store nectar and convert it to honey.

**Log Gum:** a hollowed out section of a tree used to hive a colony of honey bees.

**Migratory Beekeepers:** apiculturists who move hives of bees to one or more locations during a season, often to pollinate a specific crop or to take advantage of a honey flow.

**Nectar Flow:** see *honey flow.*

**Neonicotinoid:** a member of a family of systemic pesticides that are based upon nicotine.

**Nosema:** a disease caused by the microsporidians *Nosema apis* and *Nosema ceranae* that effects the midgut of the honey bee.

**Nuc:** abbreviation for *nucleus colony.*

**Nucleus Colony:** a new hive of bees created by the beekeeper and typically containing three-to-five frames of bees, brood, honey, pollen, and a queen. A nucleus colony is a miniature version of a full-size established bee hive and is often used to replace lost colonies or expand apiaries. Sometimes called splits or artificial swarms.

**Outer Cover:** The outermost cover of a bee hive that protects the colony from precipitation.

**Pollen:** dust-sized particles produced by the anthers of plants for the purpose of procreation. Pollen is picked up by the hairs on the honey bee's body where it may be transferred to other blossoms the bee visits, or brought back to the hive for the colony to use as food.

**Propolis:** plant resins that are collected by foraging worker bees, processed and used by worker bees as both a building material within the hive and as a way to keep the interior of the hive sterile.

**Queen:** a fully developed female honey bee capable of mating and laying fertile eggs.

**Queen Cell:** a peanut-shaped, vertically oriented cell within which a queen bee develops from egg to adult.

**Queen Excluder:** a device used to prevent the queen from moving from one part of the hive to another. While there are various styles of queen excluders, they all feature openings large enough for worker bees to pass, but too small for the larger queen to fit through.

**Render:** the act of melting down beeswax scrapings, cappings and combs, and removing the impurities.

**Reversing:** a hive manipulation that expands the area used by the bees for brood rearing and honey storage. Reversing a hive typically involves exchanging a hive body filled with brood, honey and pollen from the top of the hive with a mostly empty hive body located on the bottom of the hive in order to create room above the brood nest for the queen to lay eggs and move upward during the course of the season.

**Robbing:** the removal of stored honey within a hive by members of another colony or hive. This will tend to occur during a period of dearth when a colony is too weak to defend itself, or when the entrance to the hive is too large for the colony within to defend effectively.

**Skep:** a straw or wicker bee hive, common in Europe from the Middle Ages into the 19th century and exported to the New World.

**Small Hive Beetle:** a parasitic beetle whose larvae feed on the honey, pollen and brood within a hive. Feces from the feeding larvae cause honey in the combs to ferment. Bees finding themselves in such a situation are likely to abscond, and abandon the hive.

**Smoker:** a metal cylinder equipped with a bellows into which a burning material is introduced with the intention of producing smoke that can be directed toward honey bees in an effort to make them docile and easy to work with.

**Splits:** dividing a colony up for the purpose of creating a second colony through the introduction of a new queen. A split with a laying queen is also called a *nucleus colony*.

**Super:** see *Honey Super.*

**Supering:** the act of adding empty honey supers to a colony for honey storage.

**Swarm:** the act of reproduction when a colony divides into two. The queen leaves with 40-70 percent of the bees to find a new cavity within which to start a new hive and leaves behind a number of virgin queens that have recently hatched or are about to hatch out of their birthing cells.

**Top Bar Hive:** A hive that just uses top bars, instead of a full frame, upon which bees are able to build their combs, raise their brood, and store their honey and pollen typically without the aid of foundation and instead usually with a wooden wedge or guide on the bars from which the bees build their comb, just like they do in nature.

**Trachael Mite:** a microscopic mite that invades the tracheal tubes of the honey bee to feed and reproduce.

**Varroa Mite:** an Asian mite that parasitized the Eastern honey bee *apis cerana*, before jumping species in the mid-20th century to afflict European honey bees, *apis mellifera,* and spreading across the world. Since the European honey bee has not developed resistance to this mite, varroa typically overwhelms colonies within two years if left untreated, resulting in colony death primarily from the weakening of the bees immune system and the transmission of diseases.

**Vermont Beekeepers Association:** the only state-wide association of beekeepers in Vermont.

**Virgin Queen:** a queen that has not mated and is unable to lay fertile eggs.

**Warrè Hive:** A Warrè hive is a vertical top bar hive that uses bars instead of frames, usually with a wooden wedge or guide on the bars from which the bees build their own comb, just like they do in nature.

**Wax Moth:** a moth that parasitizes weak or dead hives and lays eggs which hatch into larvae that consume beeswax combs and their contents.

**Worker Bee:** a female honey bee with an undeveloped reproductive system that carries out the majority of the work necessary to maintain a healthy colony.

# ACRONYMS

**ACBA:** Addison County Beekeepers Association
**AFB:** American Foulbrood
**APHIS:** U.S. Animal Plant Health Inspection Service
**BCBC:** Bennington County Beekeeping Club
**BIP:** Bee Informed Partnership
**BVT:** Bee Venom Therapy
**CCD:** Colony Collapse Disorder
**EAS:** Eastern Apicultural Society
**EPA:** Environmental Protection Agency

**LCBC:** Lamoille County Beekeepers Club
**NHB:** National Honey Board
**NHBS:** National Honey Bee Survey
**SHB:** Small Hive Beetle
**UGAN:** Union Ganadera Apiar National
**USDA:** United States Department of Agriculture
**UVM:** University of Vermont
**VAAFM:** Vermont Agency of Agriculture, Food and Markets
**VBA:** Vermont Beekeepers Association
**VSQ:** Vermont Seal of Quality

# GEOGRAPHICAL INDEX

*Note: all locations are in Vermont unless otherwise noted*

# SUBJECT INDEX

# INDEX OF PEOPLE

# ABOUT THE AUTHORS

**BILL MARES** has been a backyard beekeeper for over forty-five years. Raised in Texas, educated at Harvard, Mares is a former journalist, state representative and high school teacher. Mares has authored or co-authored seventeen books on a range of topics, including "Bees Besieged." He's been president of the Vermont Beekeepers Association and the Eastern Apicultural Association. He received the Divelbiss Award for from EAS in 2012, and was named Vermont Beekeeper of the Year in 2013. He lives in Burlington with his wife of forty-eight years, Chris Hadsel.

**ROSS CONRAD** of Middlebury learned his craft from the late Charles Mraz and his son Bill. Conrad is a former president of the Vermont Beekeepers Association, a regular contributor to Bee Culture Magazine, and author of *Natural Beekeeping: Organic Approaches To Modern Apiculture* published by Chelsea Green. He has given bee related presentations and led organic beekeeping workshops and classes throughout North America for many years. His human-scale beekeeping business, Dancing Bee Gardens, supplies friends and neighbors with honey and other bee related products, 5-frame nucleus bee colonies in the spring, and rental hives for local pollination.